SERVANT THEOLOGY

INTERNATIONAL THEOLOGICAL COMMENTARY

George A. F. Knight and Fredrick Carlson Holmgren,
General Editors

SERVANT
THEOLOGY
A Commentary on the Book of
Isaiah 40 – 55

GEORGE A. F. KNIGHT

THE HANDSEL PRESS, EDINBURGH
WM. B. EERDMANS PUBL. CO., GRAND RAPIDS

The first edition of this book,
published by The Abingdon Press,
Nashville, Tennessee in 1965
has been completely revised and
updated as a new edition
first published 1984

by

The Handsel Press Ltd.
33 Montgomery Street,
Edinburgh EH7 5JX

and

Wm. B. Eerdmans Publishing Company,
255 Jefferson Avenue S.E.,
Grand Rapids, Michigan 49503

ISBN
Handsel edition: 0 905312 31 7
Eerdmans edition: 0 8028 1039 X

Printed by Clark Constable, Edinburgh, London, Melbourne

CONTENTS

ABBREVIATIONS

ANET	*Ancient Near Eastern Texts Relating to the Old Testament*, ed. by J. B. Pritchard (2nd ed.; Princeton University Press, 1955).
AV	Authorized or King James Version of the Bible
DI	Deutero- or Second Isaiah, or Isaiah 40 – 55
DSSI	Dead Sea Scrolls Isaiah, technically known as IQIsa
ftn or *mg*	Footnote or marginal note to the text of the RSV
LXX	Septuagint (the Greek Version of the Old Testament)
NEB	New English Bible
NT	New Testament
OT	Old Testament
RSV	Revised Standard Version of the Bible, or, The Common Bible.

J and P are basic traditions to be found in the first five books of the Old Testament.

EDITORS' PREFACE

The Old Testament alive in the Church: this is the goal of the *International Theological Commentary*. Arising out of changing, unsettled times, this Scripture speaks with an authentic voice to our own troubled world. It witnesses to God's ongoing purpose and to his caring presence in the universe without ignoring those experiences of life that cause one to question his existence and love. This commentary series is written by front rank scholars who treasure the life of faith.

Addressed to ministers and Christian educators, the *International Theological Commentary* moves beyond the usual critical-historical approach to the Bible and offers a *theological* interpretation of the Hebrew text. The authors of these volumes, therefore, engaging larger textual units of the biblical writings, assist the reader in the appreciation of the theology underlying the text as well as its place in the thought of the Hebrew Scriptures. But more, since the Bible is the book of the believing community, its text in consequence has acquired ever more meaning through an ongoing interpretation. This growth of interpretation may be found both within the Bible itself and in the continuing scholarship of the Church.

Contributors to the *International Theological Commentary* are Christians — persons who affirm the witness of the New Testament concerning Jesus Christ. For Christians, the Bible is *one* scripture containing the Old and New Testaments. For this reason, a commentary on the Old Testament may not ignore the second part of the canon, namely, the New Testament.

Since its beginning, the Church has recognized a special relationship between the two Testaments. But the precise character of this bond has been difficult to define. Thousands of books and articles have discussed the issue. The diversity of views represented in these publications make us aware that the Church is not of one mind in expressing the 'how' of this relationship. The authors of this commentary share a developing consensus that any serious explanation of the Old Testament's relationship to the New will uphold the integrity of the Old Testament. Even though Christianity is rooted in the soil of the Hebrew Scriptures, the biblical interpreter must take care lest he 'christianize' these Scriptures.

Authors writing in this commentary will, no doubt, hold varied views concerning *how* the Old Testament relates to the New. No attempt has been made to dictate one viewpoint in this matter. With the whole Church, we are convinced that the relationship between the two Testaments is real and substantial. But we recognize also the diversity of opinions among Christian scholars when they attempt to articulate fully the nature of this relationship.

In addition to the Christian Church, there exists another people for whom the Old Testament is important, namely, the Jewish community. Both Jews and Christians claim the Hebrew Bible as Scripture. Jews believe that the basic teachings of this Scripture point toward, and are developed by, the Talmud, which assumed its present form about A.D. 500. Christians, on the other hand, hold that the Old Testament finds its fulfilment in the New Testament. The Hebrew Bible, therefore, 'belongs' to both the Church and the Synagogue.

Recent studies have demonstrated how profoundly early Christianity reflects a Jewish character. This fact is not surprising because the Christian movement arose out of the context of first-century Judaism. Further, Jesus himself was Jewish, as were the first Christians. It is to be expected, therefore, that Jewish and Christian interpretations of the Hebrew Bible will reveal similarities *and* disparities. Such is the case. The authors of the *International Theological Commentary* will refer to the various Jewish traditions that they consider important for an appreciation of the Old Testament text. Such references will enrich our understanding of certain biblical passages and, as an extra gift, offer us insight into the relationship of Judaism to early Christianity.

An important second aspect of the present series is its *international* character. In the past, Western church leaders were considered to be *the* leaders of the Church — at least by those living in the West! The theology and biblical exegesis done by these scholars dominated the thinking of the Church. Most commentaries were produced in the Western world and reflected the lifestyle, needs, and thoughts of its civilization. But the Christian Church is a worldwide community. People who belong to this universal Church reflect differing thoughts, needs, and lifestyles.

Today the fastest growing churches in the world are to be found not in the West, but in Africa, Indonesia, South America, Korea, Taiwan, and elsewhere. By the end of this century, Christians in these areas will outnumber those who live in the West. In our age, especially, a commentary on the Bible must transcend the parochialism of Western civilization and be sensitive to issues that are the special problems of persons who live outside of the 'Christian' West, issues such as race relations, personal survival and fulfilment, liberation, revolution, famine, tyranny, disease, war, the poor, religion and state. Inspired of God, the authors of the Old Testament knew what life is like on the edge of existence. They addressed themselves to everyday people who often faced more than everyday problems. Refusing to limit God to the 'spiritual,' they portrayed him as one who heard and knew the cries of people in pain (see Exod. 3:7-8). The contributors to the *International Theological Commentary* are persons who prize the writings of these biblical authors as a word of life to our world today. They read the Hebrew Scriptures in the twin contexts of ancient Israel and our modern day.

The scholars selected as contributors underscore the international aspect of the Commentary. Representing very different geographical, ideological, and ecclesiastical backgrounds, they come from over seventeen countries. Besides scholars from such traditional countries as England, Scotland, France, Italy, Switzerland, Canada, New Zealand, Australia, South Africa, and the United States, contributors from the following places are included: Israel, Indonesia, India, Thailand, Singapore, Taiwan, and countries of Eastern Europe. Such diversity makes for richness of thought. Christian scholars living in Buddhist, Muslim, or Socialist lands may be able to offer the World Church insights into the biblical message — insights to which the scholarship of the West could be blind.

The proclamation of the biblical message is the focal concern of the *International Theological Commentary.* Generally speaking, the authors of these commentaries value the historical-critical studies of past scholars, but they are convinced that these studies by themselves are not enough. The Bible is more than an object of critical study; it is the revelation of God. In the written Word, God has disclosed himself and his will to humankind. Our authors see themselves as servants of the Word which, when rightly received, brings *shalom* to both the individual and the community.

—George A. F. Knight
—Fredrick Carlson Holmgren

INTRODUCTION

No section of the Old Testament has attracted more attention than has Isaiah 40–55. The literature on it is more extensive than any one man could hope to read and digest in a decade. Yet Deutero-Isaiah will continue to attract exegetes so long as men study the Bible, for these sixteen chapters are as decisive and significant for an understanding of the Christian faith as are the sixteen chapters of Paul's Epistle to the Romans. Yet far less *theological* interest has been paid to Deutero-Isaiah than to the Epistle to the Romans.

The reason for this is that few scholars have cared to venture beyond the critical issues which lie behind these chapters; nor have they ventured to expound them as part of the biblical revelation as a whole. Most agree however that these chapters come from the period at the end of the Babylonian exile.

To interpret any portion of the Old Testament we must take seriously the historical events in the midst of which its prophets and writers lived and spoke. We might ask ourselves what Jeremiah and Habakkuk would have given to have possessed our sixteen chapters, for these two prophets would surely have found in them the answers to their torturing problems. Their task was to interpret the mind of God as the might of Babylon closed in upon little Judah a century after Isaiah's death. If Jeremiah or Habakkuk had been able to read Isa. 40–55, the tortured cry of 'Why?' would hardly have been wrung from their lips as they witnessed the destruction and violence of their time. Deutero-Isaiah's answer to their problem was not, of course, in existence in their day. (Hereafter we use the letters DI to represent the author of our book.)

We can see that God, in his wisdom, continued to raise up an interpreter-prophet to expound his actions at each of the great crises in Israel's story — at the Exodus, at the loss of the ark to the Philistines, at the creation of the monarchy, at the crisis connected with Baal worship, at the fall of the Northern Kingdom, at the fall of the Southern Kingdom, during the exile itself in Babylon, and so on. It would surely be strange then if God had omitted to raise up a prophet at the vitally significant moment of the return from Exile, since this

1

marks the climax of Israel's historical experience. Moreover, each one of the Old Testament prophets spoke out of the midst of a situation in which they were wholly involved, bodily, mentally, and spiritually, in the crisis in question. The prophets took no balcony view of events, but belonged with their brethren down in the arena, where the heat of the battle was most intense. There they were able to feel the response of their own people to their words, as they all faced the particular situation together. In fact, the prophets needed just such a living contact with the minds of their fellows if their own minds were to work fruitfully upon the events which they knew God meant them to interpret.

We receive the impression that DI has steeped himself in the works of his illustrious predecessor. Isaiah had proclaimed certain things about the *'etsah*, or plan, of God that was yet to be worked out in Israel's life and experience. DI now proceeds to show how that *'etsah* was taking form and reality in his own day and generation and even declares that it will continue to work in Israel's life in a unique and extraordinary manner in days to follow.

After the beginning of this century, many scholars became so concerned to place the separate paragraphs of our chapters in their various *Gattungen*, or types, that they lost all sense of the unity of the book as a whole. It is of course instructive to see now DI's work can be classified within the various categories that are to be found either within Israelite literature, or else in Ugaritic or Babylonian. But DI was first of all a theological giant. He conceived his work in terms of a literary and theological whole. Thus while he made use of a number of ancient forms of artistic writing for the sake of variety, he has threaded these units together to form one closely knit argument and developing thesis.

DI is obviously well versed in the literature of his people; yet his references to past events presuppose that his readers know what he is alluding to. 'Readers' is used deliberately, for DI's work is a written unit. It does not appear to have been spoken piecemeal in short, memorable, prophetic utterances, as most of the prophecies of Isaiah of Jerusalem were. As we read DI's work with attention to detail, we become aware of the brilliant manner in which his argument advances from point to point.

Ever since the German scholar Bernhard Duhm in 1875 isolated the so-called 'Servant Songs', a disproportionate amount of interest has been paid to those chapters, to the detriment of the book as a whole.

The reader will notice that herein the 'scissors-and-paste' method adopted by many commentators is not employed. The so-called 'Servant' passages (42:1-4; 49:1-6; 50:4-9; 52:13 – 53:12) are to be understood best when we read them in the setting in which DI actually placed them, for they each in turn advance the total argument just where they stand. Therefore the 'Servant Poems' are not discussed as such. The whole sixteen chapters together are in fact a poem about God's relationship to his 'Servant' Israel, in whom he has determined to glorify himself.

This is a theological and exegetical commentary. To say that it is theological, however, does not exclude the necessity for its being critical first. But since this commentary is meant to be of practical use to the nonspecialist within the Christian Church, there is no need to fill its pages with discussions of questions that are ably dealt with elsewhere in the many existing 'Introductions' to Deutero-Isaiah. This is not meant to be an Introduction. For example, an introductory critical commentary that informs us that the Hebrew word *shalom* 'peace' (47:7, 48:22; etc.), has its roots in the worship of a Canaanite god of that name is not helping the reader to get past the prolegomena to biblical study. Important, nay essential as those may be, sufficient of that study is being made elsewhere. Here we spend no time asking where the land of the Sinim is to be located geographically (49:12), or in discussing the New Year festival held in Babylon in DI's day. Such questions ought to be faced in a critical commentary, and these exist in sufficient number. Here we take for granted the results of the work of the critical scholar. Our task is to apply the knowledge he has given us to the problem of what DI is actually seeking to say, and to the elucidation of a text which is the unique revelation of God to man.

The text of DI is part of Holy Scripture. As such it is the book both of the Synagogue and of the Church. Therefore Jew and Christian alike come to its study already conditioned by the book itself. That is to say, both of them can be comparatively objective about the prolegomena to the study of the book, but find it difficult to be so in the case of its interpretation. Interesting evidence of this fact is offered when we read the semi-official interpretation of Isaiah made in the early Christian centuries in the Aramaic Targum of the Synagogue. Some of its peculiarities will be noted later.

Then again, the chapters we assign to Deutero-Isaiah do not contain static statements about God. DI is not a collection of doctrines which could mean the same in the twentieth century as they must have

3

meant in 540 B.C. In fact, it is the very vitality of the book that prevents the Jew and the Christian from reaching an identical exegesis of it.

The text of the OT is the vehicle of a two-way traffic between God and man. It informs us, in the first place, about the thoughts of its writers on the ways of God with Israel. These thoughts can be relatively objectively studied; and the scholar, with evidence of much self-satisfaction, is able to set forth in scientific form the growing understanding of God that is apparent as the story of Israel proceeds. But, second, the text of the OT is the vehicle of the Word of God to Israel. Moreover, that Word is heard not just through the intellectual grasp of God's thoughts which the prophets were able to make, but rather in and through the misunderstanding, the folly, the resistance, the unbelief, and even the apostasy of that Israel whom the prophets represent.

The reader of DI's pages today is a member himself of this covenant people of God, this backsliding, apostate people. The degree to which he hears the Word of God addressed to Israel through these pages is therefore bound up with his degree of awareness of his own apostasy, and with his acceptance of the forgiving and renewing love of God that the pages of DI reveal.

On the other hand, the interpreter must rigorously free himself from any tendency to allow dogma to dictate the exegesis. To a degree that the linguistic and literary critic can ignore, objectivity for the theological commentator means allowing the Word of God, as it meets him from the pages of the text, to judge himself — with his theological position and confessional standpoint, even his sociological setting — instead of his judging the text of the biblical book in question and reading into it his own human limitations.

Therefore the text of Isa. 40–55 offers an encounter not just with the faith of a man whom we name by the initials DI, but also with the Word of the living God. We meet this Word in the pages of his chapters as it begins to become flesh in an historical situation that we can pinpoint and quite accurately describe. Realizing this we obviate the danger of seeking for Christian dogmas within the text, or of trying to interpret what DI has to say in a christological manner. The interpreter who attempts the latter can only bring himself under censure for offering his readers a reading into rather than an exegesis of the text. For it is Israel that we read of in DI's text, and not the person of Christ.

DI's great contribution to our biblical faith is his insistence that the living Word of the living God began to be united — though still in a proleptic sense — with the very flesh of God's son Israel at that specific period in which DI himself was participating.

This fantastic union would eventually and necessarily be realized by means of the Word which he was even then uttering on God's behalf. For the Word cannot return unto God void. The day must come, in other words, when the people of Israel would become the locus of the Word itself. That is why the main theme of these sixteen chapters is not the return from exile, as is usually taken for granted, though that is indeed a central issue. The main theme is the revelation DI makes of the nature and purpose of God in His immanence in Israel as the Servant of the universe. Unless we discover that reality in these pages first of all, we need not look for some kind of theology of liberation, as this generation is doing, far less a theology either of salvation or of re-creation. Thus the work of DI is essentially *theology*. His pages have to do with what *God* has said or is saying to man, not with what man has to say about God. The latter is not theology, it is religion. Religion is a human creation. Israel's cult, Israel's philosophy of religion, Israel's view of reality, Israel's concept of history: these are all interesting subjects and worth our study today. But we do not meet with them here. What we have here is *theos-logos*, the Word of God to man. DI evidently believed that God was using his heart, mind, faith and commitment to speak that Word to Israel, even as he set it down in rhythmic verse, in sequential order, in prayerful hope and understanding. As such, then, these sixteen chapters are not 'prophecy' in the old-fashioned meaning of the word. They constitute revelation of the very mind of the living God.

I am very aware that some of my hypotheses may appear to the informed reader to be biased or even tendentious. Yet I am in good company in this respect; for I know of no commentator who agrees completely with other commentators! At least, however, the reader, meeting such moments, should be stimulated to ask himself the question: 'Is that what this prophet really meant to say?'

Isa. 40 – 55 is a document of fundamental theological importance. The roots of much of both Jewish and Christian theology are to be found in it. Therefore its study is both essential and very rewarding.

CHAPTER 40

1 It is often said that the main factor in revelation in the OT is the action of God within the life of Israel. This is true only to a point, however. For accompanying the action must go the Word. In fact the Word is noticeably conjoined with the action at each of the great moments in Israel's story. This is because a prophet is normally found at each such moment interpreting the action that he is witnessing. Moreover, the prophet in question is more than a mere mouthpiece; he is the channel through which the Word reaches into history; and without his faith and obedience, we cannot see how God would have acted in any of the historical situations recorded in the OT.

DI is here the channel for the inbreaking of a new divine Word into Israel's consciousness. This particular Word, which comes down like the rain from heaven (cf. 55:10), results in that historical incident in which the Israelite exiles in 539 B.C. are set free from servitude in Babylon by King Cyrus and are permitted to return home to Jerusalem, there to rebuild their ancient city and to reconstitute their ancestral worship.

The Word is the ground and basis of all life. So at least believed the author of Gen. 1:3 who declared 'And God *said*'. Sharing in such a heritage, DI now conceives of this reality pictorially. Thus he interposes angelic personalities between the Word of God and the word of the prophet. It is as if the whole universe is filled with God's Word. Here at v. 1 the air is filled with living creatures. As the servants of the Word, these exist to execute God's will and purpose both in heaven and on earth. Here we are in the same atmosphere as at the call of Isaiah (6:1-4). In DI's thought, we should notice, there is no line drawn between heaven and earth.

In line with this general biblical revelation, we hear the twice repeated command to *comfort*. The word does not mean to comfort or console another in his trouble: it means to comfort him out of his trouble into joy. The angelic forces (the verb is plural) are here to bring joy to God's special people. The latter have, of course, been such ever since God chose them in the days of Moses. All the peoples of the earth belong to God; all men are his creatures. Yet Israel is God's own

7

possession among all peoples (Ex. 19:5). They are in fact *my people*. The word found here, *'am*, is that normally used for the people of Israel alone. Obviously they are no longer 'Not-my people' of Hos. 1:9, or even just 'this people' of Isa. 6:9. So what we have here is the word of grace revealing God's constant concern that Israel should hold onto the covenant relationship by which Yahweh has bound her to himself. Though the destruction of Jerusalem, the scattering of *my people*, and the harsh subjection of the nation to the rule of the Babylonians had seemed like a breaking of the covenant which God had made of old, yet our author now declares that behind and through and within that overwhelming tragedy God is still present as Israel's God, and the basis of God's purpose for the whole universe is still his Word of comfort to his covenant people.

2 DI is fully aware of the teaching of the great prophets who preceded him. We shall note his dependence upon them and agreement with their words as we proceed. Hosea for one, closely followed by Jeremiah, has already used the astounding metaphor of marriage to set forth the distinctive relationship between Israel and her God. 'Speak to Jerusalem's heart' as the Hebrew has it (RSV *speak tenderly*) is a figure of God's husbandly love as later described in Isa. 54:1-8. It is also taken over in the NT to describe the relationship between Christ and the people of God as, for example, in 2 Cor. 11:2; Rev. 19:7; 21:2-9. This means that the special relationship that exists between Christ and his Church in the NT is recognized to be in continuity with that between God and Israel in the OT.

At this point, however, it is not God himself but the angelic agencies who are to *cry to her*. God is evidently convinced that Israel is capable of making a response, hopefully one of joy and obedience; for it is God who has completed the act necessary for her redemption and not she herself.

The word *warfare*, or better, *time of service*, as the RSV margin has it, in the sense of 'forced labour', has special meaning for our generation who have known an era of slave labour camps and depressed exiles cut off from all that they hold dear. It is basically the word for army or military service, and is to be found in the divine name 'Lord of hosts'. DI's use of the word is thus in itself part of the Good News. For the dispirited Israelites would naturally remember that the word belongs in this title of their God. He was truly their *Lord*, and as such was in full command of his hosts. The idea of forced labour, however, does not compel us to believe that in Babylonia the Hebrews were as cruelly and oppressively treated as they had been in Egypt before the Exodus (cf. Ex. 1:11-14). The Greek translation, *tapeinosis*, emphasizes instead the sense of moral degradation and mental humiliation which the exiles had perforce experienced. By contrast, in his famous letter to the exiles Jeremiah presupposed that his readers could live and were living normal lives though in a strange and alien land (Jer. 29:1-14.)

Yet the word has another overtone. The conscript soldier in Israel performed a religious duty when on service. His obedience when under arms could be likened to the service enjoined upon the fully grown male Israelite when he took his turn at the sanctuary (cf. Num. 4:3). Putting these ideas together, we might say that the forced labour that Israel had been doing for the last fifty years in a land of alien gods was in reality a service she had to render to God. Now, however, the angelic message sounded, and Israel's long term of military conscription was *ended*. This last word is an instance of the perfect tense of the verb used to declare a future action, in that God has declared it will happen.

The one Hebrew word rendered by *iniquity* is pregnant with a double meaning, for it means 'iniquity plus its punishment'. So DI with just one word can imply that sin indubitably brings its own reward, like the biblical proverb 'Be sure your sin will find you out' (Num. 32:23). His next word, *received*, refers to something like 'satisfaction', so 'expiation has been made'; and of course it is God alone who can accept Israel's sin. It is true that she had suffered *double*, twice over, for all her sins, so it appeared that she had made double payment for her past disloyalty. But even if she were to suffer ten times as much as she had done, she could never pay for them in any sense at all.

In the OT sin is not fundamentally a thing, an object, that can be dealt with objectively. Sin as a thing in itself cannot be atoned for. In the last resort there is not even such a thing as sin — there are only sinners. This is because sin is primarily a breaking off of personal relations. Sin is rebellion; it is pride; it is the belief by man that he knows better than God (cf. Gen. 3:3). Therefore God alone is in the position to deal effectively with it. On such a basis, therefore, DI could see how God could accept the forced service of the exile as if it were indeed divine service, the work of one that God had required in payment for her apostasy. On Israel's part, the basis of her sin lay in her breaking off relations with her divine Husband, the figure DI uses in later chapters. Those relations only God himself could now restore, even though Israel had now completed her service to that end. *Double* therefore does not imply that Israel had now expiated her own sins plus those of the gentiles among whom she had been dwelling. Rather the word is a strong Hebrew expression for something like 'she has suffered terribly', as indeed was true. Again, the word 'cup' is probably understood after *she has received* to be a double cup, a twice-filled cup. We find the idiom at 51:22, and at Jer. 25:15 and Lam. 4:21-22. It also forms the background to similar NT usages at Matt. 20:22; 26:39; 1 Cor. 11:25. *For* means 'in payment for', as the Hebrew shows.

We have before us, then, three thrilling statements, all of them proclaimed so matter-of-factly: (1) Israel's forced labour is ended; (2) Israel's punishment has been accepted; (3) Israel has now received from *the Lord's hand* the payment which he has exacted. Only later, at 47:6, does our writer identify this hand of the Lord with the instrument that he uses, viz., Babylon. If Israel had indeed deserved to be doubly punished, then in forgiving her in this total manner God must have been pouring upon her a double portion of grace. Two centuries before, Amos had declared that since Israel had received more light than her neighbours, in that God had given her special revelation in the Torah, Israel was doubly responsible when she rebelled against that light (Amos 2:4, 6; 3:1-2). But this was all now a thing of the past, declared DI, for *her iniquity is* now *pardoned.*

Israel is here addressed as *Jerusalem.* The city of course symbolizes the people, even though the latter are presently some seven hundred miles from home, and the walls of the city are lying in ruins. But this figurative use of the word Jerusalem is important in the context of DI's exposition. Like all cities, or ships in modern English, Jerusalem was regarded as a feminine entity, and so was known as 'she'. The feminine singular can be shown in the Hebrew verb, though it is not possible to do this in English. DI employs this figure consistently when he has in mind to speak of the people of God as Yahweh's bride.

3 Obedience belongs at the heart of worship. This reality must be applicable to the whole of God's universe and not only to man. An angelic voice promptly passes on the divine command that has resounded in the heavens. It is as if the host, *tsaba*, above was with military precision obeying the Lord of hosts, just as Israel was meant to do below when she was called to bear obediently the forced labour, *tsaba*, which God had laid upon her.

Now all the heavens are ringing with shouts and commands as

God's generals prepare the way for the King of kings, and DI's language soars as he speaks of the majesty and dominion of God. What follows is of course poetry, and no poet expects his words to be taken literally. What the poetry expresses, however, is no less than this: when God completes the rescue of his bride from her exile in Babylon, his action will have cosmic significance. His method in rescuing her DI discusses only later.

4 When in DI's day an Eastern monarch travelled through his dominions in his slow and simply constructed chariot, sappers were accustomed to go ahead virtually in order to build the road that the king had to travel. Later Persian monarchs ordered the construction of a fine network of royal roads that led to the far ends of their kingdom. But Babylonia did not possess such roads in 540 B.C. So DI knew how these sappers in a primitive sort of way had to level the hillocks and build up the ditches and fill in the holes so that the royal chariot might make some kind of speed. With this picture in mind, he then invites us to imagine what is involved in the astonishing idea that the living God will march before his people across the deserts and hills that lie between Babylon and home.

The command *prepare* means to push obstacles out of the way. However, the words *in the wilderness* come first in the command. This is to remind his hearers that God has already come through the wilderness of Sinai along with his people in the days of Moses (Ps. 68:7). Israel ought then to be confident that nothing now can stop God this time. Yet the Hebrews used the word *wilderness* in a metaphorical as well as a literal sense. The wilderness represented for their thinkers and prophets the concept of chaos and disorder; it figured for them that area of life where God's ordered world was set at nought; thus it could even be a state of soul as well as a geographical area. The fact therefore that the angelic host was ordered to prepare a way through chaos is significant for a theological understanding of this important chapter.*

DI returns later to this issue. All four of the Gospel writers, on the other hand, regarded this passage in the theological light suggested

---

* The Qumran sectaries later understood this 'way of the Lord' as 'the study of the Torah by which God gave command through Moses for acting according to everything that is revealed from time to time, and according to what the prophets revealed by His holy spirit'. See Matthew Black, *The Scrolls and Christian Origins*, p. 120.

above (Matt. 3:3; Mark 1:3; Luke 3:4; John 1:23). Evidently they recognized that, poetry though it was, this voice speaking five hundred years before their day was heralding both a factual and an eschatological situation at the same time. Yet this reference to the Exodus shows that not just here but throughout his whole work DI is concerned with the Mosaic tradition, though nowhere does he make any direct quotation from the Pentateuch. He seems to take for granted that his hearers know the traditions as well as he does. He handles these in freedom and seems to be unhampered by any preconceived dogmatic interpretations. On the other hand, this is where he lays the emphasis: he argues, that since God has acted before and has already used Moses to interpret and declare the meaning of his actions to Israel, God can therefore be trusted to act again in the days to come in similar ways. Thus these coming actions must not be regarded merely as local events or as ends in themselves; rather they are actions which will affect in their outcome the whole of God's creation.

5 Next follows an even more astonishing declaration: *The glory of the Lord shall be revealed. Glory* is the word that earlier writers had used to describe the visible manifestation of God, who is yet essentially invisible and incomprehensible. No man can see God and live, DI's predecessors had declared. But later OT writers postulated a concept which they called 'glory' and regarded it as the visible medium through which God's presence reveals itself to man.

[Glory was therefore frequently visually conceived in terms either of light or of fire, as at the Mount of Revelation in Moses' day (Ex. 19). Psalm 97 for example interprets the visible nature of glory in this very manner. This kind of interpretation, however, is not a new thing in human thought, for such a Psalm is closely related in genre to the Psalms used by the Canaanites in their cult in earlier centuries. There too light and fire are figures for the radiating power of the being of the deity. Such figures were easy to conceive, since fire obviously radiates the heat which issues from its heart. When Israel took over the concept from the Canaanites, however, she employed it in a new and paradoxical manner. The paradox lay in her view that glory was actually revelation of the invisible heart of God. In Israel's early days it had been easy to confuse the concept of glory, envisaged as it was under the form of fire, with various meteorological phenomena such as lightning or volcanic eruptions. But as time went by, Israel's prophets had purified and moralized the content of glory. It remained now for DI to establish the ultimate meaning that the word would bear, for later in his work he maintains that the glory of God is to be understood in terms of redemptive, recreative and suffering love.]

God's glory *shall be revealed*, declares DI. By the word 'revealed' he employs a pun. The verb means 'to be uncovered'. But to go into exile was also described as being uncovered, because one went naked and exposed. *Together*, we should note in passing is one of DI's favourite words. Sometimes he appears to employ it just to fill up a line of verse to make it scan.

The angelic voice now concludes its command by giving the sanction for the orders it has passed on. The sanction is '*The Lord has spoken*'. Amos the prophet had declared 'The Lord God has spoken; who can but prophesy?' (3:8). But a sinful man may resist the will of God and refuse to pass on the Word. The angelic voice, on the other hand, is not a sinful personality. In DI's day the angels were regarded as the will of God made visible in action. In themselves, however, the angels of the OT were nothing. They were just the voice through which the divine Word came to man. Thus the whole emphasis here is upon the Word and not at all upon the bearers of the Word. Yet the Word of God is to be identified with the will of God that has now been uttered, and which is therefore now moving along its creative path. The Hebrew language has only one word for our two, 'word' and 'thing'. In translating the OT, sometimes one English word must be used in preference to the other; only the context can decide. But ideally for the Hebrew thinker the two meanings cannot be separated, just as in the OT world of thought no separation can be made between matter and spirit. When God utters his Word, then the thing *becomes*: 'God *said*: "Let there be light"; and there was light', or better 'light became'. The Word of God cannot return unto God void, but must accomplish that which he utters as his will. DI has more to say of this at 55:8-11. Thus the redemption announced by the Voice is bound to become event, and so event occurs in history. Yahweh's mouth has spoken it.

6   DI now hears another angelic voice telling him in his turn to cry aloud *his* message.

The date is now somewhere between 545 and 540 B.C. About forty-five years before this time the end had come upon Jerusalem. In those days, before there was medical care and social security as we know it, human life was nasty, brutish, and short. Thus it is likely that very few

13

of DI's present hearers would even remember the events of 587 B.C. when Jerusalem was destroyed. Most of those who had gone into exile in that year would now be dead. Those who were still alive must have had little hope of finding any meaning in their remaining unhappy years. When the brevity of the human span is seen in its stark reality against the vanity of human existence, then the meaninglessness of human life becomes even more apparent. Some of us have known the experience of going back on a second occasion a few weeks later to view a beautiful hillside that had been covered with spring flowers, only to discover that not one of those flowers has survived.

The word *beauty* in v. 6 needs explanation: the Hebrew word behind it is the word *hesed*. The old AV (KJV) translated this noun in many ways, by mercy, loving kindness, goodness or even piety. The translators of the RSV on the other hand have sought to render it consistently elsewhere by two words, 'steadfast love'. In Psalm 136 for example, we meet with the constant refrain, '*For his steadfast love endures for ever*'. But you cannot use any of these translations with reference to the short-lived nature of spring grass.

At Gen. 9:9 we meet with the basic theological statement, expressed in picture language (which DI had of course inherited), that describes the relationship of the living God to his creation. This relationship is portrayed under the word 'covenant'. The story declares that God, in his prevenient grace and loving compassion, has made covenant, not only with man, but actually with all creation. The word *hesed*, then, is the noun that describes the positive content of this covenant. We see it illustrated in God's loyal commitment in covenant, first to Abraham, then to Jacob-Israel, then to all Israel as one people, and finally to David the king. This covenant God will never break. God's plan, moreover, was that both Israel and the Davidic line of kings would reciprocate and respond within the covenant with equal love and loyalty. Within the terms of Noah's covenant the vegetation of Palestine, which experiences a hot, dry summer season, can give glory to God in its beauty for only a short period in spring. On the other hand, Yahweh had called upon Israel to reflect back to him without ceasing the *hesed* which he himself consistently showers upon his elect people.

7-8   This means that it is the Word of God alone that remains constant, steadfast and reliable. It alone is alive for evermore, on the ground that it is the Word of the *living* God. In fact, the Word *is* God, because it has issued from the heart of God. It has then become his will made known in creative activity. As such it is the Word uttered, and so has become objectively independent of the God who uttered it. The words *will stand* mean both to 'stand up', and to 'remain standing'.

9   That then is the good news. Consequently Jerusalem dare not keep it to herself. At the moment of speaking *Zion* — God's people — is dwelling on the flat Mesopotamian plain. But Jerusalem, the ancient capital city of the exiles, straddles a ridge that seen from the west seems to be along the skyline above. Of nearby hills, only the Mount of Olives is higher than Zion. So the people of God is to get back somehow to Zion and climb onto the top of its high hill, so that when she proclaims the good news her voice will carry further. She is not to be afraid about her task; she is to shout her message at the top of her voice — as surely she ought. While grammatically it is possible to translate this as 'O herald of good tidings to Jerusalem', such a rendering would leave us with the problem that the herald as well as Zion is spoken of in the feminine. Thus while the prophet is certainly the mouthpiece of the angelic message to Israel, yet it is Israel herself, under the feminine figure of either Zion or Jerusalem, who is to be the missionary instrument to all the world. Moreover, a city set on a hill itself signifies mission. We shall see, as his sermon develops, that Israel's missionary task is one of DI's major themes.

Included in Zion's constituency are naturally the small towns and villages *of Judah*. Not all the people of Judah had been removed to Babylon by Nebuchadrezzar in 587. Many peasants had been left to continue their simple and brutish life in the hill country of the little area known as Judah, then part of a province of the Babylonian Empire. However, as recent archaeological evidence shows, the country districts of Judah were at that time terribly decimated and impoverished. Yet these poor folk were also God's people and so were still one with the exiles to whom the angelic message, first of comfort, second of challenge, was now being addressed. The people of Judah, then, were to be the first to hear the good news. The remnant, now in Babylon, was to shout it to them the moment they succeeded in getting home to Judah. Little did the remnant realize, however, that they were specially fitted for their missionary task just because they had suffered doubly, as the towns of Judah had not. This too is another of DI's important themes, merely hinted at here in this first chapter of his thesis. Here at the beginning of this book, he makes a number of unexplained statements of this nature. It is as if he were the editor of a newspaper whose task it is to provide the headlines to the subject matter. In the small type below, the topics splashed across the page are then dealt with in detail.

The verb behind *herald of good tidings* means in origin to 'smooth', and then to 'smooth out the wrinkles' on a human face. The remnant in Babylon has now been given the comfort of God, and it has heard that *the word of our God will stand for ever*, v. 8. The natural sequence is that she in her turn should pass the good news on to her poverty-stricken brethren back home. What she is to say is: *Behold your God*, meaning 'Your God is here'. When she does so, then those careworn and impoverished villagers will know a joy such as they have not known for a generation; they will learn that, despite all appearances to the contrary, their covenant God is still alive, that his Word remains 'erect', unlike the flowers which droop and die, and that God is here with the exiles as they return from Babylon.

The Targum makes an important interpretation here. It translates the words of proclamation by 'The Kingdom of your God is revealed'. When we remember that this reading was being used in the synagogues in the first century A.D., we can recognize how Jesus' expression 'The Kingdom of God is at hand' is probably his way of expressing such a phrase as this.

10   The above message is no mere philosophical idea. DI is concerned not with ideas but with historical facts. The word 'God' which he has used before he now defines by the name Yahweh that lies behind the word Lord, i.e., by the name of the covenant God who had already revealed himself to Moses within history (Ex. 6:1-8). The transcendent God, he now declares, is about to stoop to enter history once again with *might*, the word DI uses where others prefer 'spirit'. This might or power he portrays by the anthropomorphic picture of God's arm ruling for him. This symbolic sense of arm occurs only in Isa. 40–66. An arm is for stretching out, it is for action, it is for doing the task determined upon by the whole man.

Yet it is not enough for Israel to know that God is all-powerful. Israel wants to know if the all-powerful is also essentially good. The answer comes in the next cry: *Behold, his reward is with him*, in the sense of 'See how he has brought his wages with him'. Lord Yahweh is a God of justice, whose power will never be used arbitrarily but always for those defined ends of love and justice that conform to his absolute will. The

16

double name, Lord Yahweh, had been a favourite of Amos' two hundred years before. He too had delighted to stress the justice of Israel's God. Ezekiel immediately before DI's day had also used this double title.

11 The connection between the words *might* and *wages* is now explained in an astonishing metaphor. The argument runs like this: (1) The strength of Almighty God is the strength of the gentle giant; the strength of tenderness and love and care. This is good news indeed. (2) God's 'wages' and *recompense* are his own abiding presence with the poor exiled Israelites, his covenant people of old. DI will develop greatly this second theme as his message unfolds. Meanwhile we see how God's action in picking up the lambs in his arms is actually an act of salvation (cf. 59:16; John 10:28). DI is not the first to make this plain. Israel had long since learned to picture strength and gentleness as necessarily conjoined in the Good Shepherd who was their God (cf. 2 Sam. 5:2). Yet the picture unfolds from a situation that appears to the human eye as what we would call a complete loss. Israel's God had been finally defeated, it seemed, when Nebuchadrezzar's god had strengthened him to destroy Yahweh's temple and people, and had brought about the negation of the promise made to Israel's father Abraham. This was the promise that through his descendants the whole world would be blessed (Gen. 12:1-3; 17:6), and that the covenant which God was making with Abraham to that end would stand forever (Gen. 17:7).

Now, declares our prophet, despite all appearances: (1) The Word of God does in fact still stand (v. 8). (2) God himself is still 'your shield; your reward shall be very great' as he had promised to Abraham (Gen. 15:1), and, in consequence, to all Abraham's descendants. (3) Therefore, as a result of God's intimate fellowship with Israel through the reality of the covenant, God himself, in the shape of Israel's *reward*, has so identified himself with her in her tribulation that the pain and suffering which Israel has been going through, and which Israel has been suffering to her cost, has now become God's costly redemptive experience. For he is carrying Israel *in his arms* and so he is meeting the buffetings of fate in her place. This verse thus foreshadows our theologian's argument at 43:24. The words *his recompense before him*, meaning his payment being the first thing we see, (v. 10) explain that God himself has paid the wages, has paid the price that Israel should have paid, but obviously could not do herself.

17

The picture here of the Good Shepherd embodies the reversal for Israel of all the horrors of the past — of the siege and destruction of Jerusalem, of the bitterness of separation from dear ones, of the agony and thirst of the desert march, of the sense of hopelessness they had known, and of the purposelessness of their life in exile. The word for lamb can also be used for a little child; in fact its feminine form in Aramaic was used by Jesus when he raised up Jairus' daughter. DI here makes the striking point that it will be no effort for God to 'lift' his *lambs in his arms*, for he can raise up — the verbs are identical — and fill in valleys with equal ease. It is still questioned whether DI was personally acquainted with Ezekiel in exile. Certainly Ezekiel delights to use the same picture as DI does, of God as the Good Shepherd of his people (Ezek. 34).

12 Many commentators have worked upon the assumption that DI is a collection of independent oracles which have been rather oddly strung together to form the sequence we now possess. Scholars have therefore classified the types of oracles under various heads, and have compared and contrasted those types with their fellows elsewhere in the OT as well as with those found in extra-biblical literature. But the work of DI is to be understood quite differently from the prophetic material left us by the pre-exilic prophets, including even Isaiah of Jerusalem, whose name has been set above the whole sixty-six chapters of the book of Isaiah. DI undoubtedly made use of the various types of *Gattungen* of prophetic utterance which were his literary heritage as a Hebrew. But unlike the great prophets before him, whose material has come down to us in short and pithy utterances consisting sometimes of only a few lines at a time, DI has penned a sustained theological treatise in verse. In doing so, he has brilliantly rung the changes of style possible in his day by weaving into his narrative several of the various *Gattungen* that the earlier prophets had employed. But the important point to note is that there is a logical sequence of thought throughout his whole sixteen chapters, and that each of the pictures he paints, independent of the whole as it may appear to be at first glance, is necessary for the continued advancement of his argument just at that point where he has placed it. It would be nonsense to declare for example that Rom. 9 – 11, being a separate *Gattung* from chs. 1 – 8, was therefore an inset in the Epistle to the Romans made by a later scribe. In the same way the verses that now follow should not be regarded as a brilliant but irrelevant picture portrait of the majesty of God. They follow naturally after v. 11. For at v. 12, DI sets out to teach what the power and the arm of the Lord that he has mentioned really mean. And his reason for doing so is to assure Israel that the loving purpose of God Almighty is such that he can permit himself to stoop to carry his lambs without losing his right to be known as the Creator of all.

Who then is the Good Shepherd to whom DI has referred above? It is he who could *measure the waters in the hollow of his hand*. Waters, *mayim*, is a deliberate choice of a word instead of 'seas', for it sounds in assonance with the word *shamayim*, heavens, and it must include the waters both above and below the firmament (Ex. 20:4). For of course DI lived in that three-decker universe which the whole ancient world accepted as a scientific description of the cosmos it knew. The ancient Hebrews feared the sea and seldom ventured on it. But they dreaded still more the waters of chaos under the earth, and saw them as the symbol of all that was evil and inchoate. It is interesting that nearly all the features of Creation which DI describes in these chapters are to be found in Gen. 1 – 3. Moreover, vv. 12-14 have formed the basis of Paul's citation in both Rom. 11:34 and 1 Cor. 2:16.

13 The one English word *counsellor* comprises two Hebrew words that seem to be defective. Yet one of them is the noun *'etsah*. Isaiah of Jerusalem long before had spoken of God's *'etsah* when he declared that God's messianic figure would utter the very *'etsah* of God (Isa. 9:6; 11:2). Yet in all DI's long and intricate argument he assumed that it is Israel herself who is to become God's messianic agent, and that she will incorporate within her own unique relationship to God the plans and purposes of God with power for the redemption of the world. This, of course, is a highly important theological assumption, and one that must be kept in the forefront in any christological discussion.

The word *directed* is identical with the word rendered *marked off* in v. 12. Thus does DI with both wit and sarcasm force his readers to take seriously the blasphemy of man. Man in DI's day was just as apt to imagine, as any astronomical scientist today is tempted to do, that humanity may one day measure the mind of God.

14 It is ludicrous to suppose, he declares, that any human mind could ever fully understand either this mysterious universe, or the depths and fullness of God's *mishpat*, his total revealed way of life for man. This word *justice*, then, *mishpat*, here obviously means more than we mean by justice as we shall see later.

19

15   Language nowhere offers more striking pictures than do these lines of the greatness and power of God. And even though we today live in a vastly more expansive universe than DI could ever have imagined, his similes resound as validly now as ever.

16   Lebanon was the mountainous area to the north of Palestine on whose slopes grew coniferous forests. These forests included the famous cedars, which Solomon had used for the interior decoration of the Jerusalem temple (1 Kings 5:8-10). Neither Lebanon's mighty forests nor its many and various wild animals could ever be sufficient for a human act of worship of such a mighty God.

17   Yet God does not so much reveal himself as hide himself in nature. For before its intricacies and wonders man's mind is both numbed and awed. Man realizes even while he muses, that since he can never know God, he will never come to know what degree of sacrifice he therefore ought to offer God. For is any sacrifice of any significance at all, if the humans who seek to offer it are themselves *as nothing before him*? The significance of the word that follows in the poetic parallel, the one translated most unpoetically by the word *emptiness*, is important. DI is once again using the language of the first chapter of Genesis. In this chapter (1:2) we read 'The earth was without form and void', i.e., *tohu wa-bohu. Wa* means 'and'; *bohu* is merely a poetic doubling of the word *tohu*, used for emphasis and effect. Our author DI employs this word *tohu*, without the unnecessary doubling, on seven occasions in his sixteen chapters. What he is obviously concerned to do by this frequent use of the word is to declare the great reality, namely, that it is God who is all in all, and that all else must therefore be less than nothing. As the Genesis picture puts it, in the beginning God created order in face of chaos. DI has much to say later about this concept of God's order. Here his emphasis is upon the fact that man and man's forms of government and ordered life are actually so far from being in conformity with God's order that they belong rather to the realm of entropy, to what tends towards disintegration rather than to integration, to destruction rather than to construction, to the concept of negation or darkness rather than to light and positive value. No more need be said at present of this idea, for DI returns to it with force in later lines.

18   In order to assure the exiles of what he has now said, that God is quite capable of accepting their suffering as an adequate punishment, of putting an end to their 'forced labour' (v. 2), and of leading them home as a shepherd leads his sheep, DI has first shown his hearers how their covenant God Yahweh is mighty beyond all human thought (vv. 12-15). This led to the view that man cannot respond in any adequate sense to God's demands (v. 16); that in fact the human order is wholly different from God's order and purpose (v. 17). Now DI shows how puerile are the efforts of men — and he obviously exemplifies the Babylonians among whom the exiles were perforce living — to conceive of divinity in any adequate manner.

19   Man has first to make his gods, or create his concepts, before he can bow down to them and worship them. DI reminds his readers, however, of the truth that we find expressed in the second commandment. So wholly other is Israel's God, so positive when man's thoughts and life are merely negative, that if man essays to conceive of God in any form at all, his thoughts must necessarily eventuate as blasphemy. The negative cannot possibly conceive the positive. Thus when man does try to create a likeness of the divine, all that he can produce is the fatuous gold-lacquered image which the Babylonians imagined to be a god, and yet which they had to chain to a wall to keep upright.

20   With biting sarcasm DI suggests that if a man is too poor to rise to a gold-plated image, then he can be happy making do with a piece of wood, provided only that it does not *move*, or fall over (see also 44:12 ff.; Jer. 10:3-4).

21   Sweeping all this Babylonian nonsense aside, DI returns to ask questions in the Socratic manner, such as every living soul must seek to answer if he is to remain a sane and purposeful creature. He implies first that the greatness of God is self-evident, and would agree that 'the heavens are telling the glory of God; and the firmament proclaims his handiwork' (Ps. 19:1). Yet natural revelation is never stressed in the OT. Sometimes it even seems to be denied (cf. 45:15). DI is well aware that the Babylonians gazed at the same sky his own fathers had seen over Jerusalem. Yet the Babylonians had developed no conception of an incomparable, wholly other God as the author and sustainer of their lives.

The word *the beginning (ro'sh)* is seemingly a technical term in DI's vocabulary which he employs to describe the beginning of revelation and God's first act of redemption in the days of Moses. DI understood God's control of the universe in the light of the Exodus from Egypt. Yet he seems to go further back than the days of Moses. For God's promise to Abraham had preceded his redemptive act in Moses' day. Ever since *the foundations of the earth*, when God put man in control of his mysterious universe under himself, God had been revealing himself to Adam's sons — as indeed Noah knew, and as Abraham, Isaac, Jacob, and Joseph had also certainly known. But since the word *foundations* may refer to the occupation of Canaan, for *ha-'arets* can mean the land (of Canaan) as well as the whole earth, it is quite possible that DI was punning. Thereby he implied that God's gift of land to Israel, theologically speaking, was one with his creation of the world. The world began, so to speak, when God's plan began to unfold in and through his people Israel.

22-23   This plan had to do not with *grasshoppers* (or locusts) but with people, the people of Yahweh. For what is the life of a locust? It is a life of destruction and the production of chaos (*tohu*); it is a life of rending and devouring. That is how unredeemed man behaves. But man is part of this universe that exists only because God wills that it should stay in being. *Princes* therefore rule only by God's abundant sufferance. In themselves such men are vanity — nay, they are even *negation*.

24   And so comes the logical question from contemplating the above. Why then should the exiles stand in awe of the silly power of Babylon? It might look as if the royal line of Babylon were well rooted in the soil of Mesopotamia, because for almost a century now the dynasty of Nebuchadrezzar had been ruling throughout the Near East, an area which included Israel's beloved Judah and the ruins of their ancient city of Jerusalem. But what is a human *root* when it has dug down merely into negation? God has only to breathe on the dictator of Babylon and he will *wither*, even as goes the *stubble* that is swirled into oblivion by the *tempest* out of the desert.

25   'Is it not rather ridiculous to liken anything at all to the God who is absolute ruler of earth and sky?' asks the Holy One. Here our poet borrows one of the favourite names of Isaiah of Jerusalem for God. DI uses it when he seeks to express the majesty and wonder of the Creator over against the sinfulness and pettiness of the creature. By its use, however, DI does not show that he 'believes in' creation, far less that he 'believes in' man. Unlike many present day philosophers he believes only in the Creator of the creation, and in the Creator of man.

26   When the sun sets in the evening, out comes the *host* of the stars. It is as if God were the commanding officer of a vast army in the heavens. When he visits his units on parade and numbers them off, he finds that *not one* star *is missing* or out of its appointed place. In fact, fantastically numerous as they are, God knows them all — and not just by number but actually *by name*.

The word for *host* here, *tsaba*, is the word of v. 2. It occurs also in the plural in the divine name 'Lord of hosts'. Those hosts were, as we see, the multitude of the stars. But often these were personalized in OT thought, as if each star were an angel acting as God's instrument on high.

But this is a sacramental universe, a fact which the Hebrews knew well. By that modern word we describe their belief that the universe is one entity and not two; that is to say, they believed we are not to speak of heaven plus earth, for there is but one unified cosmos. So it is natural that God's hosts should serve him throughout it all. That is why this word *tsaba* can be used both of the angels and of Israel. For Israel is God's host, that host which under Joshua fought its way into the Promised Land at the founding of 'the land' as we saw *the earth* could mean (v. 21). Yet the warrior God Yahweh is always at war against evil everywhere, and so he uses his hosts to this end both on earth below and in heaven above (cf. Ex. 12:41; Num. 10:14; and cf. Eph. 1:21; Col. 1:16; 1 Pet. 3:22). If God so cares for the host, *tsaba*, of stars on high that he knows each of their personalities as a distinct entity and can identify each by its own individual name (cf. Ps. 147:4), then how much more must he have counted the hairs on your heads, O you trembling *host*, *tsaba*, of Israel?

27   Naturally Israel has not yet known that God is like this. She has not yet heard the Word of God uttered through the mouth of his prophet, nor seen it take shape in a historical situation. Only then can the comfort announced in v. 1 become meaningful to her. Israel in exile had supposed that Yahweh had forgotten her. The temple was lying in ruins, and the temple was that spot alone where God and man could meet in sacramental worship. Jerusalem was now destroyed, and Jerusalem alone was God's chosen city, and as such was as much the medium of unfolding revelation as had been the line of David. The Holy Land, which God had given his people forever (Gen. 17:8; 28:13) was now overrun by hordes of heedless pagans. Much that DI has to say later is virtually a wrestling with the significance of these very problems. He is triumphantly able to show how Israel could lose her temple, her city, her land, even her very *raison d'être*, and yet discover that God could be wholly faithful to the promises he had made.

DI begins this section of his argument by addressing the despondent nation first as *Jacob* and then as *Israel*. By reminding them of their eponymous ancestor in this way, DI is alluding to the promise that God had made to Jacob. That promise was that Jacob's seed would be as numerous as the dust of the earth (Gen. 28:14). A few lines back DI had been declaring the insignificance of the nations of the earth in God's sight, and saying that they were like *the dust on the scales* (v. 15). But now Yahweh, through DI, assures his people that though they share the common human lot and as such are also dust, they are precious in his sight. Their continued existence as a people even in far-off exile ought to show them that God has not repudiated his promise to Jacob. God is such that he cannot go back on his promise, for *the word of our God will stand forever*, (v. 8). This linking of v. 27 with v. 15 is not a piece of ingenious exegesis, even though in v. 15 DI uses for dust a noun different from that employed in the tradition about Jacob in Gen. 28:14. The whole of DI's work is in reality a closely knit argument. His method is to make constant reference backward and forward as he proceeds, and bit by bit he binds his book together in one sustained and developing argument.

Then again, in the words of the divine promise, Israel's numbers are to be likened not only to the dust of the earth but also to the stars of the sky (Gen. 15:5). DI's teaching now becomes very clear. If God has indeed full control over the stars of heaven (v. 26), he argues, then he is also in control of the seed of Abraham, Isaac, and Jacob.

Making use of a poetic parallelism, DI now addresses his people by the other name that Jacob had won for himself, once he had wrestled with God and had prevailed, viz., *Israel* (Gen. 32:24-32). Before Jacob had undergone his distinctive spiritual experience which earned him this new name, though he was chosen by God, he had been a mean, selfish, and despicable man. His nature had in fact been *tohu*, negation, destructively false. But now, by God's grace and through the faith God had awakened in him in the encounter, he had become a new man altogether. He was thus worthy of a new name to describe the new man he had become. So there at Peniel God had blessed him. That blessing was the utterance with power and purpose of the Word of God which remains forever. The people who now bore Jacob's name had necessarily become the blessed people Israel, 'strong with God'. Why then should Israel, strong with God, so runs DI's argument, imagine that because of fleeting circumstances, her *way is hid* from her God? Even in Babylon Yahweh was surely still her God, and Israel was still 'my people' (v. 1).

28 The truth of this amazing good news DI drives home in a final magnificent word picture. Even as Israel cast her eyes upon all the ridiculous gods of Mesopotamia she should be reassured that her own national, covenant God was no other than the Creator of all things. *Everlasting, 'olam,* is a word that is not primarily connected with life beyond the grave. It comes from the root meaning 'hidden'. And so it speaks of the mists of the past, hidden from the thought of man, and it looks toward the mists of the future, into which man's mind cannot even begin to pry. It speaks of the God who is Lord even of the hidden realities that human beings can envisage only in terms of infinite time. Moreover the word *Creator* is that which occurs at Gen. 1:1. There we see no philosophical speculation about the origin of the earth such as we make today. We moderns speculate about how the universe came into being, and whether God produced it *ex nihilo* or in some other way. The significance and emphasis of the word before us is rather upon the continual creative activity of God — the word is an active participle — who continually does what no man and no heavenly power can do. God has given man the power to refashion stuff that is already there; but man cannot *bara'* except when God acts through him by grace (cf. Josh. 17:15, 18); only God can create. In fact this verb is reserved by both Genesis and DI for the action of the Almighty alone.

29-31 Now note DI's deliberate choice of words once again. The ideas of *weary* and *exhausted* occur thrice. On the first occasion they refer to God — in the negative — in the second and third to man, when they are shown to be a significant reality in his life. The contrast is clearly made. DI has just established the absolute otherness of God from man. Now he proceeds to depict the grace of God leaping over the chasm that he has made between himself and man. In v. 26 God has been revealed as *power* itself. Now DI tells us that God gives this very *power* of his, his *might*, meaning something like his bounding vitality, to those who are most in need of it, the *weary* and the *exhausted* among Israel. Yet once again God requires the co-operation of human faith, just as in the case of Jacob, before his gift of *strength* or vitality can be appropriated by the weary exiles. It is *they who wait for the Lord* who find a miracle taking place in their experience. If God, says DI, was able to create in the beginning and can keep on creating this vast and complex universe, then he can as easily create a new thing in the life of those who passionately seek him. He can make pinions grow where there were none before.

Faith means possessing not the mere physical energy of youth, but utter assurance that God is strong with the strength of the Good Shepherd. Anyone then, be he young or old, once he possesses *wings like eagles*, may find that he need no longer trudge along the road of life, for he will now be swept into a run by the pinions of faith (cf. Ps. 84:5-7). It is of interest to note that throughout the later biblical period and into the Christian centuries the eagle was used as a symbol of new life. The eagle can soar till it is lost to sight. Like the phoenix it was also a symbol of release from bondage and of resurrection to newness of life. See George Ferguson, *Signs and Symbols in Christian Art*, pp. 13-14, 23-24.

CHAPTER 41

1 Our chapter divisions are, of course, quite artificial. While DI used strophes that may be classified by us today under the titles of the various *Gattungen* that we have invented, yet his whole epic poem is clearly a unity. It does not even use stanzas or cantos as do Milton's *Paradise Lost* and Dante's *Divine Comedy*. Thus v.1 follows directly from what precedes.

Here is the Lord of history speaking. He who stoops to *renew* the *strength* of the *weary* can obviously as easily command the nations to *renew their strength*. Evidently the strong of this world gain their strength from God alone as much as do the weak — though they may not know it. It is as if God were calling the nations to a court of justice; and in the judicial language found at Deut. 25:1, passes judgment upon them, something which is his right to do.

2 What is this plan of God then? Again DI hints at it, without naming the person of Cyrus, king of Persia, who even as he was speaking was carrying forward a triumphant campaign of conquest in Asia Minor. But DI insists that Cyrus' advance was primarily God's doing and only secondarily the action of a man. He comes both *from the east* and *from the north* (41:25). That is actually the route that Cyrus took.

The translation of the next few verses in the RSV however is only one of several possibilities, as the reader can see by referring to other commentaries and the various versions. DI's Hebrew is so condensed and poetically expressed that no one should lay claim to making a definitive translation. But the picture of Cyrus' steady advance causing all powers to collapse before him is historically accurate if we place DI in the second half of the 540s B.C. Victory, *tsedeq*, is of course an equivocal translation. It has the pregnant sense of rightness taking effect by the power of God; so at times it comes to mean deliverance, victory, prosperity, as these represent the justification for or outcome of clashing with one's foes. Or again, in the sphere of morals, the word may be used as a virtual synonym for salvation, since salvation is deliverance from evil.

3   Once again more than one translation is possible; yet the purport of them all is the significance of Cyrus' victorious advance: (1) 'By a route which they are not aware of', i.e., Cyrus' intelligence corps finds ways by which his army circumvents the enemy. (2) 'By a route which he does not enter with his feet.' This might mean, as in the case of (1), that Cyrus avoids the beaten tracks. DSSI seems to favour this interpretation. (3) 'A path with his feet he does not tread', or in modern words, 'his feet (scarcely) touch the ground'. So fast does he advance that he goes like the wind. In other words, Cyrus is a kind of miracle man who never tires — for the reason that Israel's God is with him.

4   Israel's God who has been doing all this — we have two perfect tenses of two similar verbs in succession, of which the first may mean to initiate an action, the second to realize and carry it out — is no parvenu among the gods. It is he who has been active since the beginning because he is the beginning himself; consequently he *will be with the last*, that is, he will be there at the end. But DI does not conceive of Yahweh as static being. He is the active, purposeful, creative God. For *I am He* is the emphatic assertion of Yahweh's personality. As we proceed it will be noted that DI makes use of innumerable active participles in relation to Yahweh to describe his vitality. An active participle is part of a verb, which in turn is the action element in human speech. Yahweh then has been active ever since *the beginning*. As we saw, this is probably DI's technical term for the Exodus period when God chose Israel as his son (Ex. 4:22 and Hos. 11:1). Since then God had been calling generation after generation of Israelites to hear and obey his voice.

Our author has Yahweh make this great declaration about himself in the light of what the Israelites were probably learning at that time about the religion of Cyrus the Persian, the man on whom DI was calling his people to pin their hopes. It is a matter of controversy whether Cyrus was a Zoroastrian by religion or not. This is because we are not yet certain when Zoroaster lived. But when formulating his faith, Cyrus adapted into his system the very exalted religious beliefs of the early Persians which were similar to his own. This matter will be discussed further at 45:7. The *Gatha* (31:8), a paragraph from Persian literature quite as old as Cyrus runs: 'recognized, O Mazda, that thou art the first and the last'. But here, however, Yahweh is not called the last himself. He is to be at or with the last, or at the end, curiously enough a plural word. The term seems to signify the 'outcome' of particular historical events in space and time. Its use links the worlds of word and thing that have been mentioned at 40:5 and requires their unity. To use present-day theological jargon, this word 'end' might be translated by the phrase 'eschatological significance'.

All the prophets of the OT were convinced that this life is meaningful. To this end they emphasized the word 'now' in every human relationship with which they dealt. Not only did people matter to God, they believed, so also did things. This world, they were sure, was not just an empty dream, nor a mere passageway to the real world still to come. Since God's universe is one, on the ground that God himself is one, then the life we live now in the flesh is but one side of the coin which represents the whole of reality. The other side we have not yet seen. But the coin that has the two sides is still the one coin, so that what happens to one face of the coin affects the coin as a whole. Since this life here and now is important and significant, on the ground that God is speaking and uttering his Word within it, then what man does with his time and his things here and now must have an outcome in the world beyond. In our Lord's parable of the last judgment (Matt. 25:31-46), his whole emphasis is upon the outcome of ordinary human actions performed here and now. Feeding the hungry in this world he regards as an eschatological act. This verse then presents an awesome statement: it is that God will be there at the end, or at the outcome of all our everyday actions. Behind this solid world of things is not an it, but an 'I'. This 'I' has already revealed himself as such to Moses (Ex. 3:6; 6:2). This *I, the Lord*, must therefore necessarily continue to be identical with the 'I' by which men know him now, and by which he has revealed himself in his relationship to Israel (cf. Ps. 102:27).

DI affirms then that God's relationship with Israel in terms of 'now' must carry within it eschatological significance, since God himself will be there at the end. But having been there also at the beginning, he thus encloses all history in a ring. The rise of Cyrus was now the great historical event of the day. One could see that the whole balance of power in the known world was about to alter. Yet these catastrophic events were tightly enclosed within the divine plan, and were therefore under the control of the living God.

5-6 By 546 B.C. Cyrus had fought his way victoriously to the west coast of Anatolia, before which lay the islands of the Aegean, the Dodecanese, with Cyprus, Crete, and the Peloponnese not far away. So there arises a natural human reaction to this common enemy. Old quarrels are forgotten, and men encourage and help each other to resist the conqueror. These lines offer us a cameo, showing how men will whistle in the dark to keep their courage up.

7   Cyrus's most powerful opponent in Anatolia was King Croesus of Lydia, known till today for his fabulous wealth. Croesus' workmen had executed his orders well. This was to outdo all other kings in the production of golden gods such as the world had never seen before. Like a drowning man, Croesus was clutching at straws — in the shape of lucky amulets or silly, gold-lacquered charms — but even these fabulous gods were helpless before the advance of Cyrus, whom the God of Israel was using as the intrument of his plan. It may be that the three oracles preserved in Isa. 21:1-10, 11-12, 13-17 were all uttered by other prophetic voices about this time. Their authors belonged to the poverty stricken inhabitants of Palestine, and were not speaking from the milieu of Babylon, where DI was living. Yet together they witness to the widespread fear that Cyrus' victorious advance was creating.

At v. 7 DI makes the pun upon the word rendered in v. 6 by '*Take courage*' or just 'cheer up'; for it is the same verb as that meaning *encourage*. By this means our author makes his message more telling and expressive. Yet English cannot reproduce the vitality of DI's language. His whole picture is a comment on what he has already said at 40:19-20 about the futility and stupidity of making one's own gods.

8   Suddenly DI's message changes. He has been describing above how Cyrus the Persian monarch is the instrument of God's plan; the nature of that plan, however, he has not as yet revealed. What he has to say now is even more surprising than what he has already reported, yet it too must be part of the Good News. His message is that the poor, stricken, downtrodden, exiled people of Israel is God's real instrument. Israel is no less than, first, *my servant*; second, God's *chosen* one. Yet DI has God address Israel here as Jacob. He is evidently reminding his people that they are the true son of their father Jacob the unlikable, as we read of him in Genesis. DI's declaration can be paraphrased at this point with words from the NT (John 15:16): 'You did not chose me, but I chose you', adding, 'but I chose you, because Jacob is the grandson of Abraham my friend' (cf. Gen. 15:18; 2 Chron. 20:7; Jas. (2:23). DI employs the word 'seed' (rather than *offspring*) as a collective singular. He makes God address all Israel as one single, collective entity.

9 Though not mentioned at this point, it is now obvious that the city of Jerusalem is in DI's mind; for it is from above it that God sends forth his voice. Jerusalem, as Ezekiel had believed, was the navel of the earth. Thus from the point of view of Jerusalem, both Egypt and Mesopotamia lay at *the ends of the earth*. DI is saying that God has already been faithful to Abraham's descendants when he called them out of Egypt in days of old. He is therefore to be trusted to look after the contemporary generation that is now in Babylon. Thus the significant element in God's election of Israel is affirmed twice.

The term 'servant of the king' is a Near Eastern technical term for a royal official. Many a jar and seal revealed by excavation have these very words stamped on them. The name 'servant' occurs also imposed upon the weaker party in a covenant relationship, generally in the Near East, such as conquering kings laid upon their fiefs. Israel therefore knew what she was meant to be when God the king called her to be his Servant. She was called, in short, within the Covenant, to serve unquestioningly and eagerly, and to be ever ready to execute the will of her royal master.

Israel, however, is here called to be God's Servant in a unique capacity. So DI raises the issue of the mystery of the divine election. Why is it that God has 'elected' or *'chosen'* Israel *and not cast you off*, so that he could never have rejected her? Why not any other nation on the face of the earth? DI does not need to discuss the mystery, since Deut. 7, which has already dealt with it, was written well before the Exile. In light of such a discussion, therefore, DI cannot imply that a nation such as Babylon was outside God's purpose and care. The Babylonians were just as much in the grasp of God as was Israel, yet only at the level of the experience of the divine which they had reached. Their religion was a distorted religion, but it was not irreligion. This fact prevented the election of Israel from being made wholly in isolation; and it enabled the chosen people to make contact with their pagan neighbours. But it equated the religion of Babylon, which here has a small degree of positive value, with the negation that is the opposite of God's purpose of love. We shall see later (at 47:10) how DI deals with this interesting contradiction.

DI therefore lays full emphasis not on Israel herself as the elect, but on election as the action of God alone: *whom I have chosen ... whom I took* 'firm hold of'. The verb is much stronger than the RSV rendering *took*. The phrase took firm hold of is another of our author's highly pregnant phrases. It focuses our eye upon, first, the action of gripping the hand,

31

and, second, the action of leading by the hand that is now held tight. Then the words *you whom ... I called from* [the earth's] *farthest corners* remind Israel that God has led them before now from faraway Egypt into the Promised Land. God had thus called Israel from service to Pharaoh to enter into free, responsible service to himself (cf. Ex. 3:12). This service was the service of one whom God called his *friend* (v. 8); and as Deut. 4:37 had explicitly stated, this meant that God in his turn loved this whole people whom he had chosen. That of course was an extraordinary notion for anyone in the ancient world to entertain. Imagine any one of Babylon's gilt-plastered gods loving individual poor peasants huddled in their sordid mud huts on the banks of the Euphrates.

10   But Israel's God includes in his Word of love the call that echoes through the pages of both the Old and New Testaments: *Fear not*, or don't be afraid (cf. 41:13-14; 43:1, 5; 44:2, 8; 54:4; also 51:7, 12). This is surely good news to those (1) who are in the depths of despair and in fear of what man can do to them, and (2) who have become aware that they are standing on holy ground, because they are now in the presence of the all-holy and ever-living God who tells them, *For I am with you*. No wonder, therefore, that DI's next words are 'Don't gape in fear', or, *Be not dismayed*. For here we are presented with an amazing exegesis of election. Election, DI infers, means to be bound up *with* the God of heaven and earth. DI may be making explicit reference to God's words at Ex. 3:12, when he said to Moses 'But I will be *with* you'. And God's declaration 'I will be' is to be linked in turn with the words of divine self-revelation two verses later at Ex. 3:14. The words 'I will be' are identical in Hebrew with the 'I am' of v. 14, though rendered differently in English. Martin Noth declares 'It is in any case important to note that the verb *hyh* does not express pure "being", pure "existing", but an "active being" which does not take place just anywhere, but makes its appearance in the world of men and primarily in the history of Israel'. (G. A. F. Knight; *Exodus: A Commentary*, p. 45; *A Christian Theology of the Old Testament* and *Theology as Narration*.) The verb *hyh* bears the sense of becoming rather than of being. When this verb is used of God, it exhibits the purposeful, creative essence of his Being. Unite this concept with the preposition 'with', and the words 'I shall become with you' then appear as the essence of the divine plan that is to unfold within God's covenant relationship with Israel. In addition, since God has laid hold on Israel, something must have happened not only to Israel but also to God. The mutual relationship within the covenant must necessarily affect both parties to it. The last words of the line — 'I am supporting you with my saving right hand; rather than *will uphold* and *victorious* (see at 41:2) — define in what direction God's dynamic action is moving. God's essence is to save, i.e., to bring about a state of rightness, normality, justice, as we shall see at 45:18.

Another point to note about Israel's election is that though it is God who has chosen Israel *first*, his choice does not preclude the necessity of Israel's choosing him in return, in joyous response to his act (cf. Josh. 24:22). It is just this factor of Israel's responsive choice of Yahweh which prevents the biblical doctrine of election from postulating any view of divine predestination such as would overrule the human will. Jeremiah (1:5) could believe that God had elected him while he was still in his mother's womb, and DI can believe that Israel is called to be God's servant before she could know what her task and calling are to be. But in choosing to call the elect people first Jacob and then second Israel, DI reveals how OT thinkers such as he are able to hold this balance between predestination and free will. God had indeed called Jacob before he was born; for Jacob was the grandson of the Abraham to whom God had given his promise. Yet just like the infant child of Christian parents who has been presented for baptism, Jacob later could and did object to his calling, and could and did rebel against the gracious purpose of his God for him. Yet even while he remained in a state of rebellion, he continued to be the called of God. Then came the night when he wrestled with the angelic manifestation of God's presence 'with' him, and in full freedom of will had 'striven with God ... and ... prevailed' (Gen. 32:28). It was only then that Jacob gained the new name of Israel. In those days the name, ideally at least, was meant to be a description of its owner. That is why Jacob now received a new name, for he had become a new man.

It is not important to discover the real etymological origin of this word 'Israel'. Our concern is to know how the later OT writers used it and what *they* imagined its meaning to be: Gen. 32:28 takes it to mean 'he who strives with God'. Yet we are to note that Jacob — and therefore all Israel, the people of God *in* Jacob — is found striving with God in freedom of will only within the context of the relationship which God has already imposed upon him. Thus we may say that Almighty God can and does weave into his great plan every action of sinful Israel, even when, in complete freedom and in a spirit of

33

rebellion, she continues to obstruct and to fight against the evolution of his loving purpose. God does not therefore rule Israel so much as overrule her. Thus the exile is not rejection on God's part but an element in the saving plan. 'How could I ever have rejected you? Would I not then have broken My Covenant?' And finally God reaches his goal *despite* Israel, and in face of, and even by means of, her continuing enmity to and apostasy from him and his love. So in calling her freely to give up all fear and to trust his 'saving' *right hand*, God exhibits towards Israel his sovereign grace.

11-12 *Behold*, says God again; look and realize how all those who are fighting against Israel are fighting against the gracious purpose of God *in* Israel. This must be so, since God is 'with' her, in the unique sense noted above. The prophets had long since claimed that God can be only either with or against his people. There is no third way he can act (cf. Hos. 1:9, 10; Amos 3:1; Isa. 7:14; 8:8, 10). To be *incensed* is to grow hot and burn, or as we might say in today's jargon, 'all who get het up against you'. Since the verb can carry this meaning, some would vowel it so as to read 'those who snort with indignation at you'. Thereupon, *those who contend with you*, that is, who have brought a case against you before the world assize which DI has already described (41:1) will hang their heads with shame, and be accounted with those who are pure negation.

13 So fundamentally Israel need never be afraid. Her God is the living God; and it is the living God who is even now holding her by her right hand. The faithfulness, or reliability, or rock-like quality of God is thus conveyed to Israel whom God holds; and this becomes in turn the basis of her whole life and historical existence, no matter what contradictions she may have to face in days to come.

> Let me no more my comfort draw
> From my frail hold of thee:
> In this alone rejoice with awe —
> Thy mighty grasp of me.
> (From John Campbell Shairp's hymn, 'Twixt gleams of joy and clouds of doubt'.)

The above is said by DI not once as here, but again and again. This call not to be afraid is one of the basic elements in OT revelation.

34

14 Here we return to the feminine form of 'you', for the reason that the word for *worm* is feminine. DI now gives us an astonishing line. He has been emphasizing the wonder of God's grace for a sinful people descended from the sinner Jacob. But now he makes God say *You worm Jacob, you men of Israel*. Those who opposed God's plan are negative, in that they are against God. On the other hand, Israel has no cause for boasting, merely because she knows herself to be the chosen people. But *you men of Israel* may be better rendered by 'you louse Israel', thus putting 'louse' in poetic parallel with 'worm'. Yet what a couple of words for God to use! *You louse Israel* is a much stronger expression than our modern 'You lousy Israelites', for the emphasis is upon Israel's smallness, unimportance, and bestiality. The word *methey* in the Hebrew text has long been a puzzle. It may mean just 'men of', but if so, it is a very weak parallel to *worm*. Some expositors therefore have suggested it means 'little group of men'. Three important ancient versions translate it by a form of the word 'dead'. This translation should not be dismissed out of hand, as most interpreters do. If it is valid, then in the light of the discussion later at 42:24 and 43:28 we might say here 'you dead Israelites'. Others have invented a parallel to the word *worm* and understand the word for 'grub'. Their intention may have been correct, it seems, for it is only in this generation that an Akkadian word has become known to us — and it was the language of Israel's Babylonian masters — a word built from the same consonants as the Hebrew word for 'men of'. It is this word meaning *louse*. Perhaps then DI is merely quoting the term that the Babylonians used when they referred to conquered and depressed Israel. Yet the phrase may be an instance of DI's fondness for the *double entendre*. By it he could be suggesting that Israel in exile has become a corpse, as Ezekiel had already done (37:11-13), so that as a corpse Israel is also to be pictured in terms of worms and grubs. However that may be, it is the name that God himself gives to Israel. The word *worm*, however, occurs also in Ps. 22:6, where we have 'I am a worm, and no man'. If it is the case that our Lord repeated this whole Psalm on the cross and not just the first line, 'My God, my God, why hast thou forsaken me' (a sentence which is only the key to the whole), then we are presented with a challenging problem in our christology. For in both Ps. 22 and at Isa. 41:14 it is undoubtedly *Israel* that is the worm. An aspect of Jesus' self-emptying was his identifying himself with all Israel and her calling. But now we see he identified himself not just with Israel the first-born (LXX Luke 3:22 'beloved') son (Ex. 4:22), but actually with Israel the *worm*.

35

In the light of the above, the gracious words that follow have all the deeper intent: literally '"It is I who have been helping you" (fem.) is the very Word of the Lord, your Redeemer' — the redeemer of a louse!

These words contain an ultimate insight. They contain the truth that between God and Man there is a great gulf fixed. Men say that man is after all really quite good morally speaking, that he is able in his own strength to build an equitable society, that he is essentially capable of rising to meet God and of lifting himself by his own boot-straps. In the light of DI's words we see how such beliefs are nothing short of blasphemy. Worms cannot behave except as worms; they cannot raise themselves from crawling on the ground. On the other hand, if by God's grace man can become aware that he is a worm, then God can begin to do something with him.

DI now uses three designations for God. (1) He is Yahweh, *the Lord*, the covenant God, who has promised to be faithful to his chosen instrument, even if that people should be in reality, as DI says, a worm or a louse. (2) He is Israel's *Redeemer*. This is a word with a long association for Israel in the ordinary affairs of life under the Law of Moses. First, it could mean avenger of blood (Num. 35:12, etc). But second, the word was used for the male next-of-kin of a widow whose husband had newly died. A single woman could scarcely have maintained herself in ancient Hebrew society. She had necessarily to belong to a family group. So this *go'el* invited the widow into his home. The book of Ruth deals with this ancient practice; in it we see Boaz, as was the custom in the days of the Judges, graciously receiving the widowed Ruth into his home when the rightful next-of-kin was unwilling to do so. Third, the word is used in Lev. 25:48-49 of redeeming slaves and in Lev. 25:25-26 of redeeming even property as well as persons. It is understandable therefore why the verb *ga'al* (redeem) is a favourite word with DI, and why he uses it to describe the consistently loving and gracious activity of God. (3) God is *the Holy One of Israel*. This is a title of God first used by Isaiah of Jerusalem, when he took the ancient word 'holy' and gave it a new moral content. The word is as old as the Hebrew language, and was applied originally to cultic objects that were ceremonially set apart from profane usage. So it came to emphasize the great otherness of God from mortal man. But Isaiah gave this otherness a content that it had never possessed before. For Israel could easily have conceived of the divine otherness in terms of mere negative difference from man. But Isaiah had declared: 'The Holy God shows himself holy in righteousness' (5:16). In other words,

Isaiah made the great declaration that God's holiness is in reality his goodness, or better still, his saving purpose for man.

But DI transcends the thought of his master Isaiah. His word 'holy' stands here in the construct state. That means it is construed as virtually one word with the noun it governs. Thus '*Holy* (the word 'One' is not in the Hebrew) *of Israel*' is one concept. And the word Israel has been newly defined in terms of worm and louse. By means of the accident of this composite form of speech, DI daringly offers a paradox such as no human mind could have invented, arguing that the utterly other and good God is the God-of-the-louse-Israel.

15-16 Still another paradox follows. It is hard to imagine a louse or a worm acting as *a threshing sledge*. The threshing sledge was a flat piece of wood studded on the underside with *teeth*, or spikes. Domestic animals dragged this implement over the wheat piled on the ground of the farmyard. But Israel is here called to be just such an implement herself to *thresh the mountains* and *hills*; evidently she is called upon to grind these to *chaff* or dust; and this chaff Israel will not even need to sweep away, for the wind — God's wind — will do it for her.

What does this curious metaphor imply? First, the mountains and hills seem to be the difficulties lying in the way of God's purpose that has to come to fruition in Israel. Probably the phrase is the base of the similar NT phrase which speaks of a faith that can remove mountains. On the other hand, it is sin that is always declared to be the real obstacle to God's advance, not just mere difficulties and vexations. So again we have the kind of metaphor which the NT employs when it declares that 'the powers of death shall not prevail against it (the Church)' (Matt. 16:18). In that passage the Church is shown to be synonymous with the people of God. Here in DI's writings, it is Israel that is the people of God. Clearly Israel is not meant to conquer Babylon in battle. The idea is absurd. First, though Israel *is* the army, the *tsaba*, of the Lord, this is only in the sense employed today by that gallant section of the Christian Church known as the Salvation Army. Second, if a louse is to have all this strength, it is obvious that such strength cannot be her own but must be God's. If Israel can then actually exert God's strength through her own arms, then the next promise does not sound strange or unreal: Then *you shall rejoice in the Lord; in the Holy One of Israel you shall glory*. Thus the joy of God, as he works out his plan of salvation through Israel, becomes communicated to Israel herself. The verb *rejoice, gil*, DI uses to represent not an

37

ordinary but an eschatological joy. This is evident when we recognize that he uses the verb in a figure that parallels the last judgment motif, when there comes the separation of the wheat from the chaff. Apart from the motif of judgment, however, the theme of rejoicing in Yahweh is one that is fundamental to the OT.

There is an important issue to note here. It is that Israel is to be the instrument of God's judgment upon the nations and upon the forces of evil in the world. DI has nothing at all to say about any messianic figure such as we read of in the works of Isaiah of Jerusalem. We wonder whether DI knew the words of our Ps. 80, for that Psalm was composed either during the Babylonian exile or, according to Artur Weiser's *Commentary on the Psalms*, earlier. For in Ps. 80:17 'the son of man whom thou hast made strong for thyself' seems to be identified with the people of God whom God long before had brought up from Egypt and planted in the Promised Land. Here then the Son of man is the corporate people of Israel. But now DI adds that it is this corporate Son of man who is to be the instrument of judgment upon the nations. Ought not we today to read the words of Matt. 25:31 ff, in the light of this verse before us?

17-18   We are not told who the poor and needy are. Certainly in the first place they comprise crestfallen Israel in exile. But they also comprise the destitute cities of Judah, whose people had survived in poverty since the fall of the state in 587 B.C. (cf. Jer. 12:7-13; 14:2-9; Lam. 5:4-5). Yet the picture here must also describe all of the wretched sons of men everywhere and at all times. So there follows another eschatological picture. It is similar to many in the OT such as those at Isa. 35; Ezek. 47; and herein at 43:18-21; 48:21; 49:9-11; 55:13. In accordance with his genius, DI has already hinted that he will develop this metaphor later (see 40:10-11). Note three points once again in connection with the wilderness theme. First, it spoke to the Israelites of spiritual stagnation, of an inner state of need for God. Thus the call to slake one's thirst in God was naturally understood in a spiritual sense (cf. 55:1; John 4:14; 7:37-38). Second, however, the theme was no airy sentimental concept. It rested upon the factual memory of how Yahweh had already given his people water in the wilderness journey under Moses. Its sweetness was peculiarly welcome in contrast to the waters of Egypt, which God adulterated because of Pharaoh's unbelief. Third, the two concepts had already been combined by DI's predecessors among the prophets, whose works DI would know. They had declared that if Israel were disobedient, and refused God's spiritual sustenance, then Israel's goodly land itself would become a desert (Hos. 2:12; Isa. 5:1-7; 7:23-25; Jer. 12:7-13; Ezek. 6:14; 12:20; 33:29). (All these may be subsumed under one *Gattung*, based possibly on the words to be found in 1 Kings 8:35.) This is due to the fact that the concept of desert or wilderness could represent in Israel's thinking the chaos that was there in the beginning (Gen. 1:2), and which God continues to employ as his instrument of judgment and mercy. But now, as DI announces, Israel's God will enter into dialogue (*answer*) with his people once again, for their good and not for evil; for out of their present evil situation he will actually produce good, just as water can bring life to a parched desert.

19   Could we therefore make the inference from DI's declaration that he believed God was going to make even chaos praise him? Yet DI probably does not infer as much here. We should not press the picture to reveal more than it is — a poetic representation of God's creative purpose, as the latter increases and grows even as the power of his Word takes effect. On the other hand the chaotic hearts of men are included in the wilderness theme. DI draws no line between God's actions in creation and his actions in redemption; for in DI's view, to speak of redemption is virtually another way of referring to re-creation. God's first creation DI knew was good. He would agree with the annalist in Genesis who pictured the newly created world as paradise. That is why, once the judgment spoken of at v. 15 has fallen, DI presents us with a vision of God's purpose at its completion as paradise regained. The useful trees mentioned will then replace the thorns and thistles characteristic of the wilderness, and which are typical of 'Paradise Lost' (cf. Gen. 3:18). This theme too DI has developed from the works of his predecessors (cf. Isa. 2:1-5, 11:1-9; Hos. 2:16-19). His successors learned it from him in their turn (cf. Isa. 65:17; 66:22; 25:6).

20   Only God, he declares, can do all this — only Israel's God. And he will do it in order that the whole world of men *may see* and *know*, that is, 'take it in'. And this poor, dispirited worm Israel is to be the instrument whereby this transformation of the universe is to take place. So it must necessarily be Yahweh who is the Creator of this great redemption. He will do it by stooping to make use of that peculiar chosen people, whom he has just addressed as worm and louse.

21   The gods of the nations are now called upon to defend themselves. In his quality as King, God is also Judge. Yet DI's tenses infer that Yahweh never ceases to present such a summons. *Proofs* really means the entrenchments or bulwarks on which one relies.

22   The truth, God now declares, can easily be reached since it can be tested by facts. But of course neither idols nor those whose philosophy is idolatrous possess any clue to an exposition of the meaning of history. Yet Yahweh humbly invites man to set forth his philosophical notions. Listening to Babylon's man-made theories, however, Israel is to learn with DI's help that the Babylonian religion is in the last resort merely a form of star-gazing, and star-gazing is a futile activity. Israel's God, *the King of Jacob*, on the other hand, has a plan working out through history which will find its ultimate *outcome* or fruition in God's good time. It becomes obvious, as the court proceeds, that this plan of God has had a beginning — what DI calls his 'primal events' (RSV, *the former things*) — at that point in Israel's history when God raised up Moses to be his prophet. Israel's history, since it has had a purposeful beginning, is thus meaningful history. It is what we today call *Heilsgeschichte* or 'Sacred History'. The Babylonian nation had no beginning in this sense, and therefore its continued story cannot be regarded as *Heilsgeschichte* as can Israel's. The nations are consequently summoned to apply their intelligence to this fact, and to think through its significance for the world, just as we must do today.

23   Babylon's gods stare dumbly back at their worshippers when they ask them what the future holds. Therefore they are morally impotent. *Do good or do harm*, that is, 'Do anything at all, just to show you are alive; better to do *harm* than to do nothing. Behave as divine beings should. If you do, we'll gladly worship you, even in awe and terror. Only, act! But you can't, for you don't even exist in the first place.'

24   Thus the man who consciously chooses an idol as his god in face of that elementary fact must be *an abomination*, repugnant to both God and Israel. Originally this word meant 'belonging in the area of the *tabu*', and so, something like 'beyond the pale'. It is in this sense that Babylon had chosen her gods. DI is saying that they did not choose Babylon: it was Babylon who chose them. Yet Yahweh undoubtedly chose Israel. Thus Yahweh rightly has power over Israel. Contrariwise, Babylon assumes that she has power over her gods. For she has deified the state!

25   How different Israel's God is from any god that a man can manipulate: not only is he the living God — and thus not mere static Being — he is also the active, purposeful, creative One, who is constantly revealing himself in some form of saving activity. The evidence of this at the moment is the victorious advance of Cyrus. Cyrus *is coming . . . He shall trample* down all opposition in the creative way that the potter tramples the clay. How much more, DI means us to realize, must Cyrus' Maker be both the living the creative God. *Stirred up* is a strong term, for it throws responsibility for all Cyrus' actions upon Yahweh. In fact, if God has been calling him by name then he is no less than Yahweh's child, and Yahweh is responsible for him, as is declared clearly at 45:3. On the other hand, the Hebrew vowelling, with the RSV, is '*he shall call on my name*'. If this second reading is correct, what it says is to be regarded as the exaggeration of enthusiasm, for Cyrus never did acknowledge Yahweh to be *the* God, so far as we know. Yet DI is here looking to the outcone of Yahweh's coming action rather than to the state of Cyrus' mind either then or later. For DI's hope is that all men will know the Lord once the coming events have reached their victorious conclusion. The LXX also gives us an overenthusiastic translation, for it asserts that the inhabitants of the North and East are also to be called by God's name.

26   The Babylonian priests had given no sure oracle about the coming of Cyrus. On the other hand, ever since the days of Moses — *from the beginning* — Yahweh had planned the advance of this Persian conqueror. DI means that when God first chose Israel under Moses, he had already foreseen what he would have to do centuries later; for Israel would later need to be disciplined by exile and then renewed through the instrumentality of a particular human agent whom God would rouse up at the right moment.

27-28   Now God draws attention to the fact that none of the Babylonian gods has come alive or spoken at the court to which they had been summoned, so that there is no one else besides himself as a *counsellor* to give *an answer*, to produce a plan.

Isaiah of Jerusalem had already used the word 'plan' in his day, and now DI delights to employ it in his turn.

29   The last line of DI's effective strophe comes to a striking conclusion by the repetition of the now obvious fact (cf. v. 24) that the gods of the nations are as fatuous as are their priests. Yet the end of those gods is not to take place at once. The mills of God grind slowly. But DI's revelation of the inanity of the gods certainly spelled the beginning of the end of idolatry.

It is interesting that these verses are in the style of a Babylonian letter written from a superior to an inferior. DI must therefore have been sufficiently well educated, first, to read the Babylonian language and, second, to appreciate what he was reading. In him we have indeed Israel's Milton or Dante, for he is fully capable of writing in verse a complete theological treatise. Yet DI surpasses both those masters of the art, because his treatise is an existential and not just an academic work. Unlike the other poets, DI did not know the end of the story which he was interpreting from the beginning. The end, about which he now begins to speak, through the power of the Spirit, unfolds its meaning for him only as Cyrus advances toward the gates of Babylon, and only as he becomes aware in his heart, even before the great moment of release arrives, that God is even then using the sufferings of Israel for his plan.

CHAPTER 42

1 DI has mentioned before Israel's calling to be Yahweh's servant
(41:8-9). He may have taken the concept, not, as we have seen, from
pagan custom, but from the Song of Moses, Deut. 32:36, and possibly
from Ps. 135:14. Now he develops his theme. Jeremiah and Ezekiel
had both already described Israel by this title (Jer. 30:10; 46:27-28;
Ezek. 28:25; 37:25). DI now puts it at the centre of his argument (cf.
43:10; 44:1-2; 45:4; 49:3-7). The title was that held by a royal
plenipotentiary among Israel's neighbours, and so was a title of
honour. It implied executive power in the king's name and by his
authority, but it also implied total and absolute obedience on the
Servant's part. The root '*-b-d*, to serve, contains two elements: action
and obedience. In fact, 'Servant of Yahweh', seems about equivalent
to 'Son of Yahweh' as it applies to the king in Ps. 2:7. Yahweh used
many servants. The stars were his servants, for they were his 'host', like
the soldiers of a general (40:26; 45:12). Cyrus the king was his servant,
(44:28; 45:1), *whom victory meets at every step* (41:2). Isaiah had called
himself God's servant (20:3). But the Servant Israel is delineated here
in total contrast to all other servants of God. The word *behold*, as a
demonstrative interjection, marks the transition to a new subject and
fixes our attention on the significance of the word *Servant* as it occurs
here.

Israel is presently a pariah, sweating in a slave-labour camp and
therefore totally unlike a royal vizier. And yet, DI wants us to see,
Israel *is* a royal vizier. This is not because Israel has any value *per se*,
but wholly because God *upholds* him, or better, is grasping him firmly,
now that he has selected him from all other possible servants to execute
his will. To that end, moreover, he has put his *Spirit upon him* (cf. 11:2).
Thus it is clear that Israel is no longer 'not-my-people' but is truly
'*my people*' (40:1), as DI said at the beginning. Other nations were
accustomed to the idea of upholding their gods. Here is something new
for Israel to understand, for this verb 'to uphold, or grasp' with God
the Good Shepherd as the subject, takes on the overtone almost of
cuddling in the arms. There follow two contrasting yet perfectly
compatible concepts:

1. God's *soul*, his whole being — his *nephesh* — *delights* in Israel (cf. Mark 1:11; Matt. 17:5). In other words Israel is the elect, the chosen one, for the simple reason that God has fallen in love with Israel, it might be said. The mystery of election is well figured by such a phrase. To the eyes of an onlooker it appears to be a complete mystery why a young man should fall in love with one particular girl when she has several equally attractive sisters. DI would know the Deuteronomic discussion of this mystery (Deut. 4:36-37; 7:6-8). Part of the mystery is that the word 'chosen' implies a prior test on the part of the chooser. Moses for example is spoken of in this way (Ps. 106:23). DI applies it now to Israel with reference, *inter alia*, to the call of Abraham, whom God did indeed test (Isa. 41:8; 44:1-2; 45:4). The word Servant is used elsewhere for individuals both within and without Israel, for such as Moses, the prophets (Amos 3:7), Nebuchadrezzar (Jer. 27:6), David the beloved king (cf. 2 Sam. 3:18), and so for the messianic David who is still to come (Hag. 2:23; Ezek. 34:23 ff.). In conformity with this last view of the word Servant, the Jewish Targum that arose in the early Christian centuries interpreted the word as it occurs here by saying he was *meshihi*, meaning 'my anointed' or 'my Messiah'. That is to say, as head of Israel, David bears the messianic function attached to Israel as a whole people. Thus it is Israel as a whole, the chosen people as a whole *in* David, whom DI regards as the Servant of God. So the concept '*in* David' reconciles for modern man the problem of how the Servant could be both singular and plural at the same time, and helps us in our approach to an understanding of ch. 53.

2. The second concept is this. Israel is chosen not merely for her own good but in order to do what a servant is meant to do, to *serve*. Israel's service is to bring *justice*, the true way of life, to the rest of the world. *Mishpat*, translated here as *justice*, represents the conception of a rule or law for life. So it points to the idea that God has revealed the right way for men to live together as brethren in peace and concord. Its root meaning has to do with the idea of judging, so the noun that we have here signifies the entirety of judgments that God has already delivered (cf. 51:4; Jer. 5:4-5). *Mishpat* certainly does not mean 'religion' in the modern sense of the word, for nowadays the word religion describes only one area or department of human life, its spiritual element, as modern man supposes, over against the everyday material affairs that occupy his attention. The word is used at Ex. 21:1 and at Deut. 12:1, for example, to mean a collection of laws. Elsewhere it seems to cover at different times such areas as 'religion plus law',

'faith plus custom', even the concepts 'truth', 'revelation' and 'righteousness'. Since DI is leading up in his argument to explaining the words 'the good news', we have to regard this single term *mishpat* as including all the ideas found in the words: 'The new, righteous, saving way of life that is the revealed judgment of God'. The Servant is to be the channel whereby this revelation of God's loving purpose for all men can reach them. To sum up — in himself the Servant Israel counts for nothing; yet Israel's God, acting in conformity with his saving purpose, has chosen this pariah and is actually now holding him up; it is God therefore who has empowered him to be what he is called to be, for by himself he is quite unable to fulfil his calling.

Since, however, this wholesome way of life is not to be mediated in a vacuum, Israel herself is called to be more than the mere mouthpiece of God. Two points arise here, showing what she is meant to be. In the first place Israel is an empirical people, a people that lives within history. She is therefore condemned to face the vexations and tribulations that all men must face who live in a fallen world. Second, Israel is shown to be nothing in her own right, for she does not exist apart from her function, from her reason for existing. Apart from that she would be what the gods are — mere negation. Thus the 'Israel' idea is to be equated with the idea of mission as such (cf. Jer. 15:19), a mission, however, that is motivated by the Spirit and which takes form within a given area of space and time. The awful judgment lying upon Israel therefore is that, should she reject her calling, she will revert to sheer negation.

So then God has quietly *put* his Spirit upon his Servant to create a kind of sacramental union. The Servant then obeys the Spirit quietly and gently. On other occasions we meet with strong actions connected with the Spirit. The commonest verb used is that God 'pours' his Spirit (Isa. 29:10; Ezek. 39:29; Joel 2:28-29). DI uses this idea at 44:3, and it is copied at 61:1 with the word 'anointed'. Judg. 6:34 provides us with the fascinating picture of God's Spirit clothing himself with Gideon, as again with Zechariah at 2 Chron. 24:20. Whatever the action pictured by the use of a particular verb, DI does not conceive of the Spirit as something separate from God. To him the Spirit is *God in action*, as at 48:16, or even as *God in mission*.

2-3 What then is Israel's function? Curiously enough, it too is negation. It may be that the positive functions of God's other servant, the mighty Cyrus, are sketched as they are in 41:25, in order to offer a foil to the function that God has decreed for Israel. Three negatives in succession emphasize that Israel's wisdom, Israel's native strength, Israel's self-acquired knowledge, all of which are aspects of the threshing sledge powers of the domineering human ego, are of no value to God at all (41:15).

4 So now we are given the first indication of the important theme that DI will later unfold, that the way the Spirit chooses to operate is the way of self-emptying and not of self-assertion, and that it is by that means and not another that the Servant will reveal to the whole world the revelation for which it is longing. The word *torah*, revelation, here is not of course to be equated with the later meaning of the word when it is fully identified with the Pentateuch or the *law* of Moses.

On the other hand, since the revelation spoken of here is revelation of the eternal God, then Torah too must be eternal. The pictorial language of the rabbis, who in later centuries could speak of God studying the Torah each day in heaven, is thus not far removed from DI's world of thought. Such a 'midrash' is designed to protect the OT vision of God from misrepresentation. For God is not lawless power. He is capable of doing only what he wills to do — and that will of his is made known to man through the revelation of his loving, saving purpose. Moreover, the Servant is not only to *speak* the revelation, he is to incorporate it in himself; he is to *be* it. This gives Israel a vicarious role in the history of mankind. This surprising declaration is emphasized firmly at 49:6.

The above is not the accepted interpretation of the well-known words *A bruised reed he will not break*. The familiar English translation suggests that the Servant will not quench whatever good he finds in heathen hearts, but will gently fan it into flames. That meaning of vv. 3-4 may be obtained from the Hebrew, provided that the strophe at 42:1-4 is regarded as a separate utterance of the prophet unconnected with its context. But if we recognize that DI is offering us a sustained argument in this developing theological treatise, then we must interpret each section of his poem in the light of his whole argument as it reaches us in all his sixteen chapters. For this reason the Hebrew word that occurs in v. 3, *le'emeth*, has been translated by *faithfully*. This faithful way is evidently the way of renunciation. Thus, instead of choosing to fan the feeble flames, the Servant is meant to sit down alongside the brokenhearted just where they are to be found, in the mire of this human life of ours; and in this way, by his very presence with them, he will become the instrument by which a strength and hope that is not their own will be transferred to them. He is to do this thing, moreover, just because God himself does it (40:29; 57:15; 66:2), and the Servant cannot be above his Master. Moreover, God's *Spirit upon him* will be the guarantee that this way will be effective. V. 4 deliberately and for effect applies to the Servant the verbs that are used in v. 3 of the world as it lies in need. This means that the crushing which the Servant is to experience will not, nay cannot, go too far, for God's Spirit is resting upon him, and God is always in control. This, then, is what mission means.

5 Yahweh is the God who speaks, and in speaking continually creates — this is an active participle. This verbal form is not recognized by the RSV. That is to say, he creates by uttering his Word. We know more today about an expanding universe than DI could ever have guessed. He can only speak of God beating out the earth in the way that a silversmith makes a lump of silver expand until it is large enough to bend and so to evolve into the shape of a bowl.

6 But God is also personal. He is 'I Yahweh', rather than *I am the Lord*. This verse safeguards the doctrine of election, which DI introduced at 42:1-2 above, from leading to the conception of favouritism. God has chosen and called Israel, DI says, for a purpose: she is to be the agent of his plan of love, *tsedeq*. This same word occurs at 45:13 where it applies to the call of Cyrus. The root of *tsedeq* comprehends two notions. The first is that of being normal, although it is doubtful whether DI knew that the word he was handling had this basic meaning, for in his day that sense applied only to such things as weights and measures. The transitive form of the verb from this root could then be understood to mean 'to render normal'. This is the verb which the AV frequently renders as 'justify'. The state of sin is abnormal, however. For the norm is what man knew and experienced before he fell into sin in the Garden of Eden. Thus 'to render normal' must also mean 'to make righteous', and that is why eventually, and with the NT, it can mean 'to justify'.

Tsedeq then includes within it the concept of rightness. But God's rightness or righteousness, like his holy love, necessarily involves (1) his righteous dealing with sin and evil, and (2) his saving man out of his negation *into* God's joyous, wholesome way of life. That is why both of God's chosen instruments, both Cyprus and Israel, both State and

Church, we could say, are used by God to establish his rule of saving love. Here, the soteriological emphasis is central to DI's argument.

In a Unitarian conception of God, where there is no subject-object relation within the Godhead, the idea of creation inevitably comes to mean that the world is the necessary object of the divine activity . . . and God is subjected to external necessity. If however there are hypostatic distractions within the Godhead, we can find in God the possibility of creative action without introducing such necessity (L. S. Thornton in *Essays Catholic and Critical*, ed. E. G. Selwyn 1926, pp. 145-146). God does not require the Nature he has created for his own fulfilment or perfection. While the universe without him is mere negation, yet without his universe God is still God. On the other hand, his being-as-God is revealed to man, as DI saw, not in terms of natural theology but in terms of saving love. Such alone is the ground of Israel's election. Thus we are led to recognize that, in a sense beyond the logic of our thought, the chosen people of Israel, as God's mission through the Spirit to the world, is the necessary vehicle of his Word. For that Word was then in the process of becoming with man, since a vehicle such as a people was necessary to God for the fulfilment of his own perfect purpose.

The words *as a covenant to the people* are not easy to interpret, and so here experts differ. The poetic parallelism of the verse, however, should help us. For Israel is to be *a light for the nations*. So I would suggest our phrase means 'A people with whom God has made covenant for the good of the nations'.

Israel has been chosen, then, not with the object of being saved, nor merely in order to be the covenant people as an end in itself, but in covenant relationship with God, to be the channel whereby the world may be saved (cf. Luke 2:31-32). Humanity in God's eyes is one entity, even though, as one ancient writer was aware, it shows a tendency to fragment (cf. Gen. 11:9). As such it is the single object of God's concern. DI's language at vv. 5-6 is strongly reminiscent of the creation narratives of both P and J in Genesis. After creating the world, according to Gen. 2:7, God breathed the breath of life into man (cf. 42:5). But like his predecessor Ezekiel, DI understands the function of the breath of God or the Spirit of God soteriologically rather than ontologically, on the ground that, as in Ezek. 37, the Spirit of God has primarily a re-creative function.

7   This re-creative, or saving purpose, is actually meant to become flesh in and through Israel's obedience in mission. The illustrations used are typical of the whole biblical revelation, in that the poor and the depressed classes among men are to be the special object of God's continuing concern. So the poverty stricken exiles must have felt comforted indeed to discover that in their *dungeon* and in their *prison* God was concerned for them still. King Jehoiachin had spent many years in prison (2 Kings 25:27-30). DI's audience would all know this fact. And they would remember that in the thirty-seventh year of the Exile, King Evilmerodach had finally brought Jehoiachin out and restored him to favour (Jer. 52:31-34). The exiles would thus realize DI's right to build a metaphor from an historical situation.

Finally, another word from Gen. 1:3, viz., *light*. Light is the opposite of chaos or negation (cf. 41:29). Thus out of darkness Isaiah (9:1-2) had expected that light would shine as it had done in the beginning. Through the hands and mouths of the chosen Servant people, light is to shine once again, re-creatively, into the dark places of a stricken world. In fact, in passages we shall meet later, the word *light* may be found in poetic parallel with the word 'salvation'. It is interesting to note that this language would not come as too great a surprise to the educated among the exiles in Babylon. This is because vv. 6-7 echo a frequently repeated concept that occurs in what even in DI's day were then ancient Akkadian hymns with a royal messianic ideology.

8 God's saving purpose is now identified with the *name* that describes his essence. For the theologians who have given us the book of Exodus, the name 'Yahweh' had meant 'he who becomes', because this name is evidently the third-person form of the word of self-revelation, 'I am' (Ex. 3:14), or better 'I become'; for there is no verb 'to be' in Hebrew (see discussion at 41:10). But a number of scholars have come to the conclusion that the two Hebrew words 'I (am) He' are DI's own distinctive way of expressing in the Hebrew here what he found in Exodus. Thus, God's name is He, not 'it', or *that* of the RSV. In other words the name He actually says 'The living God'. So now God says 'I am Yahweh, "He" is my name'.

The word *glory* in its developed, theological usage at the time of DI signified the outer aspect of God's true being. Man can neither see nor know God as he is in himself. But God graciously allows man to behold his glory as he passes man by, even while remaining beyond the range of human understanding (Ex. 33:22). In the parable of the last judgment (Matt. 25:31-46), we read how Israel is asked if she has remembered her calling, which is to open blind eyes and bring light to those who sit in the darkness of the prison house. That is what Israel is elected for, as DI has said. Only in Israel therefore can God's glory be made plain, and his name be revealed.

Most commentators suggest that it is to false gods that Yahweh shall never give his glory, such as to Marduk in all his lacquered magnificence. But in the light of 40:5 and 49:3 such an interpretation cannot stand, even though the parallel in the second half of this line might suggest that it should be adopted. *Pesilim* are certainly *graven images*. However, in this verse we are presented with the paradox that God, who does not allow man to make any image of himself (cf. Ex. 20:4, Deut. 5:8), has actually elected Israel to be his image. Originally God had made man in his image (Gen. 1:27). But that image the J historian believed had long since been marred by sin. DI however now speaks in terms of the re-created image of God that Israel — not all mankind at the moment — may yet become through the Spirit's settling upon her, and because of the fact that Yahweh delights in her; or, in other words, through grace. Accordingly, the straightforward way of expressing this truth is to declare, as DI does, that the glory of God is to be made manifest in and through Israel.

9 God's glory had appeared to Israel in the days of Moses, says DI (Ex. 16:7, 10; 24:16). The manifestation of glory had thus represented the original events he mentions. But now, *before they spring forth* — a botanical metaphor, with emphasis upon the development of the plant out of the seed that has first to die — God will do *new things*, for he is about to reveal his glory in a new way. Yet these new things DI does not yet dare disclose. They are too astonishing just to be mentioned casually. DI will still need several chapters to allow him to work up to the point at which he can disclose what is in his mind. For what he is hinting here is nothing less than what we today would designate the death-and-resurrection motif as it becomes manifest in innocent suffering.

10 The mention of the word 'new' is sufficient for DI to invite all flesh to *sing to the Lord a new song*. No old song is good enough to match the marvellous new things God is about to do (cf. Pss. 33:3; 40:3; 95; 96; 98). Miriam had sung a great song in praise of Yahweh when the Exodus and the crossing of the Red Sea had taken place (Ex. 15:21).

The Babylonians were accustomed to singing enthronement songs as each New Year came round — and DI must surely have heard these sung. How can 'the ends of the earth' refuse to sing when God does new things greater by far than just bringing in a New Year? Even inanimate nature is to join in the song. Here the word *sea* may include the waters under the earth, the deeps of chaos that we have seen are the negative element in God's good and positive universe.

11-12 This interpretation is borne out by the next summons, which is to the desert to join in also. This is because the desert, where no grass grows, was another manifestation of the chaos concept to the Hebrew mind. Up to this point we have heard the call to join in the song go forth to (1) the end of the earth, (2) the waters of chaos, (3) the coasts of the ocean, (4) the wilderness. Now both (5) rural areas and (6) commercial cities are to contribute their meed of praise. *Kedar* was the home of those marauding Arabs who were Israel's ancestral enemies, and *Sela* or Petra was the capital city of Edom, Israel's brother nation, but also her ancestral enemy. Negative becoming positive indeed! *Sing for joy* is a verb expressing exultant, delirious happiness. It speaks of the battle cry of the excited warrior who knows that he is going to win. *Shout* is an unusual term which in Arabic means to bellow like a beast. And since these all are to shout from *the top of the mountains*, and are to offer glory around the whole Mediterranean Sea, the passage seems to speak of that eschatological joy which the NT can describe by the word hilarity in the Greek of 2 Cor. 9:7.

13 But Israel is not alone in her odd behaviour. Yahweh too *shouts aloud* a battle-cry as he rejoices in rescuing his people from the powers of evil. His *fury* or *zeal* is his burning purpose of love. The root of the word means to be red or black with dye. Yet it is often expounded in the OT in terms of fire and heat (cf. Ex. 19:18; 24:17; Deut. 4:24; Isa. 33:14; Mal. 3:2). And so it is but a short step to understand it as passion when it is used of God. So the Gentle Shepherd of 40:11 is also the *man of war* the heat of whose 'zeal' or *fury* is able to destroy his *foes*. This is similar to the language of 63:1 ff., a passage which is paraphrased in Julia Ward Howe's famous hymn:

> Mine eyes have seen the glory of the coming of the Lord;
> He is trampling out the vintage where the grapes of wrath are
>   stored.
> He hath loosed the fateful lightning of His terrible swift sword . . .
> Our God is marching on.

God the warrior then is marching on. Cyrus the warrior is marching on (41:1-3). But Israel also is marching on (40:31); yet only in the strength of him, who, while marching *in* Cyrus (41:4), also grants all needed strength — or Spirit — to this same weary and exhausted army, viz., his chosen people and Servant Israel.

14   The new thing to come will not be new in the sense of the Greek word *neos*, but new in the sense of *kainos*, i.e., it will represent an emergent newness. On the one hand, the new thing is to be something astonishing to Israel, for it will appear to her to be different. Yet on the other hand, it will be based on the consistency of Israel's trustworthy God and on the actions which he has already performed in the days of Moses.

Without warning now come quotation marks, as it were. God himself is speaking. 'The Exodus events were but the conception in the womb of my mighty plan. Now the time of delivery has come. Through the whole long period of gestation I uttered never a word, even when Israel was going constantly astray. I could well have burst out with zeal, but instead I continually held myself in.'

What a daring simile this is, to have God declare that he can be compared with an expectant mother. The three verbs in the sentence describing the pains of childbirth represent those pains as they climax at the time of delivery. At 66:7 this figure is used of Israel. Here it is used of God. With such language DI shocks his readers into recognizing that God is not beyond the pain which his people is even then suffering, but must be one with them as they meet the judgment which he himself has caused. This theme of DI actually contributes to the message of comfort with which he began his sermon (40:1). DI teaches Israel here that his people can be grateful even for pain, for pain puts them in touch with the living God. God himself has chosen that it is to be out of pain that new life is to spring just like the birth of a baby boy. What then may not the ghastly pains of the Exile bring forth in the providence of God?

15   The coming new thing that is about to be born will actually produce a cosmic effect. We who are wise after the event know how this happened, and how the historical event of the 'death and resurrection' of exiled Israel actually formed the mould into which God poured the historical revelation of his redeeming, loving self in action. But the Hebrews could never have employed such words as 'cosmic effect'.

Instead, in the mythological manner of the nations of the Fertile Crescent in DI's day, they pictorialized the significance of God's actions in poetic language.

16 Two significant truths seem to be emerging: (1) Inanimate nature is actually one with the humanity that dwells along with it. It knows the effects of human sin only too well (Gen. 3:17-19 and cf. v. 11 above). (2) What God has begun to do for the redemption of man in the days of Moses he will continue to do; 'so I shall never leave off now'.

17 After hearing that Yahweh is really like that, how utterly foolish it is to trust in handmade divinities. The subtlety of DI's sarcasm is observable only when we realize that the word for *molten images* is singular and that *our gods* is plural. For the plural form of the latter noun, employed as a singular concept, is that which is also employed for Yahweh, the God whom DI knows has created the heavens and the earth (40:12 ff.).

18-19 Who but God could invite the deaf to hear and the blind to see? Only God knows that it is possible for the blind and the deaf to respond. For only God can perform that miracle. Moreover we are now explicitly informed that the blind mentioned at v. 16 above are really exiled Israel (cf. also 43:8 and Ezek. 12:2). Although Israel had been chosen of God to become his *messenger*, Israel had never realized what the years of the exile in Babylon could mean in relation to God's plan. The word for *messenger* represents the Hebrew word which may also be translated by 'angel'. That is to say, the Hebrews used the one word for both heavenly and earthly messengers. We have noted before (at 40:5) that the prophets drew no hard and fast line, as the modern world does, between heaven and earth or matter and spirit.

Yet Israel herself is not the mission. God alone is such. Israel is to be the vehicle of God's mission. She is Witness to the Sender (43:10, 12). In and by herself she is not able to prove the existence of God to the heathen bystander. It is only those who are within the covenant fellowship of God who find that witnessing can create such a proof in their own hearts. Yet Israel, the covenant people, is called to witness that in fact the blind receive their sight (42:7 and cf. Matt. 11:5). If however she does that faithfully in the hearing of the heathen, she can then leave the outcome of her witnessing with assurance to God.

The shocking reality, however, is that 'he with whom the all-embracing covenant has been made' cannot grasp the majesty of his calling. These ten words seek to translate just the one word *dedicated* in Hebrew. My translation is but one of several possible ways of rendering it. If the root is *m-sh-l*, then the word has to do with 'reporting in story form'. If it is *sh-l-m*, then it might be vowelled to mean 'he who has been granted *shalom*, peace'. But in DI's day, the root *sh-l-m* conveyed the idea of wholeness, completeness, fullness, comprehensiveness, and the like. Yet 'peace' implies all these things. Solomon (from this root) was meant to be the man with the whole heart (1 Kings 11:4). A generation before DI's day, Ezekiel had declared that God said to Israel 'I will make with them a complete, total, comprehensive covenant' (34:25; 37:26). Today we have to learn to distinguish between what our newspaper means by peace and what DI meant by the word. On the other hand, others have translated this four-consonantal word by 'devoted' or 'dedicated' in that it may be vowelled in a manner similar to the Arabic word *muslim*, 'he who is devoted to God'. Others suggest that the word might be rendered by 'rewarded', or 'paid', and so 'hired', all of these being adjectives added to the noun servant. Whatever way we decide to translate it, we should note that it has become an epithet for Israel, in the same way as has Jeshurun at 44:2.

We are now presented with the strong contrast: (1) Israel is committed to be God's messenger; (2) Israel is blind. The resolution of that paradox can obviously come about by grace alone.

20 Israel's blindness consists in 'having seen many of My deeds, yet recognizing no significance in them'; and her deafness in that her ears have been opened, yet she has not understood what God has been doing through historical movements.

21 *Torah*, translated here as *law*, is the revelation that has already been given to Israel through Moses and his successors, the prophets and scribes. Torah was not the work of Israel but of God. All that Israel had done was just to receive it. Once again now the Lord has planned [rather than *pleased*] ... *to magnify* this Word that he has already spoken, and glorify it. This action of his is, of course, part of his saving purpose (the word *righteousness* here), 'saving' meaning both victorious and righteous because it contains both God's power and his love. Torah is not a static collection of laws or even of divine instructions; far less is it a moral code. It is the Word of God, even when that Word is necessarily expressed in the forms of legal enactments. Now, the Word of God endures (40:8). Of that fact DI is sure; thus Torah must in some sense be alive, for the God who has uttered it is alive (cf. 51:4). Consequently, as a living entity and like any human person, it continually develops and unfolds so as to meet with potency every possible new situation that may arise. Jeremiah certainly held this view of Torah; it was part of his faith that new things were still to come (31:33). And DI would undoubtedly know these views of Jeremiah. Part of the outcome of the living, evolving nature of Torah were the utterances of the great prophets (cf. Isa. 8:16), even when they themselves recognized that they were what they were, viz., prophets raised up within the people of God just because they had inherited the Torah that had created their people. The vitality of Torah is such, as DI understood it at this juncture in history, that it can witness to the action of God in destroying his own people and in exiling them in Babylon. Torah, as represented by the first commandment, had declared: 'Thou shalt have no other gods before me'. Israel had not heeded this Word of God. The centrality of this commandment Israel had therefore still to learn, even if it meant the hard way of destruction and the death of the nation. Only thus could the Word of God stand forever.

The whole verse is a surprising statement. It means that Torah is to flower especially at that point where Israel had failed God most, and therefore where she needs him most. Paul met opposition at a particular place in his travels; *therefore* a great opportunity for spreading the gospel was presented to him (Acts 14:3). Opposition is here seen as God's footstool. By stepping on it he attains greater ends than if there had been no footstool available. Thus DI in this parenthetical verse is in reality declaring a basic truth of the whole Bible, viz., that God uses even the sin of man for the achievement of his purpose. In this case the sin is embodied in the Servant Israel, despite the fact that the Servant is called to be the instrument of God's purpose for the world. Alone, Israel cannot meet God's needs in the development of his plan. Israel is not the power by which God attains his ends. That power is the Word. It alone can effect God's plan of redemption. But it uses as its locus to that end the sinful body of the Servant people of God.

22 Torah, what the NT calls 'the Scriptures' (2 Tim. 3:16), is God's gracious gift to this missionary instrument that Israel is called to be.

Israel must therefore necessarily pass it on to others (cf. 51:7, where Israel is called the people who has my Torah in their heart). But she believed that she was not in the position to do so. She is *a people robbed and plundered*, an exploited people, imprisoned in the Babylonian political and economic machine — DI consistently uses an historical situation to illustrate an inner state of mind. Israel is in reality prisoner of her own unbeliefs and folly and is now in consequence robbed of all initiative, *with none to say.* 'Restore!', 'Let them go!' Instead of seeking others with a missionary purpose, Israel is actually waiting for others to seek her out and set her free.

23-24 In fact the significance or ultimate outcome of such unbelief no one seems to care about. Then suddenly DI identifies himself with his sinful people as Isaiah had done before him (6:5): he now asks questions of Israel, using the pronoun 'we' to include himself with his people. Had Israel not realized that our present plight was God's doing? God had been compelled to act through his servant Nebuchadrezzar to destroy his own temple and city, to give his elect people over *to the spoiler*, that is, to be abducted — this is an abstract noun — and to be a prisoner of war, as in fact had happened in 587 B.C. Yet he had done so only after repeated warnings from the lips of the pre-exilic prophets, who had declared that if Israel was to remain God's people, then they must obey God's voice; and God had acted in this way only after several hundred years of postponement of his judgment, and after Jerusalem had been given the chance to see that judgment fall first on the Northern Kingdom in 722 B.C. Finally, God had acted, for *was it not the Lord, against whom we have sinned?* Israel had not obeyed God, who had commanded her to keep his Torah and walk in his revealed *ways*. Rebellion is the essence of sin (Gen. 3:2; Isa. 1:2), for it reveals man's basic contempt for God.

25 And so when God acted in the end, the burning *heat* of his zeal for Israel's good had *burned* his own beloved people, through the flames of the torches of Nebuchadrezzar's soldiers as they set fire to the homes and temple and walls of Jerusalem (cf. 2 Kings 25:9). This had happened *round about* him for Israel could not escape the judgment by flight in any direction. Yet even that terrible event had not spoken home to Israel's conscience, for she had gone off into exile merely bewailing her fate, and without even confessing her folly.

The problem of the hardening of the heart is one which the Bible never resolves, yet it fully acknowledges it as a reality in God's dealings with men (cf. Matt. 13:14-15; Mark 4:12; Luke 8:10; John 12:40; Acts 28:26; Rom. 11:8). God had warned Isaiah more than a century before that the more he should preach to his people, the deafer Israel would become (6:9-12); what is more, his preaching would actually create that deafness of which God spoke, and would produce a refusal to convert and be healed. That is to say, God's Word would in itself produce unbelief. Moses had seen this happen in the case of Pharaoh, as Pharaoh's heart grew harder at each evidence of Yahweh's power, to the point that the writer could say 'The Lord hardened the heart of Pharaoh' (Ex. 9:12). But then Pharaoh had not belonged in the chosen people of God, nor did Pharaoh know what it meant to be one with a nation bound to the living God by an eternal covenant. Nor could he know that such a covenant relationship was the container that gave locus to the most wonderful revelation of God ever yet made, God's covenant love and loyalty (*hesed*) to Israel. Israel's apostasy therefore was a far greater sin than anything Pharaoh could ever have committed. For Israel had actually been chosen to be the means of God's grace to all the pharaohs of this world.

How necessary it was therefore for Israel in DI's day to learn that 'your God is a devouring fire, a jealous God' (Deut. 4:24). Jealous is more nearly our word zealous. Thus the pictorial imagery of fire represents here the white heat of God's judgment of love. So greatly does this loving God loathe the sin of Israel that he must necessarily consume it. Yet we have noted how sin is not a thing in itself. Sin is rather the rebellious activity of the sinner. That is why God's judgment must fall, not on sin, but on sinners. So it is not merely Israel's sin that the flames must consume but Israel herself. Before DI's time Isaiah too had seen the significance of the zeal of God. He had said 'The sinners in Zion are afraid; trembling has seized the godless: "Who among us can dwell with the devouring fire? Who among us can dwell with everlasting burnings?"' (33:14). No one can, and yet — herein lies the mystery of Israel's election — Israel does in fact survive the judgment of love that she has rightly brought upon herself, but only by God's grace. The mystery of the hardening of Israel's heart DI is not able to resolve, even when he sees what God actually does with the hardened heart to display his grace. But this mystery becomes the passionate theological interest of our writer as his chapters unfold.

At the present juncture, however, even as DI questions his people in this pointed way, the hardening process is complete. Israel's heart has become so hardened that she is no longer able to make any response at all to the judgments of God upon her. Even whenthe zeal of God was burning into her bones, she *did not understand* and *did not take it to heart*, and so grasp its significance. Because of course a corpse (see commentary at 41:14) cannot feel the pain of the flames of the cremation ceremony. Yet, here is the unique new thing which DI has come to realize is basic to God's entire plan of action as he uses his people: in and through the fires God might possibly, and by grace alone, give new life even to the dead body of this his chosen and still-beloved instrument. And if he should do so, then would not such an act resolve forever the yet unresolved mystery of why God's Word should create, in the first place, a heart that had grown too hard to listen to him of its own warped and sinful volition? DI will return to this theme later.

CHAPTER 43

1 Theologically speaking, this is another highly significant chapter. It contains the roots of much of our Christian theology. For we are consistently to keep in mind that while DI addresses his contemporaries in and through a historical situation of pain and sorrow, he is also preaching about the meaning and significance of those same events. Thus he is here declaring the mind of God upon them — and that is theology.

But now! In contrast to what has just been said (42), God will declare a great new thing. First, the significance arising from God's rousing of Cyrus from the north is that Israel has no grounds whatsoever for lack of faith. '*Fear not*' resounds again, as at 43:5; 44:2; 54:4. 'Think, Israel! First I *created* you by uttering the Word: "The Lord has said", [rather than *says the Lord,*] just as I spoke the Word that created the heavens [42:5 and cf. Ps. 33:6]. Next I *formed* you; after that, because in Adam you had fallen into sin, I *redeemed* you. Is that not sufficient reason to know no fear, even in the dungeons of Babylon? Your case is like that of a slave girl for whom her master has paid the necessary price in the first place, but who has run away from home, and has turned up eventually in the slave market.' There the Master has recognized his Servant in all her misery, and has called out to her: Israel . . . you are mine! even as she stands shivering in her nakedness. Thereupon he pays for her a second time in order to be able to take her home where she belongs. It is true that Israel had paid double for all her sins (40:2), but now it is apparent that God too has paid double, so to speak, in order to bring Israel back home to himself once more. More than that — I have called you by (your) name: you are mine! The divine Lover has now proceeded to call Israel by her 'Christian' name, and in this way has claimed her as his own beloved (cf. 44:5; 48:1).

In Israel's early days, if a man knew another's name, he believed that he knew his friend's personality intimately. This was because the name, ideally speaking, was the true description of its owner. So God knew Israel through and through. She need therefore have no fear in committing her heart to him, since he already knew everything that

59

was in her heart. Moreover, God calls 'Moses! ... Elijah! ... Saul, Saul!' in such a manner that the individual hearer learns that he possesses an individual identity in the sight of God. He learns that he exists in his own right by the Word of God addressed to him. It is in accordance with this biblical way of thinking that the ordained minister today proclaims in God's name 'John, I baptize thee', and John thereby becomes the individual child of God within the divine family that God has already named as Israel.

2 When we recall that the pages we are studying are part of the Scriptures of the Old and New Testaments which together form the basis of the Church's faith, we are bound to take serious theological note of DI's use of the past tense in the verb *I have redeemed you*. This past tense is not a 'prophetic future', as some suppose it must be, pointing to a redemption still to come. We ought to take DI at his face value and not read into his works ideas that belong to a later period. Yet contrariwise, if we are Christians, we are bound to read the OT in the light of what the NT has to say about DI's theology; for God has chosen us to be his servants, not in A.D. 30, but 'in him before the foundation of the world' (Eph. 1:4). Paul is here probably quoting Isa. 51:16, a verse which we shall examine later.

The Christian then should avoid all such ideas as 'The Christian Faith is 2000 years old'; or, without qualification, 'Christ is the world's Redeemer today because of what he did two thousand years ago'. The NT sees the person and work of Christ quite otherwise. It declares him to be the Word that was in the beginning with God (John 1:1); to be the first-born of all creation, for in him all things were created (Col. 1:15). The Fourth Gospel believes that these words represent reality: 'Before Abraham was, I am' (John 8:58); 'I and the Father are one' (John 10:30). With the NT, therefore, we should gladly accept that same reality which DI had truly grasped, that the redemptive love of the 'I am', of the Word, has always been operative, in all ages, in that God bestowed his covenant upon man in the beginning. Thus in Christ what we behold is the *epiphany* (historical event) of his redemptive love, the appearing in the flesh *eph hapax*, as Paul declares, 'once and for all', of the eternal reality of God's saving love. The Cross and Resurrection are to be seen as effective both backwards in time before the birth of Christ, as well as into time far beyond his death. *Besides me there is no saviour* says God, even in this chapter (43:11). We recall that Jesus received his name 'Jesus' (*Ye-hoshua'*) only because it means 'Yahweh (the *Ye* in Jesus' name) will save his people from their sins' (cf. Matt. 1:21). Paul had this reality in mind when he wrote '*In* Christ, God was reconciling . . .' (2 Cor. 5:19). Thus '*Fear not, for I have redeemed you*' was as true of the saving love of God *in Christ* in DI's day as it was in Paul's.

God does not promise, however, to remove his beloved from a world of floods and diseases, of trials and tribulations. What he does promise is that when Israel passes through these things, he will walk beside her. This is a most interesting development of the argument set forth previously at 42:25. The story of the three representative Israelites walking in the fires of the exile in Babylon without being burned, and finding a Fourth walking beside them (Dan. 3) may well be a *midrash* upon the verse that is before us now. Moreover, this is a constant theme in the OT, as we see from such passages as Deut. 31:6-8; Pss. 66:12 and 91.

Again, the *waters* symbolize several ideas for Israel, ever since God rescued her from the waters of the Red Sea. For example, the waters referred to may be the waters of judgment, as the Red Sea undoubtedly was for Egypt. Or again, the theological significance of waters is frequently linked in prophetic thought with the waters of chaos that rage continually both above the sky and underneath the earth (cf. Ex.20:4; Isa. 51:10). So the *rivers* were the streams of the river of chaos that flowed underneath the foundations of the earth. Israel always sits precariously on the verge of chaos. Yet she is held back from falling into the abyss of chaos only by the might and the grace of God, for he has promised never again to allow the floods to overwhelm and destroy the earth as would be the proper expression of his righteous judgment.

We have seen that God's glory was envisaged under the form of fire (Ex. 24:16-17). A natural development of this second theological picture therefore was to speak of God's radiant, burning glory as capable of burning up both sin and evil as fire can burn up chaff. Thus fire represents the holy and dreadful presence of God, present like a refiner's fire. It is interesting to realize that the prophets of the OT drew no line between God's living, guiding presence with Israel in the burning zeal of his love, and his judgment upon Israel's sin which was constantly pictured in terms of burning fire. This is because they believed that God is responsible for all that happens in human life. Thus trials and vexations are his holy presence. That significant fact, as we can see, DI has accepted in full from those who have gone before him. Thus he can exclaim with confidence that *when you walk through fire you shall not be burned.*

3 This guarantee is expressed by God's declaration or virtual oath that he really is who he is. The declaration is opened by the word *ki*, a particle translated here by *for*, but which can be used to follow an unspoken phrase like 'I declare' or 'I swear', and so it precedes a strong asseveration. In the days of Moses God had made himself known under the name of Yahweh (Ex. 3:14; 6:2; 33:19), and in doing so he had coupled his name of self-revelation with overt acts of salvation. In this way he had shown himself to be Israel's *Saviour*. The Sudan (*Seba*) and *Ethiopia* may mean the then little-known southern area of Egypt rather than the areas covered by these names today. What DI is declaring then is that little Israel is worth more than the whole of greater Egypt. Yet the phrase is a Semitic hyperbole of the same genre as similar expressions used by our Lord, such as 'If thy right eye offend thee, pluck it out'. Again, the pharaoh of Egypt, or the pharaoh's son, was regarded in DI's day as the representative figure who could sum up in himself the meaning of Egypt. In the light of this we are to see the words of God at Ex. 4:22-23: 'And you shall say to Pharaoh, "Thus says the Lord, Israel is my first-born son and I say to you, Let my son go that he may serve me; if you refuse to let him go, behold, I will slay your first-born son".' Israel, then, was the 'son of God'. As a fact of history this son had escaped disaster, yet only at the expense of the life of the pharaoh's son. Such a thing could happen again, therefore, as Deutero-Zechariah also was to affirm some generations later (Zech. 10:11).

The above may seem to represent a strange theology. But in this world love can be known only as a personal experience. It can never be understood as a mere concept. Therefore, in the providence of his wisdom God chose to draw near to all men by entering into a bond of love with one particular people. Through his relationship of love with this people he purposed to let all men see his glory. Israel's calling was to become a kingdom of priests *vis-à-vis* the rest of the world (Ex. 19:6). Yet the other nations were *ipso facto* excluded from being the chosen nation of priests. 'Not to be chosen' does not mean 'to be rejected'. But they had to pay the cost of Israel's election. The rich countries of the West today are obviously chosen to have a very fortunate standard of living. But it is also a fact that they maintain that standard only at the cost, at least in part, of the underprivileged masses of the East. However, this situation must only be one of temporary advantage to the West. For along with privileges, there always goes responsibility. The West is therefore bound before God to pass on her good fortune to those who were not chosen to begin with, or else to suffer the fate that Israel suffered when her own God had to destroy her as a national entity for not accepting her priestly calling.

4   Meanwhile Israel must never forget her position of responsibility, to *men*, that is to *mankind* (cf. Amos 3:1-2), and so must never cease to walk delicately. She dare not judge her neighbours in their unbelief, for their unbelief has been necessary in the first place for her belief. God alone is judge of all the earth. This is sufficient answer for the modern Western sophisticate who rejects the Christian faith in favour of some form of syncretism, declaring that he could not selfishly accept salvation when the masses in China — or the Sudan — have not had the chance to hear of Christ.

Meanwhile, *you*, the individual personality or identity of Israel, *are precious* to God. Israel here is clearly depicted as one corporate entity, one personality sprung from the loins of Jacob-Israel. As such, of course, he is a child of promise — Israel is masculine in this strophe. Israel is valuable to God on the ground that he is the object of God's election-love and the instrument of the revelation of God's glory to all men. It would be well at this point to note how rarely the *love, ahavah*, of God is spoken of in the OT. This is because God's love is not a concept to philosophize upon. Love is something that happens to those at whom God's saving activity is directed even as they live in a particular historical situation. Consequently, the word we find most commonly used is *hesed*, God's covenantal loyal-love. This is the word the RSV translates as 'steadfast love'.

5   But the significance of the idea that God would give away all mankind if only he could hold on to Israel is so disturbing that God has to repeat the comforting words 'Don't be afraid!' And then he adds 'I swear that I am really with you', or 'I myself am with you', in that form of close relationship we have mentioned as 'covenant' loyalty and love (cf. Ex. 3:12; Isa. 7:14: 'God is *with* us'). For if God is not *with* his people, then he can only be *against* them. There can be no third way. Not that the covenant with Israel was a new thing in the world. Far from it. Covenants between a god and his people through the medium of the great king were known long before the day of Moses. It is the peculiar content of the OT covenant which is so challenging, strange, and new. For despite the fact that the Northern Kingdom seemed to have been cut to pieces and its people scattered to the winds as much as a century and a half before the destruction of the Southern Kingdom, the prophets were certain that the reality of the covenant still held Israel together as one people in the sight of God.

This kind of covenant therefore forms the framework of the revelation of God's unchanging *hesed*, his loyal love. Thus Israel cannot finally perish: God's people are destined to return home where they belong — all of them, even those who are presently scattered to the ends of the earth. Jeremiah 40:11 and 41:17 tell us that Israelite exiles had fled to Moab, Edom, and Ammon in the East, and to Egypt in the West, and many other passages speak of their wide dispersion ever since the fall of the Northern Kingdom in 721 B.C. But God is Lord of all the forces that at present militate against the working out of his purpose through Israel for the saving of the world.

6-7 This people possesses two names. DI indicates (1) that Israel is the corporate son of God, and (2) that God however knows each individual member of this people by his 'Christian name'. In the light of (1), this people possesses a surname or family name as well as their individual Christian names. And that family name is actually 'Yahweh'. As his sons and daughters — note how women have an equal place with men in DI's thought — live within the mysterious intimacy of the covenant, their *raison d'être* is to show to all the world the glory of Yahweh their Father, for he created them for this end.

8 What a tragedy for God that the flesh, the *eyes*, which should have revealed his glory, were *blind*! (cf. 42:18-20). Whom then does God summon here to act for him? For God's commands are in the imperative, singular, masculine, and the form of the verb is unusual. The prophet himself seems to be the only one who can fit the situation. On the other hand, the DSSI reads DI's verbs in the plural. If the latter is the original reading, then it may be God's angelic hosts who are here summoned to do God's bidding once again (cf. 40:1).

9 Deaf and dumb Israel is to be led into court in the presence of all the nations. The gods have been given their chance to speak and have failed. Now it is the turn of the nations (see 41:21). By this means Israel may possibly be shamed into recognizing how deaf and dumb she really is. God will now ask any nation that volunteers to do so to step forward and recount how Yahweh acted in Israel's history in the days of Moses, or else explain *this*, the emphatic feminine singular pronoun he uses for the victorious advance of Cyrus over the Near East. Of course none of them will be able to produce any witnesses to these mighty events, for they have no one in their midst to interpret what God has been doing. Their own history has not been *Heilsgeschichte*, sacred history, nor have they prophets to interpret the meaning of events.

10   Then God turns dramatically to Israel and exclaims categorically '*You are my witnesses*, for you were there when I brought you through the waters of the Red Sea and gave you my covenant by the hand of Moses, and then led you into a land that was not yours to possess but was a gift from me to my people. This all happened in order that each and all of you [the verb is plural] may know me and *believe me*, that is, put your trust in me. Later in his thesis DI will show of course that the world as well is to have the opportunity to believe. At the moment, however, in her double capacity as *witness* — some scholars suggest vowelling this word in the singular — and as *servant*, Israel has become the one proof of the existence of God that cannot be gainsaid by formal reasoning.

The word *know* can of course be used in ordinary ways. The Hebrew verb *y-d-'* according to circumstances may have to be translated by perceive, learn, understand, have skill. But it can also speak of existential knowledge. As Jeremiah says: 'And no longer shall each man teach his neighbour and each his brother, saying, "Know the Lord," for they shall all know me' (31:34). Possibly the reason why DI does not elaborate on Jeremiah's words is that there was no need to do so. Jeremiah's hope may well have been the common property of the exiles.

Israel then is to 'put your trust in me'. This verb means 'to take a firm stand upon', from the original root whch meant 'to be firm'. DI was not a philologist and is unlikely to have known this fact; the content of the idea of 'believing in' that he offers is another thing. He would be acquainted with the common figure of speech where the God of Israel is described by the epithet of rock (cf. Deut. 32:18; Isa. 17:10; Ps. 18:2). The following suggestion therefore may not be wholly fanciful. To 'put your trust in' God, as DI sees it, is not to demand any special activity on Israel's part. All that Israel has to do is to place her feet on the Rock which is already there; then she will discover that she too is as 'sure', *ne'eman*, as the Rock beneath her feet. To believe in God is to make the existential discovery that God is faithful and reliable; it is not necessary to make an act of belief oneself.

11-13   Now, no other god ever produced a saving purpose like
Yahweh's, for no god is saving love as such except Yahweh alone.
Yahweh is no parvenu barbarian god. And so he says 'I had but to
speak the Word: "Let there be deliverance from Egypt", and there was
deliverance. It was I who did it', he might go on to say, 'not the gods of
Egypt, for I, Yahweh, am God! I am He, not It. I am the living One,
active, creative, purposive; in fact mine is the only purpose. This means
that there is no power that can *deliver* or 'snatch' you, Israel, out of my
hand; there is no power to deflect, far less to *hinder*, or 'reverse' my
purpose when I have begun to act. This is because the Word of
salvation, once uttered, cannot return unto me void (see 55:11)'. Why
in heaven's name, therefore, should Israel have to be called blind,
when she has already witnessed God's mighty acts?

This is an important passage. It suggests the ultimate victory of God
over all opposition. It declares that God's essential purpose is that all
men should know him and believe in him. And it also reveals that
Israel will definitely be used by God to this end, since God has chosen
her for this purpose and will not change his mind.

The passage also suggests, however, the extraordinary freedom that
God has given to Israel. Israel is free to witness against God as well as
for him. On the other hand, if Israel is rebellious and witnesses against
her Lord, then it is her very rebelliousness which becomes the medium
through which God reveals his grace. Incidentally, God chose a whole
nation as one entity to be his witness; individuals could easily be lost
from sight in those turbulent days.

14-15   'Thus the Lord has said', as the Hebrew has it. This is a
frequently recurring formula. The verb is always found in the 'past
tense', or rather, the 'completed action' form. Thus it is wrong to
translate the phrase by 'Thus saith the Lord'. The AV translation
suggests to modern readers that the prophets were mystical dreamers,
to whom God gave visions of the future. The very idea is anath-
ematized at 47:13. DI himself tells us what the function of the prophets
is. They are messengers of the Word, and by the power of the Spirit,
interpreters of the actions of God in history (43:27; 44:26; 48:16).
From an understanding of what God has 'said', and so 'done' (for the
two actions are one), in the days of Moses and the patriarchs, the
prophet can now pronounce what God, since he can only be true to
himself, will do in the future. God's sending Cyrus to *break down*, or
better, to overwhelm the fugitives (rather than *bars*) from Babylon

(v. 14), is wholly consonant with what he has already done in overwhelming the chariots of Pharaoh at the Red Sea (v. 16). It is for all your sakes (plural), as individual children of God, that God is now acting, because he has already done this very thing for your fathers in Egypt. Thus 'for all your sakes' is as much a promise for us today as it was to Israel in 540 B.C.

16-17   The argument rests upon history. At the period of the *former things* (v. 18), God had revealed himself to be the Redeemer of Israel. But of course God does not change. Thus he is the eternal Redeemer. What God is now about to do is therefore consonant with the nature of his revealed Self. Our theologian-author here describes this contemporary historical event by means of ecstatic reporting.

18-19   The divine speech begins here, following from 'has said' at v. 16. What Cyrus is going to do under God is something far greater than the events at the Red Sea of old. And so Act II is now about to open. To emphasize it, DI makes God forbid Israel even to think back to those mighty events of old. 'Look at me in action now', he says. 'What I am about to do is something which, though new, will not be a surprise; for it will spring organically out of the old, as the butterfly develops from the caterpillar. Thus I am going to lay a route, (*make a way*), not this time in the sea, but over *the wilderness* that separates Babylonia from Palestine.'

20-21   'My action is to have cosmic significance; even the brute beasts will cooperate.' In the wilderness shall waters break out, *and rivers in the desert*, (35:6). Observe how close our verse is to Isa. 35 and other similar passages, one of which we shall meet later at 55:12-13. But this is not the place to discuss the authorship or provenance of Isa. 35. *Rivers in the desert* are of course fundamental for the preservation of any form of life in the wilderness.

The whole of the above section is obviously to be understood metaphorically and not literally, even though the declaration is based upon the literal emancipation of the exiles by Cyrus and their literal return to their homeland in Palestine. Several factors should be noted before making an interpretation. The wild animals are here to serve God's purpose as it becomes embodied in returning Israel. *Yeshimon, desert* (v. 19), was the name of an area so completely barren that no sheep could possibly graze on it. Deuteronomy 32:10, a verse in the song of Moses which DI quotes so frequently, declares that 'he found him in a desert land, and in the howling waste of the wilderness'. That is both literal fact and at the same time a picture of what life is like without God. Moreover it is what life could become once again for Israel, should she rebel once more against God's good guidance and stray from the straight and narrow road. Once again she would be lost in the desert. Yet, as DI declares, if this happens, in his grace God will not immediately lift her out of the desert and set her back on the road. He will lay new roads for her *in* the desert, and open pools of water for her to drink *in the desert* just as he had done before at that time when he gave Israel water from the rock that Moses struck (Num. 20:7-11). And he will do so in order that, walking beside her as the Good Shepherd, he may gently lead her back to where she belongs.

Thus Israel will retain her free will even in the desert, for God never forces his people to return home to his care when they do not wish to do so. The whole eschatological picture is virtually theological teaching drawn from an existential situation. Here we have the second or third indication of DI's important thesis still to follow, viz., that God is able to bring salvation to others out of the suffering and even death of his chosen people. We return to this theme at 55:1.

22 It is Israel that is now in the dock; both the gods and the nations have had their turn. How tragic it is that for the fifty long years now that Israel has been in exile she has been blind to this underlying purpose of God. With a series of verbs in the negative, God points out how Israel has *not* declared the praise of her Creator. Israel has actually 'grown tired' of God, *have been weary* of him. What an admission this is that God has to make! And not for the first time, either. We read with astonishment God's question to Israel two centuries before: 'In what have *I* wearied you?' (Mic. 6:3). DI knew that Israel was not in Babylon by chance. God had put her there to be his Servant in that particular situation, in fact, to be the means of offering to the gentiles the full life he wanted them to live. But now the eternal plan and purpose of God had failed. And it had failed through Israel's growing tired of God.

23 And so the curtain is here drawn back to reveal the pain in the Father's heart. For he is united in covenantal bond with this ridiculous people as the Holy-One-of-Israel, a people that chose of its own free will to turn its back on God's cosmic purpose.

The next lines are not easy to translate. They must almost be paraphrased at times rather than translated, and no two expositors have produced exactly the same rendering in English. Yet two points should guide us in translating the equivocal Hebrew. (1) The words are addressed to a historical situation such as we can envisage, in so far as we know the details of the exiles' life about 540 B.C. (2) The words come in sequence as part of the sustained theological disputation that we call Isa. 40–55, and are therefore to be understood not as an isolated utterance, but as the link in the argument that now introduces DI's coming exposition of God's saving method of suffering love.

DI makes God point out that ever since the temple had fallen in 587, Israel in exile had not been able to offer sacrifice. This was a great deprivation for her, for sacrifices were God's own choice of the means of grace for Israel.

24 Since the Exile had put an end to those daily and expensive offerings, the opportunity had arisen for Israel to realize that she could now hold intimate communion with God without the instrumentality of the sacrificial cult. Her prophets had sought to teach her so: 'Has the Lord as great delight in burnt offerings and sacrifices, as in obeying the voice of the Lord?' (1 Sam. 15:22). 'Will the Lord be pleased with thousands of rams? . . . What does the Lord require of you, but to do justice, and to love kindness (*hesed*, and so rather the covenant fellowship with himself), and to walk humbly with your God?' (Mic. 6:7-8). Yet that glorious opportunity, arising out of the discipline of the Exile, has been missed. Throughout the years of exile God had not looked for Israel to serve him with what it was now impossible for her to offer. *You have not bought me* . . . On the other hand Israel, who had been called by God to be his Servant, had insolently forced God to be *her* Servant! (For our translation of *burdened me*, see Wilhelm Vischer, *Das Kerugma des Alten Testaments* p. 21; and Vischer, *Valeur de l'Ancien Testament* p. 150. The verb and preposition rendered by 'to make into a servant at the cost of' in v. 24 are identical with those used at v. 23.) 'You have made me the servant who bears your sins, you have exhausted me with (or made me suffer at the cost of) your iniquities' is a completely possible translation of the second half of v. 24.

There is no discussion here on the origin of sacrifices, or as to whether God had originally demanded them or not. On the other hand, sacrifice is obviously an instrument in the covenantal plan of God. Sacrifice is a concept therefore that must not be discarded because circumstances now prohibit the actual slaying of beasts upon an altar. Israel ought therefore to have been making the discovery that since the principle of sacrifice must still hold, it was she herself who had to become the beast that must now be sacrificed. But Israel had not made that forward step. In fact she had given up her obligations to the covenant when she broke her word to keep it. Yet God had not broken his. In consequence it was he alone who was now bearing the sacrificial cost of the union, this union which the Holy-One-of-Israel had forged and laid upon Israel his chosen Servant. God thus necessarily experienced and bore upon his own flesh — for in DI's day the glory of God was regarded as the spiritual counterpart of flesh — the pain that Israel had refused to bear, and which was concomitant with being the Servant of God to the world. It is God himself then who is thus in an ultimate sense *the Servant* that Israel had been called and chosen to be.

The above words are not theological speculation. No human mind could have invented the thought contained in v. 24. These can be no less therefore than revelation, revelation into the very heart of the living and loving God, who in his condescension has stooped to unite himself with this intolerably insolent people that he now calls his own. Theological discussion of revelation should always be secondary to a recognition of that revelation in one's own experience. This is just what DI does. Hereafter he has to think deeply before he dares return to this extraordinary theme, which he does only ten chapters further on in his thesis. But the above passage is so iconoclastic of all man's preconceived notions about what is proper for the divine Being and what is not that it has been passed over in silence by the great majority of scholars. The traditional theological view about God in the works of the Fathers of the early Christian centuries, and even at the Reformation period, is that God must necessarily be impassible. The conception of God's impassibility might be acceptable if it arose in face of the idea that man's sin can thwart and frustrate the Almighty. But the work of DI reveals to us the sufferings of a God who wills to suffer. In his capacity as Creator and Redeemer of his world he sees that his ends can be met only in, through, and by means of the sufferings that the sins of the men he has chosen in love have caused him. On the other hand, DI's God is he who knows the end from the beginning. Therefore his sufferings cannot efface the joy he carries in his heart. He knows that in the end he will win his whole world to glad acceptance of his proffered love.

25 Some NT scholars believe that the *ego eimi* used by Jesus — '*I am* the Light of the world', '*I am* the Way . . .', etc. — finds its source here. So they would translate here by 'I am', "*ego eimi*", with reference, as we have said before, to Ex. 3:14. But 'I, I am He, who am wiping away . . .' is the literal rendering of the Hebrew. The poetic parallelism of the second line then develops this great picture. The living God so forgives that he forgets! It is as if he were saying 'I do not accept your sins as sins any more. So far as I am concerned they do not even exist. It is the very essence of my nature to do this — *for my own sake*'. Here is a doctrine that goes beyond anything that even Isaiah or Hosea had declared before the Exile. For it opens up the new reality now to be developed, that (1) God's complete forgiveness is the real moment of Israel's renewal, and (2) renewal takes place through God himself becoming the Servant of man.

26 But while God may forget, Israel dare not. For it is when she 're-calls', *zachar*, God's saving acts of old that Israel actualizes them in the present, that is to say, even in the Exile, where she does not have the cult to aid her in this act of recall. But when she does this, she can become existentially involved once again in the saving power of God's redeeming acts, and find that the significance of the chronological moment of long ago is as real now as it was in the days of Moses.

27 Once again, therefore, God gives Israel the chance to present her own selfish case, for he is the kind of God who will not browbeat his blind Servant into acquiescence to his will. But God solemnly reminds Israel that even Abraham was a sinner — recall how he lied to Abimelech (Gen. 20:2). Or if we regard Jacob as Israel's *first father*, as more than one tradition asserts, then the evidence of his despicable nature is stronger still, as we saw at 41:8. Even the prophets, your interpreters (rather than *mediators*) as they are called here, were sinners all, from Moses to those of the Exile (cf. Isa. 6:5), for all were involved in the corporate sin of that corporate entity known as the people of Yahweh. The hardening of Israel's heart was such that Israel had reached a point when a slight healing of her wound (Jer. 6:14; 8:11) would have been worse than useless. (The RSV translates Jeremiah's twice repeated indictment by the words 'They have healed the wound of my people lightly'.) This is because the means of grace that were available in Jeremiah's day through the temple services and the sacrifices of the cult could be of no possible advantage to a people that

was no longer in the moral position to use them. Even a century before
Jeremiah's day Israel had been wholly sick, sick all over from head to
foot, as Isaiah had put it clearly (1:6). But now, a whole two centuries
after Isaiah had said those words, Israel was not even to be considered
sick.

28   Israel was now in reality a dead corpse, as 41:4 suggests. There is
only one thing you can decently do for a corpse and that is to bury it.
Yet the only undertakers available to God are the heathen.

Is it not a blasphemous idea itself that the Holy One should hand
over his beloved *to utter destruction*? The word is 'put to the ban' or
totally destroy, as Joshua did to Jericho (Josh. 6:17) on the ground
that Jericho — apart from Rahab — was wholly evil and was imbued
with the spirit of a god of nonbeing. This reference to 'extirpation'
looks even more horrible when we meet the words *princes of the sanctuary*.
For while this title covered the whole priestly class, it also included the
king, for he was in reality the chief priest and intermediary between
Yahweh and Israel. And the king in Judah at least, we should
remember, was of the dynasty of David. And to David God has
promised through the lips of Nathan that he would be his Father
forever (2 Sam. 7:14; Ps. 89:20-29). Yet the specially chosen line of
David was included in the extirpation order, even though God had
promised to uphold it forever. The heathen (rather than *reviling*) were
those gentiles who did know Yahweh, such as Nebuchadrezzar and his
soldiers who were the intruments of the destruction of Jerusalem.
Jeremiah had already said this very thing (25:9). But Holiness can do
nothing else than this awful act. Holiness cannot remain bound up in
the Holy-One-of-Israel relationship with a people that has become a
corpse (cf. commentary at 41:14; Ezek. 6:5; 37:11). Holiness must
necessarily loathe and hate the corpse to which it is tied, for a corpse
renders him who even touches it unclean, or unholy, according to the
priestly laws that were being codified in DI's day. It was therefore
essential that Israel should suffer the curse that goes with being bound
to the living and utterly pure and holy God (Dan. 9:11). For God is not
one to be mocked.

But while Holiness must react in what may seem to us a negative
manner when it comes in contact with what is foul and evil, since
Holiness is God himself this negative reaction must be part of God's
positive and creative or even re-creative purpose as it works out to its
ultimate victory. Although it may now be anticipating DI's argument,

it would help to note what DI reveals to be God's final answer to the impasse into which the covenant fellowship has fallen.

DI must have been acquainted with Ezekiel's great vision in ch. 37 of the book that bears his name, as it describes in pictorial form his certainty of what God will do with the dry bones of his people Israel. Yet DI must have known that even God could not perform this act of resuscitating a corpse — stinking as it was now after almost fifty years, buried as it was said to be in the soil of this strange grave of Babylon, to use Ezekiel's tremendous imagery in that seminal chapter of his — merely by uttering an arbitrary divine fiat like a powerful dictator. This is because God would violate his own freedom should he behave in this manner, and violate too the freedom of those very Israelites whom his action was intended to save. God must proceed to this action, which is basic and central in the history of the world, only if that action remains in conformity with his chosen method of self-giving, and with his promise to be with his people forever (cf. Ex. 3:12; Isa. 7:14).

It was manifest by now that the one partner in the covenant, Israel, who had been called to be the Servant, was not in the position to raise herself out of the state of death she had now reached. Therefore it must be God alone, the other partner in the covenant, who would do this thing for her. Accordingly, in the freedom that only perfect love knows and expresses, God himself stoops to share with this stiff-necked Servant people the experience of being damned (*herem*) and dead. In doing so, he is of course serving them within the bonds of the covenant in the only way left for the Lord of the covenant. Since the wages of sin have been death at all times since the fall of Adam, the living God — what an unspeakable paradox — now takes those wages to himself. In so doing, he himself become the Servant of the people whom he has bound himself to love and to cherish in a bond that can never under any circumstances be broken or annulled. In this way he removes from Israel's heart the curse that she has necessarily brought upon herself, and is able to set her free, helpless as she is to do so herself, from the law of sin and death. The promised deliverance from the death of the Exile — the theme which DI leads up to in a later chapter — is a deliverance whose significance continues to unfold as the years go by in the history of this covenant people. The deliverance is an historical incident which we can date accurately just as we can date the resurrection of Christ. This historical incident becomes the sign and seal of the power of God, that he will be able to act in a like manner when he comes to redeem not only his first-born son (Ex. 4:22), but also all his sons of every nation of men. DI sees that the resurrection of the people of God must follow upon their 'crucifixion', when they suffered under Nebuchadrezzar in 587 B.C., and so his mind becomes for us the channel of the revelation of the pattern of God's redemptive work at all times. We can understand how Paul can use for this decisive moment in the world's history the words 'in accordance with the scriptures' (1 Cor. 15:3-4), for it is the same God who acts with infinite compassion and absolute loyalty to his covenant in the days of DI as in the days of Christ. Since God is faithful, it is only to be expected that the revelation he gives us of his love and holy purpose in 539 B.C. should be one with that which he makes of himself *eph hapax*, once and for all, when 'in Christ' he both reveals himself and acts to reconcile the world unto himself (2 Cor. 5:19).

CHAPTER 44

---

1 The grace of God is nowhere more clearly seen than in this section. One would think that 43:28 had related the end of the story, so to speak, and that *Heilsgeschichte*, sacred history, had come to a full stop on account of the intransigence, disloyalty, and rebellion of God's covenant partner, his Servant Israel. But God now takes up the theme of his purpose through his chosen instrument without any pause, and as if the extirpation order were no hindrance to his plan. God is of course almighty. DI therefore sees that God cannot be thwarted even by the sin of man, even by the deliberate defalcation of the essential instrument he had planned to use. But in this verse God seems to bypass the whole problem he now faces, for he insouciantly continues to call Israel his Servant even as she declines the honour.

2 He just reminds her that she was created for that end; and that he has been helping, forming, fashioning, and training her for her office ever since she was born, that is, since the election of Abraham. Then instead of scolding, which would only have produced resentment, he repeats his call, one that can melt the hardest of human hearts: 'Fear not'.

It is interesting how frequently DI refers to the song of Moses in Deut. 32; for it itself is a prophetic interpretation of what God had *done* at the Exodus. It is also interesting that DI's hearers must have been well acquainted with the song to have understood his references. For the name *Jeshurun* is used for Israel at only three other places, at Deut. 32:15 and 33:5, 26. Both of those chapters are in verse and are very ancient. (William Albright, *From the Stone Age to Christianity*, dates it 1100 B.C.; Otto Eissfeldt, *Einleitung in das Alte Testament*, between 1070 and 1020 B.C.) In both chapters the word Jeshurun appears as a poetic name for Israel. The root of the word seems to be the word for 'upright'. If such is the case, then the poetic writers employed the name to designate Israel under her ideal character, in the light of what God her Lord saw she could and might be. Moreover, Jeshurun occurs here in parallel with the ideal description of Israel's God that is found under the term 'Rock', a name for God which has already been noted as characteristic of Deut. 32. If the above reasoning is correct, that DI is drawing his material from the ancient poetic sagas of his people, we have in our hands a clue to his choice of the name Jeshurun. He evidently wishes to declare that Israel is not to be dismissed out of hand as God's failure, in that she cannot keep her bond. The noun Jeshurun may be built linguistically like the tribal name Zebulun. If so, it is in the form of an endearing diminutive. This is what the LXX has had in mind in translating Jeshurun by the Greek word for 'beloved'.

3-4 However we understand this strange word though, one thing is clear. God is determined to resuscitate Israel's faith and to raise her from the death of her corpse-like state to a new life of responsibility. The symbolism has appeared before. Thus Jacob's descendants, that is, those whom DI is now addressing, are soon to know the power of the Spirit coming upon them again (cf. Ezek. 37:1-14). Remember that God's Spirit is none other than God himself. The Spirit is God manifest in action. Similarly his *blessing* is his will, uttered from the heart through the lips in the form of the Word; and since it is God's will that is uttered, it must be effective. The very life of God is to enter into the corpse Israel as she lies in her grave in the broad valley of the Tigris–Euphrates Rivers (Ezek. 37:12).

God's original promise to Abraham was couched in the form of a blessing whose potency would enable the seed of Abraham to multiply and be as numerous as the stars of the sky. But now that that seed had fallen into the ground and died, it did not mean that the promise too had died. God was once again about to pour out his Spirit upon Israel's seed, and the promise would then be one step nearer to its final fulfilment. The combination of water and spirit, which is so important in NT thought, forms an imagery as ancient as the Tammuz ideology of Babylon, which DI would know and whose ideas he could copy. We meet it again at 55:10-11. Another important vision of Ezekiel (47), which DI would probably know, outlines the close relationship between the water of life as it pours into a desert and this language that DI uses here. But unlike Ezekiel, DI draws his metaphor from a Babylonian geographical background with its artificial irrigation channels unknown to the inhabitants of hilly Palestine.

5 The water of life converts. The Spirit changes the human heart. There is no suggestion here that only Israelites are to experience this new birth. Thus, says DI, a pagan will one day declare *'I am the Lord's'*,

or 'I belong to Yahweh'. Another proselyte will enter the family of God
by calling himself by the family name of Jacob, the Father of Israel.
Still another proselyte will tattoo his hand in the manner that a slave
had to do to show to whom he belonged, or even as a jar was marked
when it bore the name of its owner. The fourth proselyte mentioned
here will, so to speak, be baptized into the people of God with a new
name to show his new condition.

Theologically speaking, this passage is interesting. The children of
Israel are born into and claim their heritage of right; pagans are to
enter the people of God by profession of faith, just as they do today.
The people of Israel is thus ideally more than an enlarged family group
of men and women bound together by the ties of blood. Israel is
Jeshurun, the Israel that is the ideal of God. So DI now portrays her as
a supranational idea (cf. Rom. 8:14-17; 11:13-24) or even, to use
present-day language, as the Church as she exists in the mind and
purpose of God.

6   Who is this *Lord* to whom the heathen will turn in longing? For the
whole world is longing for his revelation (42:4). The answer comes
foursquare. (1) He is the *King* and *Redeemer* of Israel, that is, of his
chosen people here on earth below. (2) He is Lord *of hosts*, and so is king
of all the powers in the realms above. (3) He is also the beginning of all
things. (4) And he is the end of all things. No other four corners could
contain the whole purpose of creation and redemption as do these. It is
that foursquare God then who has a missionary purpose to work out
through Israel, and that God is Yahweh, the covenant God of Israel.

7a   Yahweh is utterly unique. There are two words for 'one' in
Hebrew. One is *yahid*, used for example of an only or unique son (cf.
Gen. 22:2; Amos 8:10) or of an isolated person (cf. Pss. 25:16; 68:6).
Here Yahweh is clearly declared to be one or unique in this sense, for he
is Lord of all and wholly other than his creation. But he is also one with
his hosts, for amazingly enough he stoops to share his redemptive
purpose with them. They are his messengers, as we have seen, and
convey his will in shared delight and joy. More astonishing still, as DI
will show later in detail, Yahweh is actually one with recalcitrant
Israel, even as a good husband is one with his erring wife. 'Therefore a
man leaves his father and his mother and cleaves to his wife, and they
become one flesh' (Gen. 2:24). This second word for 'one', *'ehad*, that is
used here in Genesis cannot obviously be understood merely in a

mathematical sense. Yet it lies at the basis of the biblical conception of the nature of God. Remember that this same word for 'one' occurs in the so-called *shema'* (Deut. 6:4), not the word *yahid* which has been translated as 'unique': 'Hear, O Israel: The Lord our God is *one* Lord' (Deut. 6:4). How this word *'ehad* is used can also be seen at Ex. 36:13. This discussion is clearly important for the biblical doctrine of the Trinity.

7b The Book of Exodus speaks of the *signs* which accompanied the election of Israel — the pillar of cloud by day and the pillar of fire by night, the fire upon the mountain, the water from the rock, and so on. The need for these outward signs was interpreted to Moses in his own original experience of the call of God. Not only did he hear a voice speaking in his heart; he also saw a burning bush (Ex. 3). The rod which Moses cast to the ground and the leprosy of his hand (Ex. 4) were also each a sign, or *'oth* given him by God. Each of these was the outward and visible sign and seal of an inward and invisible reality.

The Hebrew of v. 7b is obscure. I believe a possible translation of it, however, might be 'From time immemorial I established a people (cf. 51:16) with (that is, making use of) signs; so when these came into use, they should have been able to expound them.' For God had declared the meaning of his actions by means of sacramental signs that conveyed in themselves their own interpretation of what he was doing. In turn therefore Israel ought to have been able to understand what God would do next. For on the basis of the signs which she had been given in the past, she should have been able to interpret the future. God's nature was consistent with that revealed in Moses' day; and Israel was still the object of his love, since he had created her to be his people from time immemorial.

8 So, possessing this saving knowledge, it was ridiculous that Israel should be afraid. God's revelation of his saving love in her history had been consistent. 'Ever since "that time", have I not been letting you know', that is, since the time of redemption in the days of Moses; 'and have I not been explaining to you what my will is for you, Israel?' What DI means is that everything which has happened in Israel's history is interpretable on the basis of what God did at 'that time', (RSV *from of old*), that is, at the time of the Exodus. This is astonishing, but DI believed it to be the truth. But what is still more astonishing is that Yahweh permits his own uniqueness to be evidenced by his unique *witnesses*, the people of Israel.

9 This passage, vv. 9-20, is a brilliant piece of writing. It contains
sarcasm to a degree. Unlike the rest of DI's work, it is preserved for us
in prose. Possibly he felt that the subject was in fact too prosaic to make
verse of. Here DI subjects the idol-making of the Babylonians to scorn.
The sound of that laughter has resounded down the ages. There are
translation difficulties in the passage, however, owing to the fact that
we are not now in the position to know all the technical processes that
craftsmen employed in Babylon. The day may well come when we
shall be able to translate more exactly some of the specialized words
that occur here. But of course their exact translation does not affect the
religious issue, nor do any of these doubtful words have theological
overtones.

DI's previous lofty passage had ended asking whether any divinity
exists other than Me. Nor is there any other Rock. (At least) I don't
know of any (v. 8). But the Babylonians knew of many others. And so
DI has to take up this point and deal with it finally and thoroughly
before he can proceed with his main argument.

10-11 Imagine a man fashioning a 'divine being', *'el*, in the hope that
the thing he has made with his hands will aid him in life! A free
translation of v. 11 might be 'See how all his fellow guildsmen and
craftsmen are abashed when their god turns out to be subhuman. They
call a meeting, and all stand around in horror and mortification'.

12 DI first speaks generally of craftsmen and guildsmen. Then he
takes a specific example from an ironworker. His example is meant to
destroy the argument once and for all that idols can be of help to man.
So he portrays a smith in action. Being only human this individual
soon grows tired and weary and very thirsty in the heat of the smithy.
How on earth, DI implies, could a man who grows weary produce a
god who does not grow weary and could even give health and strength
to his worshippers? DI must surely have had in mind here what he has
already said about Yahweh, how Yahweh never grows weary, and
how he alone gives strength to *his* weary worshippers (40:28-31).

13 DI's next example is the work of a carpenter. Here especially we
are not sure of some of the technical terms. But what is important is the
emphasis DI places on the highest form of humanity that the carpenter
can imagine. How uncouth and pockmarked most peasants and slaves
must have looked. But a young man who lived in a house, one of the

royal court perhaps, could have been as attractive and wholesome as one of those young athletes of Athens who at this very time were drawing the admiration of Greece's greatest sculptors. We can wonder whether, when DI wrote this line, he had in mind the awesome words of Gen. 1:27, which both he and his hearers seem to have known: 'So God created man in his own image'. But here the carpenter creates his god in the image of man. Even though it is man as he is at his best, this is the reverse of the faith of the Bible.

14 The carpenter is shown working with all reverence at his task and choosing the very best materials available. The *cedar* tree did not grow in Babylon. It had to be fetched — at a price — from the Lebanon mountains. The various kinds of *oak* trees were probably evergreens, and thus were endued with a special divine essence, for they did not die at the end of the season. Once they had grown *strong among the trees of the forest*, the chief forester would allow them to be selected for felling only by special permission. Finally we read with astonishment that our woodworker was skilled enough to try to acclimatize cedars, probably doing so in the royal estates near the city of Babylon. On the other hand, the subject of the verb *plants*, 'he', may be God, nature, what you will, and so could be translated by the passive voice, such as 'got planted' or 'planted itself'.

15-17 Now follows a picture both humorous and pathetic, and one which speaks for itself. The word *'el*, god, is best translated as 'divine being', since DI surely meant us to be shocked by the contrast he was drawing. Here a man grovels before a divinity, half of which he has used to fill his stomach! Notice the simple pleasure at the sense of well-being that a full stomach gives a man when he has leisure after a good meal to sit and gaze into a fire. Like his smith brother, our woodworker too needs to rest. The word for *fire* used here is a rare word. In 50:11, DI chooses it again to refer to false worship. Evidently he does this to draw a contrast with the faith of the prophets. They believed that Yahweh is the sole fire (*'ur*), for he alone is light (*'or*). These two words employ the same consonants in Hebrew and so lend themselves to punning. But finally our craftsman in his human weakness seeks deliverance and strength from his own creation (cf. Hos. 4:12; Rom. 1:21).

18-19 Here is a clear statement that the Lord has blinded the eyes and hearts of the heathen, so it is beyond their competence even to become aware of the falsity of their notions (cf. 2 Thess. 2:11). Thus DI points to a fact that the Church must constantly take into account, that people are born into a religious heritage, whether it be in the Congo or in Afghanistan, which to them makes a complete and logical system of belief.

20 But that does not alter the fact that these beliefs may be so wrong that for him who holds them it is a case of feeding on the ashes of his fire. We translate v. 20: Only a deluded mind could lead him thus astray. His faith cannot save his soul; neither is he able to say, 'Is this thing in my hand not the result of mere wishful thinking?'

Let us note two issues in passing. First, soul (*himself* in RSV), here means the whole personality, the body included; for the Hebrews knew that man is primarily a body (Gen. 2:7) into which God has breathed life. Man needs his flesh (Ps. 63:1), even his kidneys ('soul' in the RSV) to praise God (Prov. 23:16, Heb.), just as much as his heart. And so the salvation that man needs is found in the competence only of a God who has created both matter and spirit. Second, the last phrase may be a proverb which DI's hearers would know already and which he would thus be quoting with telling force.

21 Once again DI leads forward logically in his argument. He both answers the problem he has raised in vv. 9-20 and at the same time connects the solution with the point he had reached in his previous argument at v. 8. If it is God who has blinded the hearts of the heathen, as he has just said, and if it is God who has rendered them logically satisfied with their particular *Weltanschauung*, or world of belief, then how are they ever to know the true God as he really is, and gain that true or whole way of life which DI has spoken of before? The answer to that seems now to be clear: it is to come about through Israel's wholehearted service to Yahweh, for it is she who has to take this whole way of life to the ends of the earth (42:4). But DI is not satisfied with such an easy answer to this fundamental problem. One does not convert a people convinced of the validity of their beliefs to a new way of life simply by preaching to them. History has proved that a hundredfold. Something more fundamental is needed than mere words to reach home to the hearts of a sinful and prejudiced world.

At this point we are made aware of the depth of DI's theological grasp. He sees that Israel's God cannot be postulated as the mere object of human thought. He does not speak of God as Supreme Being, as the Absolute, as that Power which controls all things in heaven and earth. Such a 'thing in itself' as a Supreme Being has nothing in common with DI's God. Modern man, if he uses such language, reveals that he believes himself able to picture this Being whom he thus defines. But if man can even imagine his God, then that God is an idol, the result of mere wishful thinking. DI's God, however, is apprehended by man's mind solely by virtue of God's own free decision and saving activity. It is the nature of Israel's witness to that freedom and that activity that becomes the all-important factor in the matter of the divine revelation to the world.

So DI slowly, gradually, and logically moves forward in his argument from this point until he can make clear what the new factor in witnessing to such a God must be. Meanwhile Yahweh promises Israel he will not forget her. The Hebrew for *you will not be forgotten by me* is a curious composite form. It seems to be a pun, a mixture of two possible meanings. First, it contains the above translation; but second, it can mean 'You may not forget'. The LXX favours the second meaning. But DI has the ability thus to create a vital double meaning of a word that he is handling in his own native tongue.

22 The position of Israel in God's scheme is central. God must necessarily woo her back to himself if he is to go forward with his plan that through her his glory might be revealed to all nations. So DI repeats that vitally important evangelical truth which he has already uttered and discussed. It is that God forgives us *before* we repent, not when and *if* we repent, as many imagine the content of the gospel to be. Perhaps the metaphor of the cloud here is copied from Hosea, who used it three times, for it is a striking one. When you are walking in fog or cloud there seems to be no end to it, and you can be very depressed. But the warmth of the sun can in a matter of minutes completely dissipate the fog and leave not a wrack behind.

23 There is nothing in heaven or earth that man desires or needs more than this total forgiveness of God. It is here shown to be the one factor that permits Israel's life to proceed at all. Were there no forgiveness, then her communal apostasy would have landed her in the *tohu*, the negation or chaos, in which, morally speaking, Babylon was even then wallowing without knowing it. No wonder DI uses such extraordinary language at this point in his argument. For it is an extraordinary thing that he is talking about, something that is almost too good to be true. What he is saying is that *the Lord has [already] redeemed Jacob* in the days of Moses. Why will Jacob not grasp that mighty fact? Moreover, just because of this objective and incontrovertible reality, God is now going on to do something else, for he is now 'letting his glory be seen in Israel', rather than, *will be glorified in Israel*. This is the tremendous theme that DI will now continue to unfold as his chapters proceed.

The very heavens must have begun to appear bluer for those forlorn exiles once they took this good news to their hearts; and since salvation in the experience of many Old Testament witnesses produced in them transports of gladness and joy, it is no wonder that the redeemed here should expect the heavens to join them in their joy. They had now learned that *the Lord has done it*, not man. The hills are therefore invited to *break forth into singing*. What is more, even the chaos (*depths*) that undergirds all life is ordered to join in!

24   Chapter 44 comes to a climax with a series of magnificent utterances expressing the nature and purpose of God in terms unsurpassed anywhere in the OT. By following his order of thought, we can note the emphasis that DI makes. This is what the Lord has declared (as we have seen '*Thus says the Lord*' is in the original Hebrew), that is, the covenant God, who is alive and utters his will by word of mouth, Israel's *Redeemer*; for to love and to forgive is the essence of Yahweh's nature. Yahweh's plan was predetermined before Israel came into existence. This of course is easy for a God who is the creator and author of all things. Hebrew has no word for the Greek idea of cosmos; instead it just says *all things*. Here then we have the concept of 'God in creation' united with that of 'God in history'.

With a touch of genius DI now interjects a question he puts on God's lips: '*Who was with me?*' Up to this point he has led us to believe that no one can possibly be *with* the Lord God Almighty. But he is now approaching in his argument the most amazing volte-face imaginable. For he will soon be saying that while no god could ever be with Yahweh, yet paradoxically Yahweh is *with* Israel, to the extent that Yahweh is even *in* Israel. This argument is developed fully in ch. 45.

25   Remember that for the whole ancient world the word spoken with intent had power. The curse and the blessing were each like arrows sent flying through the air and were bound to hit their target. Once shot off, these arrows could not be recalled. We would be foolish to

83

suppose that this concept has no reality in our day. The modern psychiatrist knows better than to try. For he might have to dig deep into the mind of a neurotic patient to discover what barbed words were shot into his childish mind by a cruel parent thirty years before, or what shocking incident scarred his soul while he was still a little boy, only to be buried deep in his subconscious mind. And so once the arrow is shot the damage is done. Nothing can recall the arrow once it is sped. That looks like common sense.

Yet DI did not believe that this was so, even though it appeared to be a fact of nature. He maintained that an aspect of God's almightiness is that he is able to deflect the arrow in its flight and make it reach the target that *he* wills, not the speaker. God, he believed, does more than just war against evil. As Creator of all he is also Re-creator of all. In other words, God is able to bring good out of evil. *Omens*, words spoken with intent and packed with power to affect the lives of men, flying through the air like atomic warheads, God nullifies or diverts. For DI the foolishness of God is indeed wiser than men. DI not only sweeps away the wisdom of the complicated and integrated hierarchy of Babylonian priests and philosophers and discounts their whole system of astrology, as we have seen before; he also offers a positive philosophy of history in place of their ideas. He can do so because for him faith is not a form of gnosis but is living by the Word of God.

26 He also declared that Israel had been given a glimpse of the divine counsel, *'etsah*, whose fulfilment nothing can deflect (40:8; 45:23; 46:10; 48:14; 53:10; 55:11; cf. Ezra 6:14). Thus if Israel would only act in faith and obedience — if in other words she would just let herself be the Servant and the vehicle of mission in one — then God would guide her arrows to their target.

Recalling that *messengers* can equally well be translated by 'angels', we get a vision of the great purpose of God working out both in heaven and on earth at once. God fulfils his plan as it is brought into action by principalities and powers in the heavenly places within the realm of history. Here again, as at 42:19, we find that the prophetic mind draws no line between God's messengers in heaven and those on earth; for the hosts of Yahweh were to be found both in heaven and on earth (cf. Ps. 33:6 with Ex. 12:41; 1 Sam. 17:45).

Right at the centre of God's cosmic plan there stands a city. This particularism of the biblical faith is strange to the wisdom of the Greeks. In the days of David, God had chosen Jerusalem to be that spot on earth where all things must be fulfilled (cf. Luke 9:51; 18:31). The Chronicler is very interested in this theme, following upon the Deuteronomist before him; and many Psalms sing of its reality (cf. Pss. 87:2, 132:13). Before the Exile, Jerusalem had been that one place in all God's creation where God had put his name to dwell, so that he could be present in the sanctuary in Jerusalem in a special way (1 Kings 8:13, 27-30). Nebuchadrezzar had destroyed that sanctuary, however, and for fifty years now it had seemed as if the arrow he had shot had continued to speed on to bring about the final ruin of the people of God. But God could deflect Nebuchadrezzar's arrow even after fifty years of flight. God, says DI, needs Jerusalem for his purpose now just as truly as ever before. So Jerusalem *shall be inhabited* again along with the whole area of depopulated and ruined Judah.

27 Such a mighty project, as it must have seemed to the exiles who knew that Jerusalem was lying in ruins, was obviously a small thing, declares DI, for a God who can command the *deep* of chaos and *dry up* its tidal currents, the *rivers* that flow along the sea bed.

28 At exactly the right moment therefore God has raised up an instrument to perform his will. The cosmic Plan will now continue on its way serene and unimpeded by the sin of man. Once again God will set his name to dwell in the chosen city of Jerusalem, and once again the temple will be standing to receive that name as its dwelling place on earth.

So at last Cyrus is named, in the very last verse of the chapter. Such is the genius of DI, who knows how to pursue his argument step by step as he moves from theme to theme. At this point he shows us how Cyrus is actually the particularizing, the historicizing of the cosmic purpose at that moment in history. Yet that same Cyrus never knew that he was being used by Israel's God. Moreover DI tells us nothing at all about the character and nature of this powerful man. Obviously neither the faith nor the nature of Cyrus is important in itself. Yet if we turn to a pagan source to learn of the wars of Cyrus, the historian Xenophon can give us graphic word sketches of Cyrus and show us how he was indeed a character who impressed himself greatly on his generation. In DI's eyes this mighty warrior has value solely as the instrument of the purposes of God.

A corollary of this fact is also of great interest. It is that the pagan state can evidently be used as God's instrument of mission, just as much as can the church. For Cyrus — the state — is the instrument of the recreative Word of the living God in action in a historical situation. On the other hand, while God used Cyrus for the rebuilding of Jerusalem, it was not he but Israel, the people of God, whose hands in the final event actually did the rebuilding of the city.

Cyrus is called *my shepherd*. This one word in Hebrew can also be vowelled to mean 'my friend'. At 48:14 Cyrus is known as 'he whom Yahweh loves'. DI means that Yahweh chose Cyrus from all other possible alternatives to be his instrument. In this way God has continued to choose the unlikeliest of persons to be his instruments down the arches of the years. He chose the writings of his servant Nietzsche, for example, to prevent the Christian religion from becoming a mere system of ethics. It might be said that because of his servant Karl Marx, the Church awoke to the social implications of its own Gospel to a degree that it might never have done if he had never penned *Das Kapital*.

DI now presents a combination of concepts. First, in the Tammuz ideology of the Babylonians the king was regarded as the shepherd of his people (cf. Jer. 3:15; Zech. 13:7), and also in Israel many hailed the Davidic line in similar terms (cf. Ezek. 34). The people of Israel now in exile would naturally make this association of ideas, even though at this point DI himself is making no reference to the line of David. But secondly, as the instrument of Yahweh, Cyrus is to act even as the Shepherd of Israel acts. All unwittingly Cyrus is to become the instrument of him who, as DI has already proclaimed, is about to carry the lambs in his bosom home to the ruins of that Jerusalem which figures centrally in God's cosmic plan (cf. Matt. 16:21; Mark 10:33; Luke 9:31; Rev. 21:2). Cyrus is thus no less than an 'arm of the Lord' (cf. 63:11-12).

CHAPTER 45

1   Sidney Smith writes: 'It was an Assyrian, and therefore, probably a Babylonian, custom that client kings who had revolted and then been captured, might be punished by being fastened to the bolts of the city gates with chains in such a way that, bound round the middle, they were forced to adopt a sitting posture; this gave rise to ridicule, for they looked like squatting bears'.(*Isaiah, Chapters XL-LV: Literary Criticism and History* p. 73.) This may be the background of DI's vigorous statement, that God *will ungird the loins of kings*, but it is not necessary to elaborate. The words are a poetic exaggeration typical of the Eastern mind. Yet the phrase is a plain statement. It means to render the kings helpless, for one had to buckle up the outer robe before it was possible to move freely. It is more important, however, to note that God grasps the right hand of his pagan servant Cyrus in the same manner as he grasps the right hand of his chosen servant Israel (41:13; 42:1).

2   Now follows a still more vivid Eastern hyperbole. DI says God is about to *level the mountains* before the feet of Cyrus just as he is about to do for Israel (40:4). He will do so, of course, because Cyrus is God's instrument; in fact he is actually God's 'anointed'. But the Babylonian king was also the anointed of Marduk. 'Whose right hand I, Marduk, have grasped' are words to be found on a clay cylinder unearthed in Babylon. (See what is known as the 'Cyrus cylinder' in James Pritchard's ANET, p. 315; D. W. Thomas, ed., *Documents from Old Testament Times* pp. 92-94.) DI was obviously a man of education. We have seen before that he knew court etiquette and the liturgical language of his captors. But what is amazing is that he dared to seize upon expressions embedded in an alien mythology and a pagan ritual and apply them to the God who repeatedly declares 'Apart from me there is no other god'.

In Israel's heritage several types of persons were anointed to office. For example, according to Ps. 105:15 the patriarchs were anointed to their task. Most important was the fact that the king was anointed (2 Sam. 19:21; Pss. 2:2; 18:50), as was the king's cultic successor in the days after the return from Exile, viz., the high priest (Lev. 4:3). In like

manner, then, all Israel, perhaps represented by one person, king or
high priest, could be regarded as the corporate priest to the Lord (Ex.
19:6; Hos. 4:6). So it is important to recognize that the word *anointed*
represents the Hebrew word for 'messiah' as it is rendered elsewhere
in the English versions. At this point one should be watchful about
reading into it any technical meaning along this line; for as DI uses it, it
is the pagan king Cyrus who is here entitled Yahweh's anointed. Could
it then be said that no tyrant who ever reached his throne or created an
empire by wading through the blood of the conquered has thus placed
himself outside the care of the God of Israel? For God is able to weave
that tyrant's wickedness and follies into the grand unfolding purpose
which he has continually in mind.

The wording used here by DI reminds us of themes found in the
Magnificat: 'He has shown strength with his arm, . . . he has put down
the mighty from their thrones, and exalted those of low degree' (Luke
1:51-52). None could be mightier than King Croesus or the king of
Babylon; none could be of lower degree than exiled and imprisoned
Israel.

3 So also with the words 'He has filled the hungry with good things'.
For Cyrus had by now looted the vaults of this same Croesus at Lydian
Sardis, and these contained *treasures of darkness*, indeed 'hidden hoards
of mammon'. This last word is usually translated as 'hidden treasure',
but it is quite probably the basis of the NT word 'mammon'. Finally
the Magnificat declares: 'He has helped his servant Israel'. How he will
do so DI will tell soon.

Why then had God used Cyrus in this extraordinary manner? The
word *lema'an*, meaning 'in order that', now occurs three times in rapid
succession to show us why.

The first occurrence runs: *that you may know that it is I, the Lord, . . . who
call you by your name*. It is doubtful whether Cyrus ever did come to
acknowledge Yahweh. In fact we are almost sure that he never did. Yet
Cyrus is merely representative of the great powers of the earth, who
Yahweh intended should one day acknowledge him as Lord.
Implicitly, from DI's point of view, Cyrus did in fact acknowledge
Yahweh later on when he encouraged the rebuilding of the Jerusalem
Temple.

4 Yet DI explicitly admits that God could say of Cyrus *though you do
not know me*. The second *lema'an* reads: *For the sake of My Servant Jacob,*

and Israel my chosen, I call you by your name. Just as at Christian baptism the child is given a name, a Christian name, so that in God's sight he becomes unique and beloved for his own sake, so it is here; and this is what DI means when he adds 'though you were quite unaware of me', for no child is aware of God when he is brought as a babe to the font. The emphasis here is that it is *God* who chooses Israel for his own good, and not Israel who chooses God. This means that God's action in election and adoption is one of grace alone.

5 Moreover, we observe this grace even more clearly when we notice the deliberate parallel in language between 45:1, where it is Cyrus who is the chosen one whom Yahweh has been girding, and here where the chosen one is Israel (cf. 41:13; 42:1). For with this parallelism it becomes clear that the instrument which God chooses for himself is not chosen for any intrinsic value it may possess.

6 The third *lema'an* says in effect: 'So that men — all men everywhere — might realize that Yahweh alone is God'. Once again, DI turns back to the underlying missionary purpose reposing in God's choice of Israel and in his employment of Cyrus. These actions of Yahweh are evidently not just ends in themselves. Both of them are means to the end that the whole world should know Yahweh as God. Election for DI is therefore election *for* an end beyond itself.

7 Finally, to crown the whole climactic expression of God's purpose, DI makes use of the finest religious concepts that Cyrus' Persian world had ever produced. The controversy has not yet ended as to whether King Cyrus was a Zoroastrian by faith or not. Probably he was not, for Zoroaster seems to have been born after Cyrus' day. But Zoroaster did not introduce into Persia a wholly new set of concepts: what he did was to develop the dualism native to the early Persian ideology. In that world view the gods Ahriman and Ormuzd issued originally out of 'time', Zurvan; yet Zurvan was nothing more than the starry hosts on high. Thus the hosts, about which both Isaiah of Jerusalem and our prophet have so much to say when they declare that these serve Yahweh and obey him as his minister, in ancient Persian thought were actually exalted to the highest place of all. Zoroaster took over the ideas that were native to the Persian view of reality. He deified the concepts of both light and darkness. Ormuzd, the god of light, he designated the apotheosis of the good, and Ahriman he called the god of evil. Man sees that the two powers are obviously always struggling with each other for mastery in this mysterious universe. The important addition that Zoroaster made to this basic view of things, however, was to assure his followers that the good would in the end prevail over the evil.

But to DI any form of dualism is merely ridiculous, in the light of Yahweh's continued declaration that he alone is God and that apart from him 'there is nothing else' (v. 6). So now he makes one of the great categorical declarations of the Bible. He says of Yahweh: '*I form Light, and create Darkness*'. In both the Old and the New Testaments light is regularly employed as a symbol of God's creative and saving purpose (cf. Gen. 1:3-4; Pss. 19; 27:1; 37:6; 104:2; Isa. 2:5; 42:6; John 1:5; 2 Cor. 4:6). Equally, darkness is symbolic of all that is negative and contrary to the divine will (cf. Gen. 1:2; Eccl. 2:14; Ia. 9:2; Joel 2:2). Throughout the whole OT, however, God is in control of darkness even as he is in control of light (cf. Gen. 1:4-5; Deut. 5:23; Job 12:22; Pss. 18:28; 104:20; 139:12). Both light and darkness are therefore instruments of his will. They are neither twins nor mutually exclusive divine powers that will keep on warring to the end. So DI's next line, in parallel with v. 7a, proceeds to explain the concepts of light and darkness in theological rather than in mythological language. The RSV's choice of words, 'weal' and 'woe', sound nice, but are not accurate. *I make* harmony, he says of God. Harmony represents the seminal Hebrew word *shalom*, commonly rendered by 'peace'. Here it occurs as the opposite of *raʿ*, *evil* — a thing which Yahweh actually has to create. Therefore the concept of good must materialize before the mind's eye in the form of integration or perfect harmony. *Shalom* is paralleled with 'good' at 52:7, with 'joy' at 55:12, and with 'righteousness' at 54:13-14. Evil too is comprehensible to the eye of the mind in terms of disintegration; for *raʿ* is closely related to DI's favourite concept of chaos, a concept which he holds in common with the priestly writer of the first chapter of Genesis. The RSV's attempt at alliteration by using 'weal' and 'woe' is unfortunate, for the English reader is prevented from grasping the important meanings of the Hebrew terms.

So Yahweh 'forms' light and harmony, which are integral to his nature as the living God, but he has to '*create*' darkness and evil, for they are not of his essence as God. Here we have a reference to why God created evil in the first place. God uses evil to subserve his total plan so that it can work out to its triumphant conclusion. Without darkness the concept of light is unthinkable. Without evil, the goodness of God is incomprehensible. The OT of course has no conception of goodness as such. Goodness is not a static quality that can be observed and measured. Nor is it an object that can be packaged for the mail. DI understands goodness in terms of God's actively creative, saving love. He sees it in terms of concern, of compassion, and of the pouring out of the self that others may be saved. This reality becomes ever more clear as we continue our study of DI's thesis.

But if saving love is indeed the great reality behind all things, then there must exist some other entity from which man requires to be saved. Moreover, that entity must be part of the creation of God, even though it is not to be classified as an object any more than goodness. For God is of course *all*, and there is nothing else but *He* (43:10). Thus if concern and compassion are radical expressions of the nature of the living God, then something else must have enslaved those for whom his compassion is displayed, even though that something else must also have been created by God.

God's essential purpose is that the light should reach all men (42:6), and that all men should know his name (45:6). If they should thus come to know him, they would be saved from the powers of evil, of *tohu*, of negation, of self-destruction and pride. The transitive (Hiphil) form of the verb *yasha'* can be used for the action of bringing men out of chaos and evil into that which is normal. That is why the Hiphil active participle can be applied to God and to the divine activity. For God is no less than *Moshia'*, or Saviour (43:3) of Israel. The new state of being into which God saves Israel can then be known as peace — as *shalom* is usually translated — yet not as peace in the modern connotation of the word. Here the word signifies not just the opposite of *tohu*, negation, but everything that *tohu* is not; for that which is wholly good can never be described in terms of evil, not even in terms of evil's opposite. *Shalom* speaks of that perfect harmony, wholesomeness, wholeness of being, which is present as the norm in God's loving purpose for man and for his universe. And since that norm already exists in heaven and God offers it to Israel on earth — as DI had learned from the works of Isaiah before him — then it will be on earth that God must eventually triumph over evil in all its many manifestations, and must establish the reality of *shalom*. Finally DI declares *I am the Lord, who do all these things*. An alternative reading from the NEB presents the translation as 'I, the Lord, do all these things'.

8   It is important to note that the Hebrew word *righteousness* used in
v. 8 occurs in two forms, one masculine, one feminine. In line 1 it is
masculine, in line 2 (of the Hebrew) it is feminine.

In the cultures and mythologies of the ancient Near East (with the
exception of Egypt), in which Israel necessarily shared, what comes
from the 'sky' or 'from above' is normally expressed in terms of the
masculine. What belongs to 'earth' or comes 'from below' is expressed
in feminine terms. In the ancient world the king was responsible for
justice, wisdom and the quality of life of his people. So with the god of a
nation, for it was the god who granted these very things through the
king. So Israel had learned to use this masculine word *tsedeq* to express
the idea of a general world order, one that realized itself in the various
fields of wisdom: the cult, fertility, justice, kingship, etc. But now DI
takes this technical term and here places it in the framework of God's
covenant love. So it comes to mean virtually 'God's action to bring
about a whole new way of life'. Yet it occurs in parallel with the term
yesha', which expresses the idea of 'saving love' also in the form of
action. Now, since the very idea of selfishness is foreign to the revealed
nature of God, God does not pass on 'salvation' to Israel through his
'sacramental union' with her within the Covenant just in order that
Israel might rejoice in 'being chosen', or 'being saved'. When God's
tsedeq reaches Israel, 'rained down from above' as it is, Israel thereby
receives the power to do what God does. Israel discovers 'saving love'
springing up within her own heart, a love which, through the
Covenant, is now aimed at the peoples of the earth. This secondary,
human activity is expressed by the feminine form of the word *tsedaqah*
(see discussion of this term in Anton Schoors, *I am God your Saviour*).

This distinction between the masculine and the feminine forms of
this noun reveals a deep unity of thought throughout the whole book of
Isaiah. *Tsedeq*, to describe God's action, occurs 25 times from ch. 1 to
ch. 66. *Tsedaqah*, the feminine, occurs 22 times to describe man's
response. Again, when God gives *my tsedaqah* to Israel, as he does 10
times in chs. 46-66, one senses that God's initial act and Israel's
response are included together. It would seem that Paul, steeped as he
is in the thought of these chapters, puts *tsedeq* and *tsedaqah* together in
the one word *dikaisosyne*; for the latter, he says, is *ek theou, from God* (e.g.,
Phil. 3:9) even as it is at Isa. 46:13. In a word, *tsedaqah* does not
describe the state of 'having been saved'. Rather, once Israel has begun
sharing in the divine activity through the Covenant, it describes
the power that Israel has now received to do what God does, viz.,

seek in love to save the pagan world. It is not of herself: *I the Lord have created it.*

9   DI now shows a degree of anger and impatience with the exiles who are so slow to believe his good news. We can only surmise that he has to meet all kinds of objections to his thesis. For example, some would surely object to his interpretation of Cyrus' advance on Babylon. Others would certainly challenge him on the question of the providential care of God for those exiles who could see simply no evidence of it in their present fate. Perhaps some of them, loyalists and conservatives by nature, brushed aside his teaching because it contained no reference to a messiah of the line of David. Certainly the exiles would be split into parties and factions, as happens to all exiled groups in the strange atmosphere of a foreign land. Yet to all of them DI offers the one reply: 'We and our little plans and preoccupations do not count at all. It is to God and his plan alone that we must hearken and obey, and nothing else'.

10   The insolence of Israel's attitude toward God is borne out by such questions as 'What right have you to beget children?' rather than '*what are you begetting?*' DI reminds them that the Lord, as both father and mother of his people at once, has given them birth for a purpose that reaches the stars (cf. Rom. 9:20 ff.). So DI blasts this fifth column, whatever its policy was, as he does again later at 49:15; for it represents a display of that ultimate lack of faith which, almost identifiable with the sin against the Holy Ghost of the NT, is a form of virtual suicide. Not to accept life as God has decreed it is in a sense to take one's own life. If Israel persists in this attitude, then she is sinning to a far greater degree than the Babylonians, for they know nothing of a life planned and given to his loved ones by the Almighty, to be lived out in trust and obedience.

11   It is now God's turn to take up the questioning of the exiles. DI is obviously being careful to clear up every possible objection to Israel's calling as a Servant before he comes to explain the nature of the office.

The text of this verse is obscure. We might render it by 'Do you have the presumption to question the paternity of my children, or to give me orders about what I make and do with my hands?' For of course, Israel is 'my son' (Ex. 4:22); and God's hands had rescued Israel out of Egypt.

12   Today, for example, we take it to be the right of parents to give their children the education of their choice. So God has the power as well as the right to educate his children as he chooses (49:2; Jer. 27:5). The verb *created* used of man is very emphatic here, and means so much more than the previous *made* of physical matter. It draws attention to the fact that God the Almighty has total rights over his creature man.

13   So then which of his creatures dares question Almighty God about his use of Cyrus? Even more significant is God's action in raising up Cyrus, for by the use of that strongly anthropomorphic verb DI is emphasizing that God has the right to smooth the path of Cyus even as he has already promised (40:3) to smooth the path of Israel. God says, 'I have raised (Cyrus) up in my plan of salvation' (the noun *tsedeq*), even as he has long since raised up Israel also for such an end. Which of the exiles without the enlightenment of the Holy Spirit would ever have thought out that startling equation? For on the face of it, and in view of Israel's knowledge to date of the ways of God, the equation sounds little less than blasphemy. However, its two parallel lines converge not at infinity but at a particular moment in time and at a particular spot on earth. This convergence actually happened in the year 538 B.C. It was then that Cyrus issued his famous decree, which included permission for all displaced persons to return to their homes. As the book of Ezra informs us, permission was also granted to the Hebrew exiles to rebuild their ruined city of Jerusalem, and this they actually did with the aid of a grant from the royal treasury. These things happened just a couple of years or so after DI spoke these words. Two parallel lines did meet, but not in infinity as would be expected. They met at that very material spot known as Jerusalem and at a time which can be accurately dated. That is to say, a miracle, the impossible, did in fact happen. Cyrus enabled the rebuilding of Jerusalem, yet neither for payment (RSV *price*) nor reward; for that enlightened monarch knew nothing of the significance of the moment that he was living through in the sacred history of Israel.

The significance here of DI's understanding of God's ways with Israel must not be passed over. He believes that God, as Creator, is always creating. Thus the recreation of Jerusalem cannot be the last word in God's ongoing Plan. Just as God's primary activities in saving Israel from the hand of Pharaoh at the time of the Exodus were a pointer to Cyrus' messianic activity in 538 B.C., so the latter is also a pointer to a further redemptive act not yet foreseen when God will use still another messianic figure. 'I the Lord have created it.' God has now spoken in a fact of history, 'When I speak and act, who can reverse it?' (cf. 43:13c).

14 This verse is closely related to 43:3. The phrase *the* workers (rather than *wealth*) *of Egypt* conjures up pictures of the lash of the taskmaster known to Israel from the days of Moses. *Ethiopia* means all Upper Egypt and beyond. The tall Sabeans were probably the black-skinned handsome negro peoples to the south. These three names thus cover all that was known of the African Continent south and east of the Sahara desert.

Now comes the question: is it Cyrus the conqueror of the known world that these peoples are to pass before, as at a later Roman triumph? Many expositors think that this is the case. But the pronoun — or suffix in Hebrew — *you* occurs in the feminine singular and is repeated as such five times in this short and self-contained strophe. *You* must therefore refer to Jerusalem, the mother of Israel, the feminine city that has been referred to already in v. 13. Again, are these peoples regarded as coming in fetters, as conquered nations, as transports of prisoners of war? Surely not, for this is not a historical statement that is presented to us, but rather a vision. It thus conforms with the hopes of the many other prophets, both before and after DI's day, who believed that the whole world of men will come eventually and bow down before Israel, bringing their gifts with them (cf. 49:23; 60:9, 10, 14, 16; Zech. 6:15; Rev. 21:26). Notice that it is not before God that they are to bow, as Isa. 2:1-5 and other passages declare. It is to be before that Israel whom God has already addressed as worm, or louse. At first impression the picture seems to offer a very dangerous, man-centred and unbiblical notion of the ways of God. It is true that Israel did at times fall into the temptation of imagining that the day would come when the nations would bow before her. Yet such a reading of this verse is corrected by its last words. Note that these are uttered by the heathen nations who stand and watch: 'Indubitably the Divine Being is in you'. Note that they do not say that 'Yahweh is . . .' for the nations do not know his name. Moreover, the RSV is wrong in rendering their words *'God is with you only'*. The preposition here is not 'with' but 'in'. Thus from the lips of the heathen world comes virtually the dramatic statement: 'God was in Israel, reconciling the world unto himself', as we paraphrase with reverence the words of Paul (cf. 2 Cor. 5:19; also 1 Cor. 12:12 ff.). Israel in herself is nothing but a worm, a louse. How then could the nations bow down before her in adoration? But if God is *in* her, that makes all the difference. It is God who is all in all. Israel remains as nothing. 'There is no other god at all', the heathen actually declare at this point. Thus it is preposterous even to suggest that apostate Israel could compete with Almighty God for one moment as he uses her to reveal his glory to the nations.

15 One of the pitfalls into which biblical interpreters can slip is to isolate a verse and seek to expound it out of its context. For centuries, theologians have sought to relate, for example, Isa. 7:14 ('Behold, a young woman shall conceive') to the birth of Christ, without relation to the two verses that follow it and with which it forms an integral whole. Such a course is virtually dishonest exegesis. All exegetes can make mistakes, but all ought to deal resolutely with the text both as part of its context and in respect to its historical setting. Our v. 15 is another verse that theologians have frequently handled in isolation. Taken out of its context and removed from its strophe, the verse speaks of the *Deus Absconditus*, the Hidden God, of whom much has been written in semi-philosophical terms. Theologians have discussed God as if he were an abstraction, as we sometimes blame the Greek element in our heritage for teaching us to do. But this verse obviously follows directly from the previous line. There we read that the God who is *in* Israel hides himself as the *God of Israel*, and as such he is Israel's Saviour. But that reality does not leap to the eyes of men without the help of faith. In fact, to say that Yahweh is *in* Israel, reconciling, might appear to be merely another scandal, stumbling block or even blasphemy, when one sees her lying helpless in the darkness of Babylon. For God is light and power; he is the creator of the ends of the earth; how ridiculous even to suggest that he is even now *in* Israel. If he is indeed in her, then he is hidden by that ridiculous situation rather than revealed to the eyes of men. Yet DI makes the lips of the heathen witness to the reality that God is truly present in his self-emptying, when he is *in* a people that is both louse and prisoner in the dark. In such an Israel he hides himself, yet that act of hiding is his revelation of himself. For it is just such an incarnational act that reveals him to be no less than *Saviour*.

16-17 There is nothing that the unbelieving nations can do when the truth of this extraordinary reality is made manifest but hide their faces in shame for even imagining that divinity in any form could ever be found in an idol. But once Israel herself becomes the flesh in which God Almighty hides his Godhead, she becomes caught up herself in God's *everlasting salvation* (*'olamim* is here used for the first time in the OT to represent endless time or eternity), and thus naturally she will never be *confounded*. 'You', one and all, represents the Hebrew plural, and so refers no longer to Zion as a whole but now to each individual Israelite. The essence of God's hiddenness is here declared to be actually the mystery of his incarnational act in the body of the corpse Israel. Yet his very hiddenness is to be understood as an activity and must not be seen as a state of being. For, as the Hebrew has it, Israel is saved *in* the Lord, who is the Lord of creative activity.

18   There now follow three 'Words' of revelation, at vv. 18, 20 and 22. The first of the three Words bears upon it the divine signature. Its content follows in natural sequence from the previous strophe. It is that, whether we call him creator or potter, God will not rest till his world becomes once again what it was created to be. It was not created to be chaos, that is to say, for the continuance of the reign of sin, disease, and war. It was created *to be inhabited*, that is, for civilized life, literally 'for dwelling'. We saw at v. 7 that the opposite of evil is order or peace (*shalom*). *Shalom* includes *inter alia* the concept of ordered community life. But it does so only when men who possess *shalom* in their hearts put it into effect in their community life. And so this first Word reveals that God's purpose is one of peace in the widest sense of the term. It is a peace which *he* gives, not one which man tries to produce (2:3-4); and once this peace is given, man is able to know God intimately (Jer. 31:34), and will want to love his neighbour as himself.

19   Now, this Word that DI mentions is neither new nor unexpected; it was not suddenly revealed as an afterthought on God's part, nor was it once uttered long ago and then kept *secret* till Jacob's descendants might learn about the promise God made to their forefather Abraham (Gen. 12:3). 'I did not say to them, "Seek me in the Void", in the land of darkness. What I speak is saving love; what I declare is Reality.' Since this is the Word of the living God, that Word must some day resolve itself— an explosive situation! — in living form. So we are back once again to our prophet's central theme, that Israel is God's chosen instrument. God's purpose cannot therefore remain hidden in darkness, nor can it remain a mere unspoken Word. For his Word has in fact been uttered long ago and is now hidden in Israel. To begin with, God had acted *for* Israel; now, once his acted Word has gone forth, he is also working *in* Israel. That Word is even now becoming flesh or event, in the manner that every word spoken with intent behaves (cf. 55:11; John 1:1 ff.; Matt. 12:36). However, DI develops this theme more fully in ch. 55, so at the moment he leaves us to meditate on it.

20   The second Word is a command. It is based upon the first Word which is one of revelation. *Assemble yourselves and come* (close) Israel, for mighty things are just about to happen. God declares the urgency of the situation by calling the exiles even now, proleptically, *survivors*, escapees. Note that they have not yet started to escape. But if God has now said the word 'escape', then escape they shall. One important result of their escape, one element in the total redemption that is about to come, will be the sounding of the death knell of heathenism. The reference in v. 20*b* is probably to the annual New Year festival in Babylon when the gods were carried in procession through the streets. But in total contrast to that sorry rite, Yahweh, declares DI, is about to carry Israel away (cf. 40:11; 63:9).

21   DI will return to this theme in the next chapter. But to produce the cumulative effect which he is so good at creating, he feels compelled to return first to his refrain of the greatness and uniqueness of Yahweh, who has been revealing himself ever since the days of the Exodus in Israel's life. None of the goods is as alive and full of creative love as is Yahweh, who announced his saving plan for his whole cosmos at that point in history which DI calls 'that time' (RSV '*of old*').

22   On the basis of God's saving nature, and of his uniqueness as God alone, the third Word becomes one of loving invitation. '*Turn to me and be saved.*' For it is the good will and blessed purpose of the one and only God that *all ends of the earth* should *be saved* (cf. Pss. 22:27; 65:5).

23   This truth is expressed now in clear and vivid terms prefaced once again by God's own signature, one that he has actually made on oath, so to speak. For his part, man must always swear by something greater than himself. 'By heaven, I'll . . .' he is ready to say (cf. Heb. 6:13). But God can swear only by himself, for nothing exists apart from him (cf. Gen. 22:16; Jer. 22:5; 49:13; Amos 6:8; also Deut. 32:40). Here God does this very thing. Moreover his oath precedes a word of universalistic hope. This word is so striking and so exciting that many of the early Church theologians regarded it as a clear promise from the lips of the living God expressed in living words. For living words, like arrows shot from the bow, must hit their target in the end, since it is God Almighty who has sent them forth, and since the Word of our God must stand forever (40:8; cf. Rom. 14:11, which quotes from the LXX version; Phil. 2:10).

The Targum on this verse translates 'He said to me that by the Word of Yahweh he (Yahweh) would bring righteousness', and the previous verse by 'Look unto my Word and be ye saved'. The Targum on Isaiah was the interpretation of the book that was made in the vernacular of the Jews in the early Christian centuries, but which assumed written form only about the seventh century A.D. Yet the tradition it embodied effectively conveyed the accepted interpretation that had been offered ever since at least the first century before Christ. The various Targums preserve the concept of the vitality and essentially creative nature of God's Word, as does the prologue to John's Gospel. In this later Jewish Targum, we are given an interpretation of the text of DI which goes beyond what the Hebrew text actually says. Its authors have understood that DI was putting together two fundamental concepts. One is contained in the sentence *Besides me there is no saviour*, to be found at 43:11 and elsewhere. The other is that God's saving activity that is meant for all peoples will one day be found *in* Israel.

24 As we reach the powerful climax of this profoundly important chapter, we note that the words *it shall be said of me*, though obviously meaningful enough, are a reconstruction of a mutilated text. The significance of DI's great assertions however is not affected by this minor textual difficulty. We proceed: It is *only in the Lord* (note the vital preposition 'in' again) that Israel will acknowledge she has found *righteousness* (the feminine plural form of the noun *tsedaqah*, thus meaning 'creative loving acts to others'), and *strength*, a word normally used of God alone. In fact, in some instances in the Psalms and elsewhere, God's strength is a way of speaking of his Spirit in action in the life of man. DI's unique God is strength or power itself. As such he cannot 'do nothing', nor can he produce chaos again; nor can he do everything, even though the possibility is there. For unlike the gods that man invents, Yahweh is able to do only what he wills to do. His will, DI declares, is known to man as this, that *to me every knee shall bow.*

Thus Yahweh's strength is to accomplish this, his declared will. Therefore in his turn man becomes real man — not merely man's philosophical idea of what a man should be — when he lives by that strength and expresses it towards his fellows in the way that God expresses it to him, in the form of compassionate, loving activity.

Thus DI sums up this section of his argument by declaring that the saving acts, which Israel is to deploy when as the Servant she seeks to win the gentiles, are fused into the strength that God alone supplies. On the other hand, the nations who are *incensed against him* shall come, into his presence it would seem, and obviously for judgment. Although DI does not speak of any punishment for these gentiles at this point in the development of his thesis, he seems to suggest, because of his universalistic view, that the nations will be so *ashamed* that they will be moved to repent and turn to Yahweh.

25   But there is no doubt about the salvation of Israel 'in Yahweh' (cf. the NT phrase 'in Christ', Eph. 1:1). So it is not surprising that their salvation will be marked by boasting aloud *in* Yahweh; that is to say, when Israel enters into the joy of her Lord, she will confess that he alone is all in all, and that her salvation now seen as power to save others comes from him alone.

CHAPTER 46

1 In the city of Babylon DI and his countrymen watched each year at the Akitu festival the annual procession of gods through the streets to the great E-Sagila shrine. See ANET, pp. 315-316. Marduk was the most important of those gods. He was known also by the name of *Bel*, which is just the Hebrew *Baal*, a generic title for any god (cf. Jer. 50:2). Marduk was the tutelary god of the city of Babylon. *Nebo* is from the same root as the Hebrew *nabi*, a prophet. Nebo was Bel's son, and was known as the speaker of the gods, like Mercury or Hermes in later centuries (Act 14:12). Nebo was worshipped at Borsippa in a magnificent temple called E-Zida. Many kings were called by his name, such as Nebuchadrezzar (Nabu-protect-the-boundary). Nebo was Babylon's saviour god.

The conversation overheard in this verse is almost certainly apocryphal. Here is my translation of it:

> 1 '*Bel's knees are giving way!*' '*Nebo's toppling over!*' '*They've actually put their graven images on beasts and cattle!*'
> '*What loads your bundles are!*' '*They're only burdens for weary beasts!*'
> 2 '*The men have stumbled and their knees have given way too!*' '*They can't rescue their load!*'
> '*(The gods) themselves have gone off into exile!*'

No displaced persons, aliens, foreigners would dare make sarcastic remarks such as these as they elbowed their way on the sidewalk when the procession of gods was going by. The Israelites would more probably have been numbed by the magnificence of Babylon's gods, and would keep recalling how their own God had been defeated fifty years before. Even more certainly they would be numbed by the magnificence of the city of Babylon as their thoughts strayed to the heap of ruins on Zion's hill. But DI at least kept his sense of humour, as we see here. First it is the gods who are nearly 'toppling' as the cart carrying them hits a rut or a cobblestone.

2 Then DI's sarcasm swings to the human beings as they stumble and try to rescue their precious load. For effect he reverses the order of the verbs, identical as they are, which he uses for tottering gods and stumbling men. And then a ludicrous thought strikes him: the gods are fleeing the city. Cyrus is at the gate! All that those poor human beings are trying to save are their gods' shells; the gods themselves have already fled and are in exile from their home city. And Nebo was the saviour god! Yet he couldn't save himself. When Cyrus did actually enter Babylon, he took the city by surprise, and the gods did not have time to escape. However, Cyrus respected the beliefs of the Babylonians and at once offered worship to the ancient gods he had conquered. But DI's purpose here is to preach, and this he does by means of sarcasm. He is not concerned to try to be a foreteller of the future like a Babylonian stargazer. He knows that that is not what a prophet of the Lord is called to do.

3 What DI does is to make the procession an object lesson. He addresses the exiles by the title of *remnant*, for that is a description of Israel which conveyed to them overtones of love and compassion. The pre-exilic prophets had used it (Amos 5:15, Micah, 2:12, and Jeremiah with reference to Judah when the Northern Kingdom fell). DI's hero Isaiah (37:32) had used the term for the survivors of the Exile. This overtone of love is now carried forward by the figure of mother love and of the word *womb*, which has the same consonants as the verb meaning to show compassion. There go the gods, carried by their devotees. But you *have been borne* by your God ever since your birth, as a mother carries her child (cf. Deut. 1:31; Isa. 63:9).

4 What is true of the past is therefore certain to be true in the future. Yahweh will continue to *carry* Israel all her days. This is because God will never change. He will still be '*I am He*'. Here are set down two great affirmations of our biblical faith: (1) Man-made religions are a burden to those who hold them, but the God of the Bible upholds those who trust in him. (2) One need use only the present tense when speaking of Israel's God, for in both the past and the infinite future, God is always the same: 'I am'.

5 While it is a trifle wearisome that DI should return to this topic and should ask once again who can be compared to God, remember that the remnant must have needed much persuading. DI evidently felt that the occasion of the procession was too good an opportunity to let slip. Surely the exiles could now see with their own eyes what heathen gods looked like. There was an aura of mystery about Bel and Nebo so long as they remained hidden in a gaudy temple.

6-7   But here they were on the street, and anyone could see they were merely gilt-covered dolls. More of his sarcasm follows as he points out to the exiles 'Fancy when they set it down, it stands!' But Nebo, the saviour is no saviour, for he cannot rescue you from any kind of trouble when you cry to him.

8   The moral of all this follows naturally. Not to believe in Yahweh's providential care is in reality to rebel (not *transgress* with RSV) against the covenant relationship binding Israel to her God. Not to believe in Yahweh's plan means to have lost one's footing. Israel's God is her rock, as DI has quoted before from Deut. 32:15. Yet there we read how Israel scoffed at her Rock.

9   Within the bonds of that relationship God had long ago revealed himself in the mighty acts of the Exodus period. It had been the God of Moses who at that time had revealed himself as the 'I am' (Ex. 3:14). Thus, explains DI, it could not have been Bel or Nebo who brought Israel out of Egypt, for these gods do not even exist.

10   Then DI goes on to declare that the Exodus revelation was only the first of God's mighty acts. What followed thereafter was that the significance of God's actions slowly unfolded to the faith and consciousness of Israel. DI probably meant that it was the great prophets who expounded the developing significance of the covenant relationship. The Hebrew word for 'significance' is usually translated as '*end*'. But it means more than that for DI. The prophets saw God's world sacramentally, so to speak. They regarded any historical event through which they were living as if they were observing a coin. From where they stood they could of course see only one side of their coin. But that coin had an '*aharith* on the back — its meaning or, as we might say today, its eschatological significance. The meaning of all events, DI declares, God will therefore undoubtedly reveal in the end. Then the eyes of believing men will see how everything that has happened has fitted into the plan or purpose which has been working out all the time to its final solution.

11   There was no reason to doubt that Cyrus, pagan *bird of prey** as he was, could not fit into God's plan: he was actually 'the man in My Plan' for the moment. How many pagan vultures there have been since Cyrus' day. If Cyrus belonged in the plan, then they must all belong in it too.

12   After Israel had seen with her own eyes how 'in everything God works for good with those who love him, who are called according to his purpose' (Rom. 8:28), that she should express unbelief at this point was rebellion indeed. She was in fact a 'stubborn-minded people'. No wonder she was not conducting herself with love to others (*tsedaqah*, rather than the RSV word *deliverance*).

Stubborn of heart or stubborn-minded is a very strong word (cf. 48:4). It is actually a double pun. In the first place, the word '*abbir* is used of man. In the form '*abhir*, however, it is used of God. Yet in DI's day the two words would be indistinguishable, for *bb* and *bh* both represent the one Hebrew consonant. '*Abhir* is translated in English as Jacob's *Mighty One* (49:26). But here is the man Jacob — or Israel — thinking that he himself is the mighty one, that he himself knows better than God. Yet what is the sin that DI says Jacob is committing at this point? It is that of not passing on to others the saving love of God which Israel has already received. DI then declares surprisingly that such is a sin equal to blasphemy, one that is evidently worse than murder or stealing, of which DI never even suggests that the remnant is guilty. Second, the word is a pun on the Hebrew word '*ebher*, meaning 'pinions'. The remnant was now clearly soaring on its own pinions (40:31), and thus was ignoring the pinions of the bird of prey whom God had decided to use. (In passing, note that the argument at Rom. 10:3 has been built up from words contained in this verse and could be regarded as a comment upon it.)

13   Consequently God has now to act at this juncture in history despite his people Israel, and not with her cooperation, as he would have wished. He says 'That is why I am bringing you my creative love' — for of course Cyrus was daily drawing nearer and nearer to the gates of Babylon. Finally we meet a surprising statement. It is the simple yet profound declaration that God is now about to set his new creative way

---

* The Greek historian Xenophon, in his *Cyropaedia* (VII, 1, 4) and in his *Anabasis* (I, 10, 12) informs us that Cyrus' ensign was a golden eagle.

of life (*tsedaqah*, the feminine noun again) within Israel, for Israel obviously cannot take even one step forward alone in her unbelief. When he does this thing, it will certainly not be with Israel's consent and cooperation, since she thinks herself wiser than God. God's action must therefore be one of grace alone. In poetic parallelism with the word for creative love, there now follows a new and significant term, the word *glory*. It is possible to translate the second half of this line in two ways: either by 'I will put saving, creative love in Zion, *for Israel my glory*', or 'by giving my glory to Israel'. Whichever way we take it, the statement comes to us as a great surprise. For it contains a dogmatic announcement which DI will develop only later in his argument. His statement is no less than this, that the glory of the Creator of the ends of the earth, the visible form of the invisible God, will be made manifest precisely through Israel's resistance to God's will, and through her rejection of God's plan, even as it was then working out in contemporary events and in the coming of Cyrus.

CHAPTER 47

1 This chapter belongs to a genre that occurs elsewhere in the OT, for example at Isa. 13–14 and Jer. 50–51. It is an elegy on the coming overthrow of Babylon. As such it is a unity, a single poem in several strophes. But it is no insertion in the text of an otherwise unified whole. It follows naturally as the obverse of the promise which came at the last verse of the preceding chapter.

Cities in Hebrew are feminine, like ships in English. It is therefore easy for the poet to identify the queen at the Babylonian court with the city over which she is now preening herself in pride. Thus the verbs here are all in the feminine singular.

A queen is addressed as 'thou' in Hebrew. So here the queen city also is 'thou' (English *you*) for she is a corporate personality or a unitary identity in the sight of God. Moreover, she is called a *virgin* even though she is married, on the ground that she has not yet been ravished by a conqueror and her *nakedness* has not yet been exposed (v. 3). Note, by the way, that DI employs the word *Chaldeans* in parallel with the word Babylonians or *Babylon* (cf. 48:20), and so the two words describe the same people.

What kind of pampered and artificial existence did the queen lead in the royal quarters? Deut. 28:56 reads as follows of a lady: 'The most tender and delicately bred woman among you, who would not venture to set the sole of her foot upon the ground because she is so delicate and tender'. We can well imagine what this queen's small-minded and circumscribed life would be like. So the glittering civilization of Babylon was small-minded and artificial in the eyes of Israel's God. Although she was the greatest city in the world, the mighty emporium of Eastern trade, beautiful and adorned with the riches of empire, her culture was describable only in terms of *tohu*, vanity, in respect of God's plan. Archaeology has revealed just a little of Babylon's former glory — her mighty temples, her exquisite palaces, the colonnaded streets of the sacred areas, the gate of Ishtar that pierced through the inner wall, the docks and warehouses along the river front, the homes of the nobles — but archaeology has produced not a trace of the slums of the rabble population. Evidently Israel's God was more interested in Babylon's

107

proletariat than was her queen, for she — and her court — provided the ordinary man with only a hovel to live in. It is evident that those clay homes of the poor must have collapsed just as soon as they were abandoned or disused.

Come down and sit in the dust. Man cannot help but pride himself in the miracle of his great cities with their mighty stores and warehouses, their lighted streets and temples. Yet as we look back through history we note how in reality few of the world's big cities survived for long. If they were lucky enough not to be sacked, then they gradually fell into decay; if in modern days they are not destroyed by fire, then they may be bombed or blasted sky-high. Although the people of God were only transient citizens of Babylon, they supposed that the city itself would stand forever. Thus they still had much to learn about God's purpose for that other city which he had chosen in contrast to the impermanent and doomed city of Babylon. Under God, DI has to expound to his people how the chosen city, Jerusalem, is the type of a new kind of human society. This theme is taken up in chs. 49; 60; 62; 65:17 ff. The Babylonians, however, supposed that their city was an end in itself. It had owed its origin in the first place to the god Marduk, and it would undoubtedly remain forever as queen of the nations, lording it over all the peoples of the earth.

This is a picture of human politics in all ages. But DI believes that the human city is, by virtue of its foundation, always under the judgment of God. DI's picture is quoted in the NT at Rev. 13. There the human polis, guided by the spirit of a god — such as Marduk — who is created by man to serve his own ends and aims, becomes known as the beast from the abyss. Yet it is here that the suffering of the Servant takes place within that presumptuous city that God will use to unmask the spurious glory of the human city, as DI will proceed to show.

2   DI must have watched with pity the simple peasant who formed the proletarian substructure of Babylonian society, as he or his womenfolk toiled in the filth of the suburban areas of the city. These areas were intersected by little irrigation canals, as in modern Egypt, where today the peasant women can be seen on the banks with their skirts tucked up to the waist as they 'step through those ditches' tramping on the family wash. *Uncover your legs* was also the fate of the adulteress, as the earlier prophets tell us (cf. Hos. 2:10; Jer. 13:26). By using such a threat, DI was thus linking the false worship of Babylon with the lascivious cults that had attracted Israel's only too willing attention ever since she had entered the land of the Canaanites (see Hos. 1 – 3). DI's elegy can be regarded as the enunciation of an eternal principle which must eventually become flesh, on the ground that God has spoken it.

3 DI here might almost be writing a commentary on his favourite source, the song of Moses: 'Vengeance is mine, and recompense, for the time when their foot shall slip; for the day of their calamity is at hand, and their doom comes swiftly' (Deut. 32:35) — words that may have been uttered as far back as the days of Solomon. At the other end of the time scale, from the early Church's liturgy of worship, come the words 'He has shown strength with his arm, he has scattered the proud in the imagination of their hearts, he has put down the mighty from their thrones, and exalted those of low degree' (Luke 1:51-52). Finally we have the words of Paul: 'For it is written, "Vengeance is mine, I will repay, says the Lord"', for at Rom. 12:19 Paul quotes from Deut. 32:35. And now this same idea occurs as, *I will take vengeance, and I will spare no man.*

4 Well might we ask the question: How could DI's God do otherwise? If he is indeed the *Holy One*, then sin must be anathema to him, and he must necessarily extirpate it from his presence, even when that sin is enfleshed in the corporate body of the queen city of the world. The beauty and majesty of this rich and mighty emporium must necessarily count for nothing in God's eyes if the civilization it embodies is riddled through with sin.

5 The future holds a kind of poetic justice for Babylon. At the present time it is Israel that is sitting in silence and in the darkness of the dungeon (42:22; cf. Lam. 3:2). Paradoxically, however, it is Israel's calling to bring forth the prisoners from that same darkness and from that very dungeon (42:7).

At the present moment Babylon's heart is hardened, and so she cannot discern the good news that God is revealing to her through his Servant Israel. God must therefore act to break Babylon's pride, for pride is the root of all sin. It is the barrier to her reception of Israel's news. God will therefore bring Babylon down to the dust and over-whelm her in her turn with the darkness of the dungeon and despair. For in his wise providence, God has so ordained it — that only when a man is walking in darkness can the Light shine upon him. In other words, Babylon's eyes must first be blinded before God can use his instrument Israel to open the eyes that are blind, to bring out the prisoners from the dungeon, and from the prison those who sit in darkness (42:7). Moreover, God is no respecter of persons. Even the queen of the nations must travel by this same terrible road if her soul is ever to be saved. God has been using her for fifty years now for his own purposes and ends.

6 Israel had refused her calling to be the Servant of the Lord, and so fifty years previously Yahweh had had to profane his *heritage*, and destroy the land and people of his choice. A man normally cherishes his heritage, of course, and finds it quite unnatural to have to pollute the land and people that he loves. So also with Yahweh. Yet Israel had had no right to presume upon her election when God had made her into his people, or to suppose that by it she was rendered exempt from the judgment of his holy zeal. That was why Yahweh had had to deal with Israel's pride in exactly the same manner as he was now about to deal with the pride of Babylon. That was why Yahweh had used Nebuchadrezzar and the armies of the Babylonian power when he disciplined Israel at the beginning of the century. He reduced Israel to the level of a pariah nation and condemned her to mere existence in the darkness of the dungeon. But now, DI said, Babylon had actually overstepped her duty as the instrument of God's righteous and saving wrath. Babylon had in fact overdone the punishing she had been called upon to administer, because she was naturally a cruel tyrant (cf. Jer. 50:17; 51:34; Lam. 4:16; 5:12).

7 DI now declares that Babylon has actually committed the ultimate blasphemy of supposing that she herself is God. The Hebrew at this point for the words *I shall be* is *'ehyeh*. *'Ehyeh* is the 'I am' of God's self-revelation in Ex. 3:14. DI has used it about Yahweh more than once before, primarily in those cases where Yahweh has declared 'I am, and there is no other, there is nothing else' (e.g., 43:11; 45:5, 6, 18, 22). Babylon here is virtually taking the Word of divine self-revelation out of the mouth of God and applying it to her own evil and proud self. It is in the light of the succeeding verse that this parallel can be drawn. Then again, the words *for ever* are part of the title of the living God, as both prophets and Psalmists in the days before and after DI's time employed them (cf. Isa. 9:6; Ps. 102:12).

110

The title of queen (rather than *mistress*) is the personification or apotheosis of this created earth on which we stand. Thus Ishtar or Belit (lady), the Babylonian goddess of war and love, is ultimately the personification of the natural processes of earth.

So Babylon as mistress of all the earth, was the apotheosis of the pride of the creature earth. This pride, DI knew, was exemplified in a concept that was false — that since earth gives birth to life, then earth must be mistress of all. As DI has already declared, it is Yahweh who is Lord of all, who is Lord of both heaven and *earth* (40:12). And DI has shown again and again in his argument that Babylon 'didn't try to realize the significance of these things' nor 'remember that it (Cyrus' advance) must have an outcome' ('*end*'). If only she had done so, DI wishes us to understand as the climax to his argument, then Babylon would have acknowledged that Yahweh alone is Lord, and she herself was but dust and ashes in his sight.

8-9 'You voluptuous woman' is how DI conceives of the Babylonian 'idea', the *Zeitgeist* or way of life, of the Fertile Crescent. For with the worship of the forces of nature there went an abominable practice. The lifeblood of the area has naturally been a peasant economy. The peasant has always lived a life very close to the soil. His virtual survival depends upon his annual crop. From earliest times he has been aware that the forces of nature seem to die in the great heat of summer. Rains do not fall at all in that part of the world until about October. The peasant therefore has always supposed that the personalized forces of nature have gone below the ground into the realm of death; thus he lives in the fear that nature might not return to life again should the autumn rains not return punctually.

Arising from the sympathetic rapport with nature which the landsman seems to feel, an understandable practice became woven into the cult. It rested upon the fact that to man is given the power to create life. By analogy man could, through sympathetic magic, create or procreate life even in inanimate nature. From earliest biblical times the 'high place' (RSV 'lofty place', e.g. 1 Sam. 9:12; Ezek. 16:23-24) was a feature of the peasant's cult. On it he worshipped Asherah, the goddess of sex and procreation, particularly at the end of the summer, by means of sacred prostitution. By means of this act he believed that Mother Earth would bring forth once again the plant life which had drooped and died in the summer heat. Such cultic actions were of course performed in all earnestness and sincerity of purpose. On the other hand, human nature being what it is, these festivals degenerated into licentious orgies. Here it is the apotheosis of this whole degenerate cult who exclaims 'I shall be for ever and ever, Queen' (v. 7). '*I am, and there is no one besides me.*' This is a parody of the words that the living God had used to manifest his nature to his chosen people (cf. Lam. 1:1, which is akin to this passage; and cf. Isa. 50:1; 54:1-17). No wonder the queen of Babylon believed that she would never be a widow, worshipped as she was in such sexual orgies; for she had at her command male consorts without number. So DI saw the coming judgment of God upon the city of Babylon as God's answer to this all-pervading sex cult which so dominated the lives of men and women.

10 The Babylonians were no atheists — far from it. But in this sentence they implicitly admit the nonreality of their gods. '*No one sees me*', says Babylon, just like the adulterer at all times. Let us take that particular sin as our example, since the LXX translates *knowledge* by *porneia*, 'lasciviousness', 'carnal knowledge'. No wonder the author of Rev. 18 can build his picture of the scarlet woman from DI's incisive description of Babylon personified.

Moreover, as a concomitant of this practical atheism, there goes also a deep intellectual pride, pride in a *Kultur* that is based upon a merely rational interpretation of life. Having ready an answer to all the problems of life, Babylon felt secure in her wickedness. She believed that she could utter such a sentence as 'I am the captain of my soul'. Moreover, she had the right to say so, for the whole ancient world knew of the wisdom of her wise men. Yet the more cultured the state of Babylon became, the less could her people realize how it was that 'your philosophy and learning are what have led you astray', to the extent that you declare with pride: '*I am, and there is no one besides me.*' DI has now revealed the heart of what idolatry really is, for it is not the worship of wood- and gilt-covered images: it is in reality a trusting not in God but in human ideologies. Suddenly, in the broad daylight of Babylon's exalted pride and glory, the night of the soul can fall. God has many means at his disposal to bring this darkness near: an economic collapse, a plague, or a pagan king from Persia by the name of Cyrus.

11 But whatever the means, DI is certain that for the clay arrogantly to rebel against the Potter is for the creature to call down upon itself the wrath of God. None of Babylon's wise men will be able to help her then, because no man can ever bribe the holy God. *Atone* and *expiate* present a striking assonance in the Hebrew.

12 Some nations even as they fall have struck out in fury with all the sorceries of science at their command still hoping thereby to *inspire terror* in their enemies. But neither the mathematics of the magi then nor the atomic energy of the scientist now can avail to avert the outcome of events.

13-14 Finally DI takes up the figure which Isaiah of Jerusalem had used so effectively before to declare the true nature of Israel's God. Isaiah had believed that God has a plan, or '*etsah*, for the redemption of the world. DI now declares that Babylon has *many counsels*, especially those given by her astrologers, but has grown weary of them all. At 10:17, Isaiah had declared that the Light of Israel would be a fire, and her Holy One a flame. At 30:30 he had likened once again the wrath of God to the flame of a devouring fire; and at 33:14 he had solemnly asked 'Who among us can dwell with the devouring fire? Who among us can dwell with everlasting burnings?' Isaiah thus agreed with Deut. 4:24: 'The Lord your God is a devouring fire'. Let us note that this latter statement equates the concept of God as fire with his zeal, that is to say, with his burning, loving purpose, eager for the goal he has in view. No genial glow is this at which they warm themselves, nor is it a fire to sit in front of (v. 14c). We have already seen what DI believes that goal to be (45:23).

15 DI therefore is sure that Babylon must first experience the fires of the zeal of God upon her flesh if the hardness of her heart is to be broken. And so in a final picture of a beseiged city whose defendants are crazed with thirst and blood, he describes men surrendering to the attackers as they advance from opposite them, but finding no one to save them from the attacker's wrath. (See Rev. 18 for an interpretation of Isa. 47 made in the light of God's zeal towards all human institutions that say of themselves 'I am'.) Nebo, the saviour god, now lets Babylon down just when she needs him most — but then Nebo is merely nonbeing, *tohu*, negation. So wisdom fails the philosopher; the study of economics and the practice of trade fail the merchant; even Babylon's religion fails her in the day of wrath. For it is only the power of Israel's God that can preserve a body from atomizing, from splitting up into its components parts. So 'each individual will stagger off straight before him' — each man is seeking to save himself. The end of the story of Babylon is therefore a dreadful *sauve qui peut*. It is a representation of the elemental truth about ordinary, unredeemed human nature; for in the final debacle, whether it is to be in nuclear warfare or in the face of disease or self-appointed ruin, sinful man finds himself utterly alone even as his little world tumbles about his ears, and as he recognizes that he has to face nemesis as a disintegrated soul.

CHAPTER 48

1 The previous chapter gives what might be called a typological exposition of retribution. The fall of Babylon still to come is there presented in the form of a theological truth: the zeal of God must necessarily show itself as wrath against sin and, in consequence, against sinners too. On the other hand, retribution alone does not effect redemption, so retribution cannot be the totality of God's action in the face of sin. Seeing this quite clearly, DI turns to the next problem. This is the problem that arises from the failure, not this time of pagan Babylon, but of God's own chosen people to be what God intended her to be. Has God not planned to use Israel as his instrument for the furtherance of his purpose, that his name might be known to the ends of the earth?

DI begins by emphasizing the privileged position that Israel holds in God's plan of redemption. The people of God are really 'Jacobs', 'heels' all — the root meaning of the word 'Jacob' — although by grace they have been *called by the name of Israel*. For they too are a libidinous people. We have only to re-read Gen. 38 to see what DI means, for there *Judah* behaves as any pagan might do who is unaware of his unique election and relationship to the all-holy God. Thus Israel practises her calling 'neither sincerely nor creatively' as the people of God should. It was her custom to call Yahweh's name to mind in order to invoke his real presence in a cultic act. But she was not giving any content to the meaning of his name or to the action she was performing when invoking him. Several times in this chapter therefore God solemnly addresses Israel with either the word 'Hear' or 'Listen', or with the clause 'You have heard' (vv. 1, 6, 8, 12, 14, 16). At each summons the sternness of Yahweh becomes ever more vivid, and the judgment under which specially chosen Israel stands becomes ever more abundantly clear (cf. Amos. 3:2).

2 The Holy One, we recall, named Jerusalem 'my city' (45:13); in this way that city actually partook of God's holiness and could be called 'the Holy City'. Yet Israel imagined that she too must be automatically holy in this sense, because God had said to her that within the covenant relationship holiness was to be her calling (Ex. 19:6). Relying on her holiness therefore, she had come to 'lean upon' the God of Israel (cf. Mic. 3:11; Rom. 2:17). In other words she had taken God for granted. What effrontery on Israel's part such an attitude was; what a misuse of her election it had become! It is possible that DI deliberately calls Jerusalem by the title of 'holy city' at this particular juncture in order to press home his point more clearly, for this is the first time in history that Jerusalem has been so called by anyone. What he wants to bring home to her is this: how will the unholy people of Israel ever become the Servant of God in the unholy land of Babylon?

3 Israel has no excuse of course for the apostasy that is in her heart. For God is a God who speaks, who reveals both himself and his purpose by means of his Word. All he has to do is to speak, or do his Word, and then that Word becomes historical event. The redemption from Egypt, for example, was his Word *suddenly* proclaimed, and just as quickly it *came to pass*. Thus Israel all along has had the chance to know God's true nature as that of loving care for her and for the world.

4 But now a strange statement follows. DI declares that God 'foreknew' before his election of Israel that Israel would resist his will. For even as Israel's Creator, he had given her a 'stubborn' heart, a 'brazen forehead', and an *iron sinew* for a *neck*. In other words, God had actually created Israel able and determined to resist the purpose that he himself was planning to work out by his election of her.

5 Despite that fact he had kept on giving her every chance, by telling her through the mouths of her prophets the significance of her choices even before she had had to make them: *lest you should say*: '*My idol did them*', or, as we might say, 'My own ideology'. So God knew that ultimately Israel would refuse the office of the Servant, and would not be willing to work in the world with and through her Lord.

6 So we now reach DI's surprising conclusion to the argument. He declares that God had first let Israel hear the word: 'Take a look at it as a whole!' That was when, through the lips of his prophets, he had called upon her to ponder the mighty events through which she had passed, and thereupon to become a witness of God's actions to her heathen neighbours (cf. 43:10). Then he puts the onus on each individual Israelite. Israel, however, had not been willing to pay attention. Her heart had been too hard. Therefore God was now about to act once more. Unfortunately this could not be with Israel's cooperation: it had to be in and through her foolish resistance to his will. This whole conception of a God's winning his victory through the resistance of his people is surely completely new in the world's thought.

On this basis then, DI can declare that God is now about to show Israel *new things*. Some interpreters suggest that these things refer to the new exodus which DI undoubtedly believed God was about to accomplish for his people, for God was certainly about to set his people free from Babylon and lead them home to Zion. Yet such an 'act of God' would be but the 'sacramental sign' of a still greater spiritual reality.

7 But DI expounds these *new things* by saying that even now they are being created. That is to say, they are no mere repetition of God's previous mighty acts. *Before today*, he says, *you have never heard of them*. They are *hidden things* (v. 6), things that could come forth only from the mind of Israel's surprising God, or out of his peculiar involvement in the life of Israel (45:14). DI's choice of the verb *bara'*, create, is that found at Gen. 1:1, where it is used for God's original creative act. DI wants his hearers to understand that when they see it, men will not be able to say 'Behold, I knew it all the time'. In passing, we should recognize that it would be ridiculous to ascribe these words to Isaiah of Jerusalem, as do those who believe that Isaiah wrote all sixty-six chapters of the book. This line alone is evidence that he is not the author of this section, chs. 40–55. Anyone who lived in the centuries before DI could not say with honesty 'I knew it all the time', and then proceed to foretell events that were to take place two centuries later. If three centuries ago Joachim Neander, in the English translation of his hymn 'All my hope on God is founded', could say of the mere matter of the universe:

> Beauty springeth out of naught.
>> Evermore,
>> From his store,
> New-born worlds rise and adore;

then how much more, DI is claiming, can God re-create the lives of men and nations to constitute his kingdom, not as of this world (John 18:36), but as something wholly *new*.

8   How tragic that the people of God should never have co-operated with God's plan to use them. Even their suffering in the Exile and the loss of the Holy City had not opened *your ear* to hear the Word of God as it was disclosed in events interpreted by the mouths of the prophets. Israel was competely deaf (cf. 42:19). This verse contains a terrible indictment — by the living God. Israel, the only nation given the chance to hear the Word, had been a rebel since birth. Her birth, by the way, is here equated in poetic parallelism with the Exodus events. Thus DI is laying particular emphasis upon the giving of the covenant at Sinai, for that was the moment when God both adopted Israel as his own, and married her as his Bride (Ex. 19:1-8).

9   God's wrath is what we see of God when his love encounters sin. For the heat of his zeal must necessarily burn up and destroy that which essays to pollute his holy love. Yet the tension between God's mercy and his wrath is necessarily acute. For seven hundred years now, ever since the days of Moses, God had 'held my wrath in check', not wanting to *cut you off* (cf. Jer. 13:11). This he had done so as to be true to himself — *for my name's sake*, ... 'because of the praise due to me'; for God's true nature is positive, creative, loving, merciful. And he had sworn to be faithful and loyal to Israel forever. That loyalty exhibits his true nature.

10   But not even the chosen people can mock God forever. So finally God had had to act, as happened at the historic moment of 587 B.C., when Nebuchadrezzar sacked the Holy City and took the cream of its population into exile. 'See how I have been refining you ... testing you' (cf. Ps. 66:10; Ezek. 22:20-22). God had never intended of course to exterminate his people. For God must remain true to his side of the covenant even though Israel should break hers. Long ago in the days of Egypt, however, he had already revealed what he would eventually have to do to Israel (Ex. 3:2), and he had also revealed how suffering is to be understood as a fiery furnace that must be endured (Deut. 4:20). Yet now in this new testing period of the exile in Babylon, even the heat of the fire of the wrath of God had not been able to smelt out any *silver* at all. DI is therefore declaring in this line that there existed nothing inherent in Israel herself that could be of use to God. There was in fact no vestige of intrinsic goodness in the chosen people, no silver at all. Herein we see the extraordinary paradox, that God has chosen a people to be his Servant who are in themselves intrinsically useless, and yet he is determined to use them.

11 The resolution of such a paradox can obviously be discovered only in the faith which DI here sets forth, viz., that God's purpose and plan are to be understood in terms of grace alone. Or in the actual words of DI, repeated for the sake of emphasis: '*For my own sake, for my own sake* I have been doing this'. Evidently refining Israel in the fire has been the only course left open for God to pursue; 'for how can (my name) continue to be profaned?' Note Ezek. 36:19-23 for this theme. DI would probably know this passage. On the other hand, God will never let his worthless people go, for never under any circumstances can he be faithless to the covenant he has made with them. Consequently he does not even consider showing forth his glory by choosing and uniting himself with any other people on the face of the earth (cf. 42:8, where reference is made to this verse; 44:23; Ezek. 20:9).

12 'O Love, that wilt not let me go', the words of a modern favourite hymn, are as true a description of the God of the OT as of the God of the NT. DI now demonstrates that this is really what God is like by returning to his great theme of God as the self-revealing 'I AM' (Ex. 6:2-3; Deut. 32:39). Yet God sorrowfully acknowledges that his people is really rebellious *Jacob*, and is only *renamed Israel* by grace.

13 Then DI reminds Israel that God can re-create simply on the ground that he has already created. God is still in command of the hosts of stars, and they obey his will absolutely.

14 The hosts below, the people of God, ought therefore to be continually aware that God is always in control. How silly to suppose that it was the angelic hosts, the sons of God (Deut. 32:8), or even the gods of the heathen nations, who had spoken the word of creation in the beginning, for the gods of the nations are themselves part of creation.

It is interesting to see how DI now leaps from creation to the contemporary scene. After all, we are all more concerned about our present problems and distresses than about even the glorious moments of the past. DI therefore turns to the vital interest of the moment: Yahweh actually *loves* Cyrus! We have seen that while 'love' can also mean 'choose', at the same time it can presuppose an intimate personal relationship, as in the case of Abraham at 41:8. Similarly Solomon was God's choice of king — 'And the Lord loved him' (2 Sam. 12:24) — for he was chosen to execute God's will in a decisive manner. Here then is the next step in the plan that has been working out since the beginning.

15 Cyrus is about to become God's *arm*, that is to say, the outward, tangible sign of God's invisible and divine will or *purpose*. Moreover, Cyrus is bound to accomplish that which pleases God; for it is the 'I AM' who has uttered his will, and who has been preparing for its eventual resolution in the paths of history. Yet before that moment of resolution can arrive, God sees fit to employ a period of preparation. We recall how God ordained that the Roman *pax* should prevail before the final act of redemption took place in the birth and death of Christ. Similarly DI regards Cyrus as God's instrument whom he is employing as he prepares the right conditions for the astonishing moments to follow. What these are we shall see later.

16 DI reiterates that God's purpose will certainly work out. Then, in a line of verse in which God plurally addresses the whole world of angels, gods and men together, DI suddenly presents us with a striking sequence of thought. First, he declares that God has all the time *been there* in Israel's story, or immanent, as we might say today. Then second, he declares that that immanence is now being realized in a new way, even as God's Spirit uses DI's own mouth and mind. 'And now the Lord Yahweh, that is to say His Spirit, has sent me' he writes. Apart from 40:6 only here does DI ever make mention of himself; otherwise he is wholly subservient to the voice of God.

The word *now*, *'attah*, is DI's choice of technical term for the contemporary moment. We have already seen that he selects the word *ro'sh*, 'head', or another noun built from it, to represent the concept of 'beginning' or the first action of God in his handling of Israel in the days of Moses. DI believes that the period between has not been mere history. It has been 'sacred history', or the history of God, for Yahweh has been immanent in it, working out his purpose for the world through his association with Israel. But DI is now keenly aware that at the very moment he is speaking, he himself is acting as the mouthpiece of God. He knows that it is God's Spirit alone and not his own human perspicacity which is enabling him to interpret events, and to be the instrument of the Word as it is even now 'becoming flesh' in that vital moment of the world's history. Thus DI virtually equates the Spirit of God with the Word of God. In the OT the concept of Spirit normally contains the overtone of power. So when DI continues with his message we are to be sure he believed that the power of God's Word was now being uttered through him, and that his Word must necessarily be effective in the days to come. The Babylonians too believed in a reality they called the word of God. So also did the Egyptians. But both those nations understood the concept very differently from DI. They thought of it in terms of emanation. The Egyptians, for example, pictured the word as a fluid that issued materially from the mouth of the god who spoke it. DI, however, must have turned from this pagan conception with impatience. For to him the Word of Yahweh was no less than the creative, and consequently recreative, power of the living God himself (cf. 42:1; 44:3).

17   The Word of God, which he has uttered over the years to Israel, ought to have been effective in Israel's life. God's *tsedeq*, or saving activity (masculine; cf. 45:8), which he had poured down upon Israel, ought to have borne fruit in *tsedaqoth*, saving righteous actions, or creative acts of compassion (feminine plural) on Israel's part (see discussion at 45:8). But it had not done so thus far, because man cannot perform saving acts, or show creative compassion for others without accepting the *tsedeq* of God. Israel had not done so. It is only in fellowship with God that life can be lived 'effectively' (cf. Pss. 32:8; 119:165).

This important point cannot be fully grasped unless we realize what DI meant by the word 'effective'. Unfortunately the RSV translates here by the word *profit*. The prophets did not conceive of the good life as a mere static condition. In fact the idea of just being good is not to be found in the OT; it is not presupposed even of God himself. For goodness in OT usage means the desire to create such things as fellowship, trust, joy, and wholeness in the minds of others, not in oneself. Jesus later speaks of a goodness that is not the goodness of the scribes. Jesus speaks of God as He who sends — implying activity and not a state — his rain upon the just and upon the unjust alike, who turns (note the action) the other cheek to the smiter, not with the object of feeling a sense of self-satisfaction at his own self-control, but in order to win the sinner into creative fellowship. Effectiveness is the hallmark of divine goodness for DI also; and so we shall see later at

52:13 that it must be the hallmark of God's true Servant as well. DI's insistent indictment of idols was just that they were ineffective (cf. 44:10). Ineffectual saints have no place within the people of God. Yet Israel had committed just this very sin. She had rebelled against her calling to be effective, in other words to be holy even as God is holy (Ex. 19:6), and to love her neighbour even as God loved her (Lev. 19:18). Was there then one thing in God's creation that was actually stronger than God himelf: the rebellious free will of the creature Israel? If the words of Mark 6:5 may apply here, it is as if God could do no mighty works in her at all.

18   How wonderful the world would have been by DI's day 'if only you had paid attention to My orders', says God (cf. Ps. 81:13). Then two good things would have eventuated. First, Israel herself, as the people of God, would have found her true *peace, shalom*. This word, as we saw at 45:7, means much more than that English word can convey. DI compares *shalom* to the influence of a river. The river Euphrates is perennial and is therefore reliable. But it owes its fructifying waters to God alone. It is not like a Palestinian wadi, which is a roaring watercourse for a week in winter and then a dry useless gorge the rest of the year. Moreover, because the waters of the Euphrates, like grace, are always there, they are of use to others; in other words, the Euphrates is *effective*. The Mesopotamian plain in DI's day was interlaced with irrigation canals fed by the Tigris in the north of the plain and by the Euphrates in the area of the city of Babylon. This Euphrates water brought life to what would otherwise have been desert. Thus we have the peaceful picture of a gently flowing river, and we are shown how true joy comes from creating life and vitality where it has not been found before. Israel's life would then have been a concert of saving actions (RSV *righteousness*), of acts of compassionate concern, *tsedaqoth* (cf. Isa. 11:9), just as all those little irrigation ditches which Queen Babylon was soon to step in (47:2) brought life to the peasants of the land.

19   That would have been the first wonderful result. The second would have been this. The promises of God to the patriarchs would have been fulfilled by now, viz., that Israel would be as numerous as the grains of sand on the seashore (Gen. 22:17; 32:12; but also Isa. 10:22; Hos. 1:10). Whereas the bitter reality was something wholly different. The sins of pride, apostasy, and disloyalty had now cut off

Israel's *name*, or essential being, from before God's face, or presence, as the Hebrew has it, and consequently from happy fellowship and co-operation with Him who had chosen her as his very own precious possession and the instrument of his saving purpose (Ex. 19:5).

20 There are scholars who remark that here we have a unique and individual oracle inserted in the text at this point for no obvious reason; for what it contains is DI's cry to the exiles at the exciting moment when Cyrus' armies reach the gates of Babylon (cf. Jer. 51:6). Yet these are not the words that anyone would use at such a moment. Even DI the theologian would have given more immediate and practical advice to his bewildered countrymen than the contents of vv. 20-21 offer. Surely these words were spoken well in advance of Cyrus' arrival and in perfect sequence from v. 19. For v. 18 has just expressed what might have been. Verse 19 has gone on to declare the awful reality of the situation as it is. But v. 20 offers the kind of surprise that God delights to give throughout the biblical revelation. Our poem suddenly takes for granted that Yahweh will save his people after all. What DI now proclaims is that God will act, not *with* his people's co-operation, but *despite* their non co-operation. Surely this is grace abounding. This is indeed the love that will not let Israel go. Israel's joy, when Cyrus should come pounding at the gate, is therefore to be no ordinary joy. *'innah* is a *shout of joy* issuing from a heart bubbling with excitement; in fact since it is a cultic word, it represents a joy that is virtually not of this world at all. The wonder of what God is doing at this crucial moment in the world's history — now, *'attah* — must in fact be shouted to the Hebrew exiles in every land and not just to those in Babylon. And what is to be the content of the shout? Is it to be 'Cyrus has set us free'? No. It is to be *The Lord has redeemed his Servant Jacob* (cf. Rev. 18:4).

21 Getting out of the doomed city is thus to be understood in terms of what has already been done in the past when Israel fled from Egypt (Ex. 14). But the Exodus had been more than a physical deliverance; it had been the beginning of a new life to be lived in covenant fellowship with God. At that time God had given his people water to drink; in fact, in the wilderness *he cleft the rock and the water gushed out*. If God had done this before, then he could easily do it again, and do it for a people who would have to face the desert once again on the homeward road to Zion (cf. Ex. 17:6; Num. 20:11; Ps. 105:41; and already at Isa. 41:17-18).

22   What does it mean to be wicked? It means to refuse the wholeness and fullness of life, the *shalom* which it was Yahweh's will to give to his beloved Servant. It means in effect to refuse to be effective. It is therefore something negative, as refusal must be, and so it belongs in the realm of *tohu*. This chapter therefore concludes with a terrible utterance. We saw in ch. 47 what the end of Babylon was to be. Equally under judgment, however, stands the chosen people; and we listen in awe as we await the sentence of God upon them. But v. 20 has just said that the sentence is to be one of grace and mercy. Verse 22 is no editorial comment, as some would have us believe, written in by a pious scribe. Actually it is so important that it is quoted later by the writer of 57:21. It is a reiteration for great effect of the subject brought forward at the beginning of the chapter in v. 1. For DI wants us to recognize with awed surprise that God is determined to reveal his glory *in* Israel, *despite the fact that* she has broken the covenant and departed from him. God will in fact do so at that very point where Israel is farthest from him in thought, intention, and co-operative faith. We are now awaiting a revelation that can be accounted for in terms of nothing other than grace.

CHAPTER 49

1 'If only you had paid attention to My orders', God had said to his Servant Israel at 48:18, then you would have been effective. Yet effective to what end? We are obviously now drawing close to the heart of DI's remarkable exposition. He has eliminated more than one side issue by now. He has dealt with the question of the validity of idol worship; he has already vindicated God's action through his instrument, the Persian Cyrus; and he has more than once shown how the great 'I AM' has a purpose working through the events of the moment. So now he draws in his net and discloses what Israel has been meant to do and be ever since God had called her to be his Servant, but a Servant very different from Cyrus. This fresh theme, however, has led some commentators to declare that ch. 49 introduces a new section of the book. Note that Cyrus is no longer mentioned in this section. Some commentators have therefore averred that we are now actually reading the work of a different author. In reply it can be pointed out that ch. 40 offers a summary of material that appears in all that follows. Remember that DI is a theologian who is concerned the *'aharith* of things, their eschatological outcome. While his method of exposition is to *begin* with history, as a good theologian must do, he then proceeds to expound its meaning in the light of God's plan; and this is just what chs. 49 ff. do.

First, we hear a voice addressing itself to the whole human race. Remember that 'coasts and islands' (one word in Hebrew) come to mean 'the whole earth' in DI's idiom. Interestingly enough, the LXX deliberately makes *from afar* refer to time and not to place. With no warrant from the Hebrew it reads: 'For a long time it will stand, says the Lord'. Now however, without warning, we find that it is the Servant who is speaking and not God, though we are not told specifically that the Servant is still considered to be the people of God. Let us now examine the text in order to establish his identity.

The Lord called me from the womb. At 49:15 DI will speak of a woman's beloved son as *the son of her womb*. It would seem that in some sense it is God's son who is spoken of here. Next we read that God *named my name* before birth, and for DI this phrase implies election in love. The

speaker's first words, then, are *The Lord called me.* Yahweh, the name of
the covenant God, is written at the head of the sentence, the Hebrew
method of showing emphasis. This is Yahweh's act, not man's; it is the
covenant God's not the creator God's, or that of the Lord of hosts. The
call is the call of election. It is the call to a specific individual who can
be identified by name, and that name is Israel (cf. 43:1). God had
chosen Israel from the days of Abraham (41:8), and it was his son
Israel whom he had rescued from the hand of Pharaoh (Ex. 4:22).
Moreover it was the covenant God known to Moses as Yahweh, the
Lord (Ex. 6:3), who had thus called Israel to be his people; and it was
with Israel alone that God had made his covenant in days of old.

2   What then does Israel confess that God has done for her? *(Firstly)*
he made my mouth like a sharp sword. DI himself had found that the Holy
Spirit was using his mouth (48:16). But how could Israel, a whole
people, comprising old and young, male and female, rich and poor, be
said to possess one mouth?

We noted in ch. 40 that God can address his people as one
individual personality, as one 'thou'. Moreover, God has already
addressed this corporate personality that is Israel more than once in
the feminine singular form. This feminine form cannot be rendered in
English, nor has attention specifically been drawn to it as yet, though it
is of prime importance as this chapter proceeds. The RSV has not
preserved the singular number at all, for the sake of rendering a
modern English translation. But when Israel is addressed as 'thou' in
the feminine, then in God's sight she is obviously the personification of
Zion or Jerusalem, as we have seen before. In the same way the people
of Babylon can be personified and typified in the singular entity of their
queen, as discussed at 47:1. Later in this chapter, moreover, we shall
note how DI uses the feminine singular in a very surprising and daring
manner (vv. 13 ff.). While the conception is a difficult one for modern
man to grasp, believing himself to be a strong individualist, remember
that this corporate personality idea was a completely natural way of
thought in biblical times. Moreover, it is carried forward into the NT.
Jesus addresses Zion in the singular (Matt. 23:37), and Paul refers to
the Church as the body of Christ (1 Cor. 10:17; 12:12 ff., especially v.
27). Paul was thus using language that was common to the whole OT.
For Israel could say of a neighbour *'Woe to thee, O Moab!* thou (RSV
you) *art undone, O people of Chemosh'* (Num. 21:29); or an Assyrian could
say of Egypt 'That broken reed of a staff' (Isa. 36:6).

Eph. 6:17 speaks of the '*sword* of the Spirit, which is the word of God'. In the same way the Babylonians used the adjective *sharp* to describe the royal word that pronounced judgment (cf. the figure at Isa. 11:4); presumably then DI, writing from within a Babylonian milieu, is implying that Yahweh had been teaching Israel his own word of judgment, possibly taking his imagery from the Royal Investiture of the Servant-Knight by the Babylonian king. Israel had to learn to be the instrument of the Word, so that the Word might be effective in human life. The life of man, however, is one of dungeons and darkness; and it is into such areas that the Word must be carried by a willing Servant. DI is therefore hinting once again that he will soon be developing the question of what must happen when the Word is confronted with the darkness.

Then *in the shadow of his hand he hid me* must point to a period of quiet and undisturbed training, as does the phrase *in his quiver he hid me away*. There was a long period after the establishment of the monarchy when Jerusalem, unlike Ephraim in the north, was undisturbed by war. *A polished arrow* is obviously an effective arrow (cf. Ps. 45:5). Israel was therefore being trained by God at the time to hit the target that he had chosen for her. Note that to miss the target is one of the many Hebrew words for 'sin' (*hata*; cf. *hamartanein* in the NT). The word for *polished*, however, is composed of the same consonants as the word for pure or clean. DI would probably enjoy the pun that would spring to the mind of his Hebrew listeners. For he would want to emphasize the second truth too, that it is only 'he who has clean hands and a pure heart' (Ps. 24:4) whom God can use as his Servant.

3 Now we have a categorical statement about who the servant is. This line in Hebrew is in three parts: (a) *And he said to me*, (b) '*You are my servant, Israel*', (c) '*in whom I will be glorified*'. It is God himself, then, who calls Israel 'My Servant'. The Servant, however, is to have only a secondary function. What DI is explaining from this 'Word' of God is that, while God is light indeed, his light cannot be reflected unless it strikes a polished surface. *Israel* has been created by God to be that surface, for to be it is to be the *Servant*. A mirror is nothing in itself. It can reflect light only when there is light to fall upon it. Then we note that the word *glorified*, *pa'ar*, is not derived from the usual word for glory, *kabod*. It is best translated as 'splendour'. Yet it must mean much the same as glory; for God had already promised to give his glory to no nation but Israel alone (42:8; 43:7; 46:13; 48:11). But now this promise of God goes one step further. It is that he will actually reveal his splendour *in* his Servant Israel (cf. John 17:1).

4   For *I said* we might put 'But I had thought'. Israel is represented as ruminating within herself. In the previous verse, however, God has just *said* an important word. It is therefore ridiculous of Israel to say anything at all in reply about what she had been thinking in herself. The Servant has just received an extraordinary call, even while she is still a pariah amongst the nations. How could the splendour of God be revealed in her? Fifty years of struggling to be faithful — more or less — in distant Babylon had made her feel that *I have spent my strength for 'negation' and vanity*. Her life in Babylon clearly exhibited the opposite of what she had been called to become. Obviously her life was now meaningless, *hebel, vanity*, the word which was so central to the thought of Ecclesiastes in later years. And *yet surely* life has a meaning for her, even in exile. Israel does not claim here to have any righteous saving deeds of her own. All she claims is that she believes that her *mishpat* is still with God.

This word, *mishpat*, unfortunately can mean many things. Initially it signified judgment. Then it came to cover the idea of justice in general, and so could be used for our word ordinance or even for a man's legal right. Then it spread into the meaning of the fitness of things that are just and right, and so became what we mean when we speak of custom or of an accepted manner of doing things. Then of course it was used to describe God's justice as it has been revealed to man. Since God's revelation is concerned with the whole man and with the whole of his life as it must be lived out here on earth, the word *mishpat* may even be translated by the German term *Weltanschauung*. Here we can take it to mean that whole, true, wholesome, and creative way of life which it is God's will that Israel should understand and live; in other words it is the meaning of my existence, as Israel says in this poem. And if the latter is to be understood in terms of God's reward to her — the usual translation of *pe'ullah*, here rendered by *recompense* — then it must surely be rooted and grounded in *my God* alone.

5   So Yahweh is still for Israel *my God*. 'I believe,' Israel is virtually saying, 'help thou mine unbelief'. God now seizes gladly on this little vestige of faith in his Servant, and at once makes a basic statement about his purpose in Israel for the world. This comes at v. 6. Verse 5 is a long parenthesis leading up to the central affirmation which follows:

and now ('attah), the Lord 'has said' — that is, here and now *in* this exile
situation — Yahweh's plan will find its way. *Who formed me* is the same
word as potter at 45:9. There potter is paralleled by creator and is
linked with those great words of redemption which are to apply even if
Israel has to go through fire and water. Here DI is reminding Israel
that the creative activity of the living God, ever since he *formed me from
the womb to be his servant*, obviously cannot end in *tohu*. His purpose must
still be to win *Jacob* back to co-operation with himself in his plan. *And
that Israel might be gathered to him* or brought home, that is, in poetic
parallelism, 'gathered home from exile'.

Note that it is Israel herself who is speaking here and actually
quoting what Yahweh has said. Thus Israel now confesses what God's
purpose *in* her is beginning to mean to her. It begins with the reality
that the glory of God is becoming apparent on earth. 'The heavens are
telling the glory of God' Hebrew poets had already declared (Ps. 19:1).
But the heavens show only the hem of his garment, DI believes. The
heavens are dead matter, whereas Yahweh is the living God. DI
therefore has to employ anthropomorphic language to express what it
means to conceive of Yahweh in personal terms. To do so, from now on
he employs a great variety of active participles to describe the living
God in action. He calls God creator, fashioner, potter, giver, spreader-
out, refiner, redeemer, carrier, sitter, judge, bringer-forth, speaker,
planner, opener, shutter, shouter, wiper-away. Such transitive, creative, purposive verbs describe the action, not primarily of One who
made the heavens with all their beauty and majestic spread, but rather
of One whose true glory can become visible only in human
relationships. Moreover, those relationships are to be with Israel
alone, not with any other. *I am honoured in the eyes of the Lord* therefore
means something like 'that I might bear the glory of Yahweh as he
reveals himself in action'. Many editors would place v. 5c after v. 3. But
in this way they empty v. 5 of its content. This is too facile a change and
shows an unwillingness to wrestle with the text against its context.
Such an interpretation of the first half of the line is upheld when it is
seen in the light of the second and parallel half: *my God has become my
strength*. For God alone, not Israel, possesses strength, and his alone is
the glory that is to be revealed on earth.

6 He has said (in the Hebrew). Note that 'to me' is not required and
is not stated. For what follows is a divine fiat for all the world to hear.
Yet at the same time it is a repetition of 'the Lord has said' of the

previous parenthetic verse, in order to give sequence to the theme. Now follows mention of the two functions assigned to the Servant Israel. (1) The Servant is to *raise up*, that is, to re-establish *the tribes of Jacob, and to restore Israel*, now *preserved*, held, in exile in Babylon. But that is too easy a thing for the Servant to do, if he is the Servant of a plan that is intended to embrace the whole of humanity. (2) Therefore the Servant is to become *a light to the nations*, 'so as to be my salvation to the end of the earth'.

DI would know the contents of Ezek. 37. There we find two distinct themes. First, says Ezekiel, God is about to resurrect the corporate dead body of Israel, and to bring Israel out of her grave in the great Mesopotamian valley. He is about to breathe into the individual corpses his own life, as he did when he first created man (Gen. 2:7), and so this resurrection will become a new creation. Second, God's purpose in this resurrection is to work itself out through all the twelve tribes of Israel and not just through Judah, that tribe which had retained the leadership of the Davidic line; it was to embrace even those tribes who had seemingly lost their identity almost two hundred years before. Thus Ezekiel looked for the promises of God, spoken as they were so long before to the patriarchs, to become flesh, so to speak, in a reconstituted Israel that was representatively the whole people of God. Here DI is speaking of the same great hope for all twelve tribes that Ezekiel had enunciated some years before in the ears of the exiles in Babylon.

Yet we are faced with a difficulty in interpretation. If Israel is the Servant, then how can Israel raise up Israel? Must not the Servant be identified with someone else who has a mission *to* Israel, but who is not Israel himself? It is clearly only a modern, individualistic reader of DI who would think in such terms and ask such questions. Till now we have been aware that the Servant in DI's sequential narrative has in every instance been a title given to Israel and to none other, except when in another respect it is used of the person of Cyrus. Again, v. 6 follows in direct sequence from v. 3, where there is the explicit sentence *You are my servant, Israel*. So the Servant here must still be Israel, difficult as that is to understand. The Servant must be the whole people of God as it is represented by the *remnant* (46:3).

However, when we recall that the NT conception of the Church is in continuity with the OT conception of the corporate personality of Israel, we find a clue to the puzzle of this verse. A local congregation may decide to hold a mission to its own people, for it has newly discovered a sense of responsibility for all those who dwell within its parish area. But the whole membership does not at once become the instrument of evangelism. It is the faithful few, the inner core, who are the first to become the vehicle of the Word to others. On the other hand, those others to whom the parish mission is being addressed will probably still regard themselves as Christians, for they have been baptized and confirmed and are to be found on the roll of church membership. Who then is to say that they are not as truly 'Israel' as are the more self-consciously confessing group who are quite clearly Israel in the sense that DI is using here? What we have is the Servant-group Israel seeking to re-establish and restore the whole Servant-people Israel to their rightful place in the plan and purpose of God.

Then again, whenever a congregation regains its understanding of what it means to be the Servant-people of God, it also regains its understanding of the world mission of the Church. It is too easy for any local congregation just to restore its lapsed and lost members; its greater task is 'to be my salvation to the ends of the earth'. (The RSV does not translate accurately here.) For without his Servant God cannot act. And so it is, even as the Servant witnesses by word and deed to God's salvation, that the glory of God is revealed — not in the inanimate heavens, but in the active, fashioning, giving, spreading-out, carrying, refining, speaking manner in which living man can reflect the living actions of the living God.

A light to the nations is repeated from 42:6, and now its significance is made crystal clear. For since ch. 42, we have learned that it is God who forms the light, not man, (45:7; cf. 60:3). Moreover, since *light* and *salvation* are set down in parallel, the one word illumines the meaning of the other. The God who forms light is light himself; and so he is salvation itself; or rather he is light in action; he is saving love in action. And yet, paradoxically, the salvation that DI speaks of can be conveyed to mankind only in the body of the Servant Israel (cf. Luke 2:32; Acts 13:47).*

Here we have Israel preserved in the dungeon and darkness of Babylon, 'looking for the consolation of Israel', to use the words of Luke 2:25 at this point. DI tells her three things about her present

* Note that the Qumran community undoubtedly regarded themselves as this true, inner core of Israel in their day (circa 100 B.C.: Black, *op. cit.*, p. 129). Thus it is quite natural for some of the NT writers to adopt a similar exegesis of DI's lines with reference to the young Christian Church of which they were a part.

situation: (1) Her time of consolation or comfort has come (40:1-2). (2) God is now about to use her despite her state of rebellion, because he has forgiven all her sins. (3) God is now preparing to make use of her even while she suffers rejection in Babylon, and will do so in such a manner that her suffering will become his instrument for the world's redemption. But as the reader is aware, DI leaves the development of this tremendous theme until a later chapter.

7 DI left us at v. 6 with a one-verse cameo of the Servant, now clearly portrayed as one who suffers. The words *to one deeply despised* are only one possible translation of the phrase, and much depends upon the interpretation of the words. The more study that has been given to the DSSI text, the less willing are scholars, generally speaking, to believe that it can add much to our knowledge, yet here its reading seems to make better sense than the received Hebrew text. The word *deeply* is the Hebrew *nephesh*, person, soul, life, and many other things in English as well. So it could be translated 'despised of soul' by himself or by others. The LXX translators later on must have read it as 'he who despises his own soul' (cf. 53:3). Yet a previously noted truth emerges again even from this difficult text. Once more we see that the Servant in himself is nothing. God is still all in all. On the other hand, the Servant is needed by God. What God needs is his obedience, and that alone. However, the servant Cyrus could give more than his obedience, unwitting as that was, for he offered God his strength and his many abilities both as a warrior and as a king. But Israel, we have learned, has neither strength nor native abilities to offer to her God. In consequence all that God wants and needs of her is an emptiness of self, for it is only then that God can reveal himself in her body (cf. Heb. 10:5). Nothing else can be the medium of divine revelation, for nothing else leaves room for it.

Yet, as the parallel passage at 52:15 ff. declares (cf. also 49:23; Ps. 72:10-11), the *rulers* who now despise the Servant will eventually make obeisance to him in the abject manner customary at the period. But note that they will bow not to Israel but to the *Holy One of Israel, who has chosen you*, who is now made manifest in and through the self-emptying of Israel. That is why God, as the trustworthy or *faithful* One, can be relied upon to uphold his Servant at that moment when the Servant is no longer 'himself'; for in despising his *nephesh*, the Servant is no longer clinging to his own ego. The words *who has chosen you*, therefore, must point to the end in view, for which God's Servant is called.

8 Just as the NT can use the word *kairos* with reference to Christ and
speak of his 'time' as being *at hand*, on the point of arriving (cf. Matt.
26:18), so DI can use the word *'eth*. Here it occurs as the emphatic first
word of this new section. *Thus says the Lord*, ' "At the moment I willed to
do so" *I have answered you*', almost 'answered your prayer'. This line
is a development of the news headline, as we have called it, with which
DI opened his announcement of God's good news: 'Speak to
Jerusalem's heart . . . that her forced labour is ended, that the
punishment due her for her iniquity has been accepted' (40:2). Now he
goes on: 'At the day' *of salvation I have helped you* (see 42:6). In fact, 'D-
day' in God's plan has now arrived (cf. 54:8; 57:17; 61:2; Luke 22:53*b*;
and Paul's quotation at 2 Cor. 6:2). Cyrus is pounding at the gate of
Babylon — or proleptically he is just about to do so. 'Now is the day of
salvation; I have come to your aid.' God then has come to do three
things in one. He has come (1) to save Israel; (2) to save her that she
might become the covenant people to mankind which he has
proclaimed above (v. 6), in order that the whole world may be saved.

But now DI takes a step farther. He knows with Hosea (cf. 2:1 ff.),
Jeremiah (cf. 4:20-31), the author of Gen. 3:16-19 and others that
natural disasters are bound up in some way with the fall of man. Evil is
in fact no more a static thing than is goodness. We have seen that DI
regarded goodness as the 'in-breaking' of creative love within Israel's
life. Israel's goodness thereby becomes the counterpart of God's
goodness to her and is visible as acts of compassionate love. Goodness is
thus inconceivable without either God or man as the instruments of
good in action. So too in the case of evil, which cannot exist *per se* (cf.
45:7). For evil is the expression of the evil purposes of living beings.
The prophets before DI's day, in looking forward to the day of
redemption, saw the latter as the day when the evil in nature would be
done away with as completely as the evil in the human heart — for
God's universe is one *uni*-verse. Thus Amos can speak of the coming
redemption of the cycle of nature (9:13), as Hosea also does a few years
later (2:21-23), and as Isaiah does even more particularly when he
promises the redemption of nature red in tooth and claw (11:6-9).

So now we can put promises (2) and (3) together: *to establish the land,
to apportion the desolate heritages*. That sentence must point beyond the
rebuilding of Jerusalem and the cities of Judah. There are those who
limit the function of the Servant to the latter task, and who would read
land as 'land of Judah'. But they are not seeing the passage in the light
of DI's great heritage of thought. For he can say of the world: God *did*

not create it a chaos, 'He fashioned it for civilized life' (45:18), i.e. to be inhabited, not to lie in ruins. DI believes that this is a fallen world, and that it must therefore be raised up. That is, the whole earth must be 're-established' according to God's initial purpose for it when he saw that it was good (Gen. 1). This verse is thus a mere extension of God's promise at 49:6, and an explanation of it. All this will eventuate once the *tohu* with which it is riddled is reclaimed for order and *shalom* (45:7). Before proceeding further, note that Trito-Isaiah advances DI's argument still another step; for he sees the renewed people of God themselves bound up not just with a renewed nature, but with a new heaven and a new earth as well (65:17 ff.).

9   The redemption *of* Israel is thus bound up with the redemption of others *through* Israel. But Israel, though a corporate body, is composed of individuals. Of course it is only individuals who can respond to God's call or who can risk their lives rescuing prisoners from dungeons. We know that many Israelites did not respond to this challenge and never gave up the flesh pots of Babylon for the rigours of life in a ruined Jerusalem. They imagined perhaps that one can be saved without sharing in God's great saving purpose for his whole creation (cf. Matt. 16:25; 27:42). For the saving activity of God is visible only as we see men breaking down prison bars, or venturing into the dungeons beneath the public buildings of Babylon or Benares, there to meet with a stench and a filth that appals. Yet without this human action God's purpose could not advance (cf. Matt. 25:35-36). On the other hand, God takes the initiative in love. The Good Shepherd, spoken of at 40:11, 29-31 promises that *along the ways shall they feed*, as they return to their Promised Land.

10-12   DI sees the exiles returning not just from Babylon, but from every point of the compass. We need not dwell on determining where *Sinim* (RSV mg.) was. For no agreement has been reached whether DI meant Syene, which is *Assuan* in Upper Egypt (cf. Ezek. 29:10; 30:6), or the Sudan, or even an area of Eritrea. Probably DI did not know himself, nor was he concerned to know.* What mattered was that these people lived at the ends of the earth, and the redemption of Israel was to reach to the ends of the earth. That is a reality which has

---

* *Sino*-Japanese War includes an English word built from *Sinim* in misunderstanding.

interested the author of the book of Revelation also much more than the geography of God's activities, as we can see when we read his beautiful development of DI's words at Rev. 7:16-17.

These last lines, let us note, speak of an action of God which has nothing to do with Cyrus and Babylon. DI has thus departed from an exposition of the immediate historical situation, and has entered upon a broader theological discussion of what God's redemption of Israel means as a thing in itself. In doing so, however, he remains true to the biblical method of the presentation of truth. The prophets never discuss the meaning of concepts or of propositions. What they do is to expound the actions of God in and from historical situations. It is thus imperative for us to make sure we know all that we can know about Israel's history. On the one hand, DI gives us no discussion of the concept of redemption. On the other, however, he expounds the historical situation in which he and his contemporary Israelites found themselves, even as Cyrus the Persian marched upon the city that held them captive.

13   This little, single-verse poem becomes a generalization from the actual incident of the fall of Babylon. Moreover, the significance of the incident has now become even greater than the redemption of all the Hebrews scattered amongst the nations. God's people, God's afflicted, are to be found, in point of time, both before and after this particular moment that is bound up with Cyrus the Persian; whereas, in point of space, the reality of the redemption is now to obtain with respect to the whole cosmos. We dare not dismiss the call to the *earth* and the *heavens* to shout for joy as just poetry. For the Hebrews employed poetry along with the parable as a vehicle to convey truth at those moments when no prose language could do so.

The words *his afflicted* force us to pause, however, and examine an important theological issue, one that is possibly the chief stumbling block at the heart of DI's exposition. How can God use to serve his ends a people who are *his afflicted* when it has been he who has afflicted them as punishment for their apostasy? How, in other words, can a sinful nation *be* the instrument of the Holy God's salvation to the rest of the world?

Israel had received from God special revelation in the form of Torah. This light had then had an effect upon her which she did not realize. In a negative sense, she had rejected and failed to use the light. Positively speaking, the light had blinded her eyes, stopped her ears, hardened her heart, so that her failure surpassed the sinfulness of any other nation on the earth (cf. Isa. 6:9-12). Yet God foreknew that this would happen. Was it fair of God to choose Israel at all, knowing as he did (1) that Israel would necessarily fail him, and (2) that his own light would blind her eyes and render her even more rebellious than she would have been without it?

The full judgment of the living God had now fallen upon Israel, and she had met with just retribution for her disloyalty. For she had failed not merely to be good, the position that all nations find themselves in; she had actually let God down as he sought to use her to save the world. Accordingly she bore the unspoken execration of all mankind as the nations of the earth dumbly sought for a salvation whose source they knew not. DI has spoken of the ugliness of sin. Now he has declared the judgment of the all-holy God upon it. For the Holy-One-of-Israel cannot tolerate union with a corrupt Israel. God must therefore reject her even when he never lets her go. So finally he did act, and Israel became what she is called here: *his afflicted* people.

DI thus comes to the extraordinary conclusion that Israel had been chosen to become — that. She had been chosen to become the scapegoat required to carry the judgment of God upon the sins of the world. God had rendered her so by blinding her eyes still further. Yet, instead of being accursed for allowing her heart to grow hard, Israel was in fact the most highly privileged nation of all. Actually her hardness of heart was necessary for her election.

Yet we are to remember that Israel had not offered herself to be the scapegoat as if that had been her own good idea and the expression of her loyalty to the covenant. Israel was in fact quite unconscious of the uniqueness of her calling. For was she not just an ordinary, despondent prisoner of war, just a pariah people that had been conquered in war?

Here is where DI makes a contribution to our knowledge of the ways of God with men that is without precedent. What he does is to combine two realities which, humanly speaking, seem to be total opposites. In the first place, DI acknowledges Israel's rebellion, acknowledges that she is a worm, acknowledges that she had suffered justly for her sins. Yet at the same time Yahweh, he says, has kept asserting that even while she has been suffering justly, he has never let her go. In fact, he has been beside her in her sorrow and pain all the time. DI even dares to use the simile, following Hosea, of a loving husband sharing, even bearing, the pain that results from the folly of his wife's disloyal ways.

But in the second place, DI asserts that the suffering undergone by Israel, which she has so richly deserved, God has accepted as if it were suffering voluntarily undergone on Israel's part. That is to say, God imputes to Israel the good intention she never had. God imputes to her the complete self-emptying, which she had to undergo when her *nephesh*, her person, was despised and abhorred by her conquerors. Thus in reality it is no longer she, the stiff-necked, proud, self-confident Israel of old with whom her God is dealing; all that man can now see is the mere broken body of Israel as it suffers the strokes of the lash of a terrible judgment. For Israel is no longer 'there', so to speak. Rather, the place where she had once been is now taken by the Word that dwells within her. For as a *nephesh* in her own right she is dead (42:6, 8; 43:2; 48:11; 49:3, 8). So her body is now merely the form through which the Word becomes flesh. Therefore it is the Word — a masculine noun in Hebrew — who has now borne the consequences of Israel's guilt. No wonder therefore the cry goes forth: *Sing for joy, O heavens and exult, O earth:* 'Burst into singing, you hills!' *For the Lord has comforted his people,* 'he has shown' *compassion* (as the Hebrew runs) *on his afflicted people.*

14 The humanity of Israel is clearly underlined in this verse. Here she is quite unable to appreciate and understand the wonder of the gospel that DI is proclaiming to her about her God. In fact, all down the ages men have found the good news of God's love too good to be accepted as true (cf. 40:27). DI here calls Yahweh Israel's *adon*. While this word normally means lord, it may also be used for husband, in the same way as the word *ba'al*, Baal, or lord, can also be used for husband.

15 The remarkable metaphor that follows is DI's way of showing still another facet of Yahweh's special relationship to Israel. For here we learn of the mother love of God. The figure occurs a number of times in the OT and serves to balance the usual masculine image of the Almighty that men have held. Thus if only the early Church had fed the ordinary believer faithfully with the truths of revelation as they are given us in the OT, as well as with those that come to us from the NT, the felt need for a mother image in the heavens might never have developed, and the Virgin Mary would not have been exalted to the position she now holds in the imagination and respect of many. For the Virgin Mary is really the representative of the feminine figure of Zion, the people of God, now fully accepting her role as handmaid (the feminine form of the masculine word 'servant', Luke 1:38). With Simeon, she had been humbly *looking for the consolation of Israel* (Luke 2:25). The word 'consolation' means the consummation of the union, when her body would be used as the temple of the Holy Spirit, so that the Word could in reality become one flesh with God's People Israel. At v. 14 Zion has just spoken in the feminine singular of her heavenly spouse. The pity and compassion in God's reply can be heard in the choice of the word 'breast-fed babe' — for that is what poor, abandoned, helpless, ridiculous Israel obviously appeared in his sight. But now, how can the omniscient One forget? (cf. Pss. 13:1; 77:9; Hos. 4:6). *But I will not forget you!* comes the emphatic reply — *you* being in the feminine gender and singular. Thus *you* is no longer the Servant in the masculine: *you is now the beloved wife*.

16 Now we have a moving picture of divine grace. For it is not possible to conceive of grace in the abstract. The picture has been adapted from a practice with which Israel would meet in Babylon. Some of Israel's neighbours, including the Babylonians, were in the habit of tattooing the name of the god they worshipped upon their hand, in order to remind them to whom they belonged, and who was the controlling power in their lives. Similarly, Israel was called to witness to God's act in bringing her out of Egypt by wearing on her hand a reminder of that great event (Ex. 13:9). On that occasion God had been the sole actor. He had done everything for Israel, and all that Israel needed to do was just to accept it in gratitude. But in this picture the tables are turned, so to speak, and we are given a picture of *God* showing Israel that he has her name inscribed not just on one but actually on both of his hands. Moreover, although the walls of Jerusalem are now lying flat on the ground, God declares that he sees them re-erected, protecting the city that he has promised to keep forever as his own. This can only mean that the walls shall be built; what God sees cannot be a mirage, for God sees both the beginning and the outcome of every situation in every age.

17-18 God in fact now sees feverish activity in progress as Zion's sons work faster at rebuilding the city than her enemies are able to destroy it (cf. Neh. 16), and all marauding desert nomads vanish in the mist. Back to their predestined home come all the sons of Mother Zion from every corner of the earth — and so not only from Babylon, as we saw before. And then comes a heartening declaration from the lips of Zion's

God. Beautiful as her walls and buildings may be, Zion's real wealth and beauty reside rather in her — and God's — sons and daughters. Unlike Queen Babylon who will soon be mourning the loss of her sons, Queen Zion, when the marriage is later renewed, as the Bride of God will possess all the children she desires (cf. Gen. 22:17). And while Queen Babylon will be putting on widow's weeds, Queen Zion will be attiring herself with the glory of her sons. (Note that Trito-Isaiah quotes this verse (60:4), but that he adds to the returning sons and daughters of Israel representatives of all nations of the earth, for they too will be among God's sons returning home to Zion.)

DI may however be saying the same as 60:4. We should examine his words in the light of what he has said before (cf. 44:5), though he is not wholly explicit on the matter. For Mother Zion here seems to be surprised at seeing some of her children, and evidently does not recognize how she came by so many. Moreover, it is unlikely that Jews were at that time living in the very far-off land of *Sinim* (v. 12 *ftn*). The DSSI actually reads 'the people of *Sinim*', from whom also 'sons' will return to Zion, as if it were expecting not just Jews but gentiles to come home to God. This scroll seems to be interpreting DI aright, and agrees with what Paul had in mind when he insisted that there is only one Israel of God, one original stock, into which the believing gentile is grafted by baptism (Rom. 11:17-32; 1 Cor. 10:18).

19-20   The same God who had *devastated your land* was now, beyond the 'death' of Zion, bringing new life abundant to the city he had chosen. It is true that for a time God had had to put away his Bride, Mother Zion (cf. Hos. 1-3; Ezek. 16) because she was unclean; she had consorted with other lovers and had given her loyalty elsewhere. But God had long since sworn to give his glory to no other than his faithless Bride.

21   Now that she had been forgiven, therefore, one of the joys of 'setting up house' again which the Lord would grant her was wondering where all her children had come from. So long as she remained an exile in Babylon she had not been in physical contact with Yahweh her Husband — for the temple, where Yahweh had put his name to dwell, was then in ruins. Without a Husband, who could have sired her with all these children? The only answer is that they must have been born of grace (v. 15), the grace of a Husband's love that had remained unchanged throughout the whole long period that she believed herself to be barren and a grass-widow in exile.

How daring this figure appears to us, with our Western conceptions of delicacy in matters of sex. Yet no figure conceived in an Eastern mind could express more movingly the reality of grace, the same grace as is described explicitly in the annunciation narratives of Luke's Gospel. We note that the figure unashamedly includes both *agape* and *eros* in the love of God for Israel; and so if DI believes that both concepts are needed to expound the love of God, then there is no reason for us either to be ashamed to make a similar identification.

22 Nothing now can stop the outworking of God's *'etsah*, or plan. DI here refers to a daring saying of Moses as the latter expostulates to God: 'Did I conceive all this people? Did I bring them forth, that thou shouldst say to me, "Carry them in your bosom, as a nurse carries the sucking child"?' (Num. 11:12).

23 In fact DI's language could easily be and has often been misconstrued. His expression *Kings . . . and queens . . . with their faces to the ground they shall bow down to you, and lick the dust of your feet* has led expositors to exclaim with disgust that what is portrayed here is a highly undesirable trait in the nature of the chosen people. But this is to misunderstand the *'etsah* of God.

Isaiah of Jerusalem has a long poem on the haughtiness both of man and nature, in which he describes how all human and nature's pride must be brought low. For God is all in all, so that *the Lord alone will be exalted in that day* (Isa. 2:9-11, 12-19). DI, whose works are included in the 'Book of Isaiah', would know this passage well. Therefore we are not in order if we read into vv. 22-23 any suggestion that here Israel is preening herself as the 'chosen people', chosen to lord it over the nations of the earth. This misinformed view of Israel's election has bedevilled Jewish-Christian relations all down the centuries.

DI's meaning, however, is to be found only when we wrestle with the text in its context (of which we saw the need at 45:14-15). In the phrase *lick the dust of your feet*, 'your' is still in the feminine singular. It can therefore refer only to Israel as the Bride of God (see 50:1). Israel is that people *in* whom God hides himself. Thus, if kings and queens *bring your sons in their bosom and your daughters shall be carried on their shoulders*, and if, *with their faces to the ground they shall bow down to you, and lick the dust of your feet*, then they are in fact bowing down to God-in-Israel (v. 7), the Husband of the Bride. Since they bow down to *you* (feminine singular) and lick the dust of *your* feet (again feminine singular), evidently DI is not thinking of Israel now as 'Jacob' (masculine) but as the Bride of God. For the Bride is the sacramentally visible aspect of the Presence of God in this world. Then *you* (feminine singular) will know that I AM YAHWEH, the Lord who is utterly faithful to his covenant partner.

24-26 DI now allays a final doubt that Yahweh may not be strong enough to effect his purpose. Yahweh, he says, is surely stronger than any human dictator, for he has made them all (45:9). In fact he *could* effect the terrible picture drawn in v. 26; and yet even if he were to do these things, they would represent even less than justice for the evil in the thoughts and plans of the nations. For God, being the living, active God, must do something, no matter how shocking that something may be. *Then all flesh*, mankind, *shall know that I am the Lord your Saviour, and your Redeemer*, the *Mighty One of Jacob ('abhir)*. This last word is the old poetic name for Yahweh that Isaiah of Jerusalem had used (1:24), and which was employed by the narrator of Jacob's story in Genesis (Gen. 49:24; cf. Ps. 132:2, 5). It was discussed at 46:12. By using this word DI is declaring that God's purpose and plan, now about to be revealed to the nations, are rooted in the far distant past of the patriarchal period, even before the 'history of God on earth' began.

CHAPTER 50

1   Our chapter divisions are of course artificial. DI is here proceeding with the question of the estrangement between Mother Zion and her Husband which occupied his attention in the previous chapter. What God is saying here to Zion's children — in the plural — is this: 'I didn't *divorce* your mother (when I sent Zion into exile), and the proof of that is that she can show no certificate to that effect'. Such a certificate was necessary by the Law of Moses (Deut. 24:1-4; cf. Jer. 3:8, where the Northern Kingdom is given such a certificate, but not Zion). Within Israel it was only the husband who could divorce his wife. All that the woman could do was to be unfaithful. No divorce therefore became legal unless the husband presented his wife with such a certificate. 'I had to deal with you in some way for your *transgressions*,' God explains. 'It was not that I was bankrupt of love. Yet I had to make a plan. My plan was to allow you to leave home, and so to let you suffer a just punishment (40:2) for your unfaithfulness; but I vowed to have you back thereafter.' 'Selling to creditors' is a figure of speech for giving into the power of a conqueror (cf. Judg. 2:14; Deut. 32:30). At Ps. 44:9-22 Israel's complaint against God for his handling of her adulterous pursuit of other lovers is clearly stated.

2   What Zion did not realize when she went a-whoring after other lovers (cf. Hos. 1-3) was how much she hurt her Lord by so doing. In love he 'came in to her', but she had gone; when 'he called, no one answered'. In this one line we are shown the pathos of the empty home, the loneliness of God's heart, the pain at the centre of the universe. Yet here we get only a glimpse of that pain, for this is only a foretaste of a later theme. Instead, God asks at this point whether Israel realizes that, as the Almighty, he could compel his wife to return home to him if he so decided. The Almighty could do anything. He 'could dry up the sea', and thus reverse the order of creation (Gen. 1:9). He 'could turn rivers into a desert', leaving death and devastation behind him.

3   He could even produce the *blackness* of chaos and thus reverse his gracious purpose of creative redemption. But that way of redeeming the world is unthinkable. For God is not like that. His method is to use a Servant who is wholly dedicated to his mission.

4 This ideal, wholly dedicated Servant now speaks. And his first word is 'Yahweh', not 'self', and his second is *has given*. The Servant thus witnesses to Yahweh alone and to his acts of grace. *The tongue of those who are taught*, or disciples' language reveals that the speaker is aware of his need to learn, and has the humility to confess that need. This word for disciples, *limmudim*, occurs substantivally only in the book of Isaiah. Its first occurrence is at 8:16-17. There the prophet Isaiah of Jerusalem declares: 'Bind up the testimony, seal the teaching among my disciples. I will wait for the Lord, who is hiding his face from the house of Jacob, and I will hope in him.' Then the word does not occur again until here, except for two occurrences in Jeremiah, where it is virtually an adjective, and where it must be translated by 'trained' or 'accustomed'. Some suggest that Isaiah of Jerusalem really coined a new and special term in this word, and sought to demonstrate by means of it that it was his own disciples who were eventually to be the 'remnant' that 'will return' (Isa. 10:21). For Isaiah evidently did not think that the time was then opportune for the full scale prophetic Word of redemption to enter into the life of Israel. That was why he had to seal it among his disciples until God's good time. If these scholars are right, then DI believed himself to be the second Isaiah, and as such authorized by God to declare that the time had come at last when the seal could be broken. If this is so, then DI believed that the seed of Isaiah's disciples was now to be identified with the whole (remnant) Servant people of God; for, as he declares later at 54:13 'All your sons will be Yahweh's disciples', in this sense of the word.

However, the Servant does not learn merely for the sake of learning, but in order to *know how to* preach a *word* to — or possibly 'help' — *the weary* 'to waken them up'. For the Servant has learned from Yahweh, learning it in fact day after day, to be compassionate towards his *weary* fellow men to the point of searching out those who are sleeping the sleep of death.

5 Once again the Servant emphasizes that *the Lord God* is doing this, not he. His task could possibly have rendered him *rebellious* or refractory, or frightened him enough to make him run away; but he had withstood the temptation.

6   Far from taking this ignominious course, the Servant had actually
tried a new thing in the face of the world's violence — obviously again
as taught by Yahweh. The vast majority of peoples in all ages of the
world have known only one answer to the problem of commanding
obedience — strike your servant and compel him to obey. However,
this Servant had learned from Yahweh neither to run away nor to
rebel, nor even to hit back, but instead to bare his back to the *smiters'*
lash. The most telling insult that the East could perpetrate on a man in
order to insult him and so to render him inferior, or even just to put him
in his place, was to pluck the hairs from his *beard* (cf. Neh. 13:25). But
the Servant had now learned to turn the other cheek. He had never
even tried to escape from the insulting spittle (cf. Num. 12:14; Deut.
25:9; Matt. 26:67) of a world that could only show its inverted
inferiority complex by mean and ugly acts — instead he quietly
accepted them. Why did he do all this? We are not told as yet. DI's
brilliant psychological understanding of his reader's mind prompts
him to withhold that secret till the moment of the great denouement
that he plans for later on.

Now how did DI conceive of this extraordinary new approach to
the problem of man's inhumanity to man? Of course it is utterly new.
He did not find it in the Tammuz ideology that some expositors have
adduced. As one of a vast concourse, he may well have stood and
watched the Babylonian high priest ceremonially strike his monarch
on the face. The latter then symbolically fell dead. For the king of
course had to die and be raised to life again: such an act of sympathetic
magic would make the world of nature come alive again with the
advent of the autumn rains. Though such a ceremony was undoubtedly a very ancient one among the Canaanite peoples, we are not
as certain today as scholars were a generation ago that the king in
Babylon ever underwent such an indignity. (See ANET, p. 334, col. 1.)
But if he did, he accepted it as a staged ceremonial act, knowing that
the eyes of all men were upon him — DI's included, perhaps. This act
may indeed have set our prophet thinking and reasoning. But DI's
portrait here of the Servant as he humbly accepts the obloquy of a
vicious-minded humanity belongs in the sphere of divine revelation —
for no human being had ever yet consistently acted in this way since
the world began.

7   We are not told *why* the Servant acts this way — except that
Yahweh had taught him so — but we are told *how* he can face the pain

and obloquy spoken of in v. 6. He can do so because *the Lord God helps me*.

8-9   Yahweh is in fact *with* his Servant in a very potent manner. He stands beside him as his Advocate in court. What adversary or accuser dare come forward to take legal action now? As Paul says in another context with regard to the Christian man: 'If God is for us, who is against us? ... Who shall bring any charge against God's elect? It is God who justifies; who is to condemn?' (Rom. 8:31, 33-34). It would take the accusers so long to stand and make their case that they would *wear out like a garment*. Moreover, this vivid analogy is introduced by 'see', in the typical biblical manner. It is the genius of the Bible to pictorialize theological issues, for ordinary men can grasp these only when they can see them in a mental picture.

Now a new picture of the Servant is building up. At v. 5 we saw that he could be God's completely willing Servant. But as such his obedience is not to be construed as merely passive. His response to evil is that of God himself, viz., positive and recreative. Verse 7 confirmed this view, for here we read that with God's help he is able actively to turn the other cheek toward wicked men. Finally at v. 9 we discover that the Servant's secret is an inner spring of joy and assurance.

10   Because of his total obedience, the Servant actually empties out his own self. In this way he leaves room for God to act through him without any block or hindrance. He who *fears the Lord* — the most representative OT expression for our modern phrase 'being religious' — now has the chance to know the Lord's will. This is because Yahweh's will has materialized, so to speak, in *the voice of his servant*. In obeying the Servant, the God-fearer will now find that he *relies*, or literally *leans upon his God*, directly! In obeying the Servant's voice, he will *trust* not in the Servant but *in the name of the Lord!*

Both Yahweh and the Servant are here spoken of in the third person. This verse is therefore DI's own note appended to the direct speech of the Servant that precedes it. In this note, moreover, he makes an extraordinary equation: the voice (i.e. words) of the Servant *is* the Word of God; he who obeys the voice of the Servant finds himself leaning upon *God*. The Servant thus enables those who walk in darkness and have no light of their own (cf. v. 11) to find their way to God who is the light himself (cf. Isa. 9:2), there to lean on him in utter dependence. This word of DI's is therefore much more than a historical note about the Israelites in the darkness of Babylonian prisons (cf. 49:25). It is a theological utterance, based indeed upon the contemporary historical situation, but one which thereafter has repercussions throughout the whole of the biblical revelation.

11 Finally DI turns and addresses the pagan world, Babylonians and all others. Probably he includes even the Persians because of their interest in fire worship. How stupid it is to worship a fire which you yourselves have kindled, he says (cf. 44:16). For Yahweh is the true light, and so Yahweh is the source of all fire, not Ahura Mazda nor any other. DI thus connects the concept of the true light available to those who trust in Yahweh (v. 10) with a terrible reality also connected with light and fire. That reality is that fire destroys as well as gives light. DI is therefore saying to the heathen world the kind of thing that we today might put in a proverb, such as 'He who plays with fire will get burned' or 'Be sure your sin will find you out'. There is a law of life that ensures that in the end evil devours those who worship it. And if such is in fact a law of life, then it comes from God. This truth DI now expresses pictorially. For along with Isaiah his predecessor, DI knows that it is *God* who is the real furnace, so that to enter the fire is to meet with God (Isa. 30:33; 31:9; 42:25; 47:14; 66:24).

The doctrine of hell is just as integral to the Old Testament revelation as it is to the New. For the God of whom Paul can say, 'Do not be deceived; God is not mocked, for whatever a man sows, that he will also reap' (Gal. 6:7), is the same God whom DI came to know and trust in the days of the Babylonian exile, and whom he found to be both light and fire at once.

CHAPTER 51

1 Before this point DI has made two opposing statements. First, he has shown that Israel, called to be Yahweh's Servant, has signally failed in her calling. But second, he has outlined what the calling of the Servant could be; and so he has pictured for us the perfect Servant, that is, one who is wholly obedient to the will of God. Here he reconciles these two disparate statements in a remarkable manner. For he now calls upon the actual, empirical, historical, wholly sinful Israel, composed of the exiles in Babylon, to trust and believe in God as Abraham had done of old. Obviously Yahweh intends to accept sinful Israel's act of faith, and through her faith to impute to her the power really to be the Servant, even though she is far from being like the ideal picture that DI has drawn.

Abraham was an individual. It is only individuals who can believe. So God here no longer addresses Israel as he has been doing in the singular feminine, thus regarding her as a corporate personality: now he addresses her in the plural. For Israel is also an aggregation of individuals. God accepts these individuals as purposeful personalities, as *you who pursue deliverance, you who seek the Lord*, meaning 'you who, by seeking the Lord, reach after God's saving Plan'. Did Israel really believe in God in this way? No matter, for a divine utterance such as this shows us the real secret of faith. Israel in exile has faith in Yahweh only because Yahweh first has faith in Israel. It is Yahweh's faithfulness, not man's faith, which is the basis of the hope of Israel. DI makes this clear by quoting what must have been a well-known metaphor, since it also occurs in the song of Moses (Deut. 32:4, 18). He does so of course by way of illustration, not to make etymologists of his readers. There, as elsewhere (33 times) throughout the Bible, God alone is the Rock. The Rock represents not the faith of DI, nor even that of Peter (cf. Matt. 16:18), nor of anyone else. The verb 'to believe', *he'emin*, basically means to find oneself standing on something secure or, to pictorialize it, to find that one's feet are upon the Rock. That is to say, when Abraham found himself standing upon the Rock, God imputed to him the power to become a rock to others (cf. Isa. 32:2). He had pursued *tsedeq*, (God's) saving righteousness, and had been rewarded with the power to display *tsedaqah*, compassionate concern for his fellow men. This at least is how DI understood the words of Gen. 15:6.

2   The potency of the ancient blessing is here accepted as a natural experience. A blessing was a word uttered with intent; it was quite distinct from mere idle chatter that was of no consequence. How much more effective must be the blessing of Almighty God.

DI has just used the word *quarry*, which sounds in Hebrew like the word 'woman'. So now he mentions Sarah, the only time her name occurs outside of Genesis. Gen. 12 has nothing to say about Sarah's faith, only about Abraham's. Yet as we read the Genesis sagas we find that Sarah, who had no visionary experience such as Abraham had, sets off from Haran with her husband to go to the land of promise. DI did not need to mention Sarah at all even to provide himself with a poetic parallel; another patriarch would have done for that. Then why did he draw attention to her at all? Evidently for two reasons:

(1)   Despite the fact that Abraham was *one* when he received his call, he was not one in the mathematical sense of the word. 'One, and all alone', 'only', 'unique' all represent the word *yahid* in Hebrew, as we saw at 44:6-7. That is the word which is used later in Genesis for Abraham's one and only son (22:2). But the word that is used here for 'one' is that employed for the oneness of husband and wife together, also found in Genesis at 2:24. The Bible does not seem to reckon with the idea of mere individuality in the modern sense. A man in OT times is always one with his tribe, his family, his wife, his children, and even his slaves and possessions. These all reflect his personality as he does theirs. Abraham would not have been the Abraham that we — and God — knew if he had not had Sarah for his wife. Without her he would have developed a different personality. His faith, DI implies, was dependent on the kind of wife he had, for he was one flesh with her in trust and love. Sarah as an individual does not need to make the decision to travel, for she makes it *in* Abraham's decision. Her part in their joint act of faith is the expression of 'loyalty-in-love'. This hyphenated concept represents the word *hesed*, which Hosea before DI's day had stressed in his own existential decision to continue in loyal love with his apostate wife (Hos. 1 – 3).

(2)   The second reason for mentioning Sarah is this: Sarah, the *quarry from which you were digged*, had a barren womb. It was a miracle of God that she bore a son at all. DI wants us to recognize that what God has done once he can naturally do again. He can raise Israel up out of the womb of death, for new life can spring forth for Israel now in Babylon as truly as new life once came from Sarah's womb.

3   Yahweh is now doing for Zion what he did originally for Abraham, Zion's progenitor. He had kept his promise to Abraham despite all appearances to the contrary. DI here returns to the feminine singular and ceases to address Israel in the plural as 'you'. He must therefore be emphasizing once again how all Israel is truly one, in the same sense as Abraham was one with Sarah, and even with Lot, and with 'the persons that they had gotten in Haran' (Gen. 12:5). At that time Yahweh had accepted Abraham as his servant and friend (41:8). Now he was accepting Zion in the same way. He was comforting and forgiving her — as DI has begun by saying at 40:1-2 — and was imputing to her his own quality of 'being rock' to others (cf. 49:6), a quality which was certainly not inherent in Israel herself. So the contrast between the one and the many in the person of Abraham, showing him to be an individual and a corporate personality at one and the same time, is DI's approach to the problem of the personality of the Servant also. Therefore his allusion to Abraham here is important for our understanding of the Servant concept later when the issue is more fully developed.

Before he develops this theme, however, DI opens a door on to the cosmic hope that his great predecessor Isaiah also had held (cf. 11:6-9). This hope is that the end of Yahweh's plan through his Servant will be much more than just the redemption of individual men. DI actually looks for the redemption of this whole fallen universe, and in saying so in lyrical vein he again uses the language of that great passage, Isa. 35, which may or may not be attributable to him. That is to say, he uses the mythology connected with the concept of the return of the Garden of Eden or paradise regained. This was a very widely held theme in the ancient Fertile Crescent. The prophets took it over, but they used it to serve a theological not a cosmogonic end. We found at 47:8 that Babylon in contrast to Zion is given the adjective '*adinah*, 'voluptuous', *lover of pleasures* (47:8), which is a feminine form of this same word *Eden*. DI may have thought of Babylon as Eden after the fall of Eve. But he is soon to describe Zion in terms of the Garden of Eden restored (54:11-14).

4   This explicit universalism (cf. 54:5), this ultimate redemption of the whole cosmos, was dependent upon something about to happen at that moment in history. DI pinned down the moment to the events of 539 B.C. This whole cosmic movement was dependent on Israel's giving *ear* or attention to Yahweh. Such a little act of obedience, at such an obscure moment in the obscure history of an obscure *people*! And yet in the providence of God that little act of obedience meant that God could act for the salvation of the world. Without it, God could not act, as he could not act without the faith of Abraham. Torah is the revelation that was given in the days of Moses, and that subsequently evolved into what we today wrongly call the law of Moses. For the noun *torah* comes from the word 'to teach'. DI, with all the prophets, used the word as a technical term for the revealed knowledge of God delivered to Israel in the form of instructions on how to live together as the people of God in obedience to his will. Through Israel's obedience, Torah will go forth 'from within God' (as the Hebrew says), not from Israel; for Israel is the mere *pied-à-terre* where the glory of God will be revealed (49:3). The double Hebrew preposition 'from with', in connection with Torah, is reminiscent of the language used to describe the relationship between wisdom and God in Prov. 8, and between the creative Word of God and God himself in Genesis and John (Gen. 1:3; John 1:1-3).

Parallel with God's Torah, his *mishpat*, his 'way of life', shall become *a light to the peoples*. This is the language of 49:6 once again. *Mishpat* has already been defined as 'true religion' or, better still, as 'total way of life' (see commentary at 42:1). For since *mishpat* is paralleled in this line by Torah, DI must intend these two nouns to complement each other. It is interesting that God's *mishpat* can be expressed only in and through Israel's life and obedience. DI sees therefore that Israel is more than the *pied-à-terre* God will use on earth. Israel has actually become the 'body' which the Torah and the *mishpat* of God occupy while the process develops even as the Word becomes incarnate before the eyes of the gentiles.

5 God is about to act at any moment (cf. 46:13), as DI knew. For DI was convinced that Cyrus' capture of Babylon, obviously now only a matter of days away, was the historical moment that God would use for his own mighty ends. Not that God would confine himself to that relatively unimportant historical incident. DI thought of God's use of the fall of Babylon in terms that we today can best understand as a chain reaction. The capture of Babylon by Cyrus was not *all* that Yahweh planned to do. The first effect of the fall of the city would be the rescue of the exiles. But then the rescue of the exiles would initiate a new understanding by Israel of the ways of God with man. That new understanding would thereupon interpret the suffering which Israel had newly undergone. Israel would then give herself in the saving plan for her neighbours till the redemption of all *the peoples* and even of the cosmos would finally be reached. Yet it was all to begin like a flash of lightning or, to use our idiom, like an atomic reactor's first explosion. *Rule* is the verb connected with the noun *mishpat* and thus means something like 'rule with the application of that justice which will regulate the whole of life'. It is most interesting to recognize that DI evidently believed that in their heart of hearts all men, even in the chaos and turmoil of their short and brutish lives, desire above all else the revelation — arm — of the living God.

6 It is a mistake to imagine that apocalyptic imagery is only a late phenomenon in Israel's story. The pre-exilic prophets used it: DI does so here also. The phrase *the heavens will vanish like smoke* could be rendered 'are (even now) dissipating like smoke'. Jesus used similar language when he declared, 'I saw Satan fall like lightning from heaven' (Luke 10:18). In such a way the prophets emphasised that what they were maintaining would surely come to pass. In the OT God does not, of course, dwell in heaven. He sits above the heavens. Heaven is as much part of creation as is earth, and will pass away at the end just as the earth will pass away.

The emphasis of this apocalyptic picture, however, is not on what we today would call the end of the world. It is upon the contrast between the transiency of this world, with man upon it, and the everlasting nature of God's continual saving activities. Neither the Exodus in the past nor the return of the exiles in Cyrus' day is to be the climax of God's saving purpose. That purpose is to *be for ever*, just as God's Word endures forever (40:8). The verb *hayah* normally means not 'to be' but rather 'to become', 'to endure'.

7 After such a tremendous utterance, how ridiculous it is for Israel, with God's Torah in her heart and actually knowing what God's saving activity is — for Israel has already experienced salvation — to be afraid of short-lived man. The Hebrew word for *men* used here, *enosh*, *mere man*, is the one which emphasizes his weakness and dependence. So DI says of this human obloquy: *Be not dismayed at their revilings*. This verb, rendered 'dismayed', is the same one that in v. 6 translates 'my saving activity shall never be "subverted"', rather than *ended*, even though in English 'dismayed' needs a personal subject.

8   As DI has said before, evil finally devours itself, even though it may be as slow a process as the disintegration of a *garment*. A garment cannot last forever, and we ought to recognize that fact as clearly as we realize that 'My compassionate love which I have put in you (the feminine form *tsedaqah*), and My saving power (the feminine form *yeshuʿah*) will go on (the verb *hayah*, to become) *to all generations*'. This must be so, simply on the ground that God is God (cf. Ps. 102:26-27). DI, in concert with his predecessors, is not concerned to show that Yahweh's transcendence is to be understood in terms of space, so that he dwells outside his universe. Both the ancient Greeks and modern man regard the spatiality of the divine Being as a problem for the mind. Rather, what DI is concerned to express is that God's transcendence is to be understood in terms of time. Yahweh is both first and last; therefore he must be the same forever (41:4; 43:10; 44:6).

9   'Arm of the Lord, awake, awake!' runs the favourite missionary hymn. Yahweh's arm is here apostrophized as if she — for 'arm' in Hebrew is feminine — were an independent entity apart from God. But no arm can act without motivation by the will of the person to whom it belongs. A man's arm in fact bears the same kind of relationship to his person as does his word or his spirit. That is why DI can call upon not Yahweh but Yahweh's arm. We can see from this verse how the Church father Irenaeus could speak of Christ and the Holy Spirit as 'the two arms of God'. For DI however, the arm signified action. He may have learned this concept from the Deuteronomist (cf. Deut. 4:34; 5:15), who speaks of God's arm as that which delivered Israel from Egypt. DI consequently daringly summons God's arm to *put on strength* again as one puts on clothing. If Yahweh's arm has done so before, DI believes, then she can do so again.

   The mythological language that follows was the common property of the ancient Near East (see T. H. Gaster, *Thespis* pp. 135-200.) *Rahab* was the West Semitic name for the monster of the 'waters under the earth' (cf. Ex. 20:4) who in herself represented the powers of chaos in which she swam. *The dragon* is a poetic synonym for Rahab. DI here takes the important step of demythologizing the monster; and instead of recounting myth, he theologizes upon the religious significance of the whole concept.

10   Here then he does not allude to the primal battle between the god of the sky and the goddess of chaos that the Babylonians believed in, that battle which underlies the theological picture presented to us in Gen. 1:1-3: he alludes to the crossing of the Red Sea. To show that he is theologizing and not repeating a myth, DI now equates *the waters of the great deep*, or 'abyss' (the *tehom* of Gen. 1:2) with the waters of the Red, or better, in the Hebrew, 'Reed' Sea through which Yahweh made *a way for the redeemed to pass over*. DI thus speaks in terms of soteriology and rejects the myth, although myth was the only science that was available to the ancient world. We ought therefore to interpret the Exodus from Egypt not by asking scientific questions as to what actually happened, but by seeing in it the arm of the Lord in action, ready to save. Since DI's hearers were certain, or ought to have been, that Yahweh had won the victory over Rahab at the crossing of the sea, he now declares that it will be an easy matter for Yahweh to do so again at any time he wills (cf. Job 9:13). In fact he can and will do so *now*, for the fall of Babylon by the arm of Cyrus is certainly contemporary evidence of the power of Yahweh's arm over the dragon at all times (cf. Ezek. 20:33 ff.).

11   This vivid section now ends on an eschatological note. *Everlasting joy* is rejoicing that will only begin, not cease, with Cyrus's act. In a sense it is parallel with the NT term 'hilarity' (the Greek behind the word 'cheerful' at 2 Cor. 9:7) which is an outrageous kind of joy that is shocking to the faithless (cf. Acts 2:13, 15). The word *singing, rinnah*, or shouts of joy, is a joy which comes from God and belongs to God. So DI in a few lines passes from mythology to theology and finally to eschatology. This fullness of meaning in DI's language is implicitly recognized at Rev. 7:16-17.

12   With such a future in prospect, *who are you* (feminine) to fear frail, mortal man, or 'what kind of person *are you* to', 'in what condition *are you* to' (cf. Ruth 3:16), as if the question is asked with astonishment. Yet *you* is plural in the phrase 'It is I, the I AM', *that comforts you*. This interesting swing from the collective singular to the plural, as noted earlier in this chapter, has a basic significance for understanding the person of the Servant. Meanwhile God comforts the hearts of the exiles one at a time, but expects them to respond in his service as a body. We can see here how the NT doctrine of the Church is in part derived from the words of DI. The word *ecclesia*, 'church' in the NT is both feminine and singular, just as Israel, Yahweh's Bride, is both feminine and singular.

13   Israel's response must take the form of opposition to the wrath of man, for man is evil. The question is of course what form the opposition should take, in face of the fact that in the end the oppressor's fury is only transitory. *Oppressor*, however, might be more cogently translated for our generation by the word 'liquidator' to bring out its terrible meaning.

14   But those who are at present the object of the oppressor's fury (the Servant people of God in exile) must ultimately know the saving power of God, simply because the oppressor's fury is indeed transient, while Yahweh's Word endures forever. *The Pit* is the lowest level of Sheol, the abode of the dead. *The oppressor* will not liquidate him; on the contrary, *neither shall his bread fail*.

15   The reference here is to Israel as the Servant, for the *your* of *your God* is expressed in the masculine singular once again. Finally Yahweh concludes this promise by appending his signature, as we might say, to the promise he has uttered.

16   What a contrast DI now draws between the God who can raise a storm at sea and the God who acts with the gentleness of the uttered Word. Yet astonishment at the contrast, which after all Elijah had already experienced (1 Kings 19:11-12), is as nothing compared with the profundity of the subsequent declaration. It is that Israel's election to be the Servant was made contemporaneously with creation itself. DI does not mean that empirical, sinful Israel was in any sense pre-existent. He means that God's purpose of love was prepared from the beginning for all eventualities. He means that the eternal Word has needed this 'body' in which it could become 'flesh' ever since *planting the heavens* (see RSV *ftn*). He means that at the beginning of God's purpose God said of Israel *You are my people*. Since God had said this *dabar* (word), and it had come forth from his heart and mouth, it necessarily had to become event (*dabar* again). For the two are one, and need but one word in the Hebrew language.

17   DI is not averse to presenting us with shattering contrasts. He first proclaims God's eternal purpose in Israel. Then immediately he reveals what Israel is really like, figured as she is once again by the feminine personality of *Jerusalem*. Even as he summons her to *rouse yourself, stand up O Jerusalem*, he knows that she cannot do so in her own strength. Herein rests the paradox of the way God works in the heart of his Servant.

DI is at one with his predecessor Isaiah, who believed that his preaching would serve only to harden Israel's heart, not enlighten it (cf. Isa. 6). The Hebrew mind pictorialized the conception of the hardening of the heart under the figure of drinking the *cup of his wrath . . . the bowl of staggering*. The concept of staggering obviously originates from the experience of the drunkard whose legs cannot hold him up. But the prophets use it with a theological aim. As such it becomes the picture of the effect of drinking a cup which the Lord has handed a man to drink. Throughout history the idea of sharing the cup has been universally employed as the symbol of fellowship and so by derivation, of covenant. We read in Nathan's parable how the lamb drank from his master's cup (2 Sam. 12:3). To the Psalmist his cup could be the portion of his heritage offered him by a loving God (Ps. 16:5), a cup running over with grace (Ps. 23:5).

However, that which was symbolic of the reality of fellowship and covenant love, if misused, could become the veritable cup of damnation itself. On the one hand, the Psalmist who received the cup in faith could exclaim 'I will lift up the cup of salvation' (Ps. 116:13). But on the other hand, if that cup should be taken in an undiscerning manner (as Paul says at 1 Cor. 11:29), the drinker thereby drinks damnation to himself. 'For in the hand of the Lord there is a cup, with foaming wine . . . and all the wicked of the earth shall drain it down to the dregs' (Ps. 75:8). No more terrible use is made of the figure than by Jeremiah (25:15-33). In that parabolic experience which he undergoes, God hands him the cup of staggering to give to all the kings of the earth, with the words 'Drink, be drunk and vomit, fall and rise no more'. DI would regard it as inconceivable to except Israel from drinking the cup, for he had no illusions about her being part of all the wickedness of the earth. Election, he knew, was not to salvation but to service. That was why Israel had now suffered the ultimate outcome of her apostasy, the total damnation which God must in fact offer to those who prefer blindness rather than sight (cf. also Lam. 4:21; Ezek. 23:31 ff.). She has *drunk to the dregs* not just the cup but the huge Babylonian *bowl*, chalice, of reeling. The word at the end of v. 17 is the translation of a Hebrew interpolation meant to interpret the Babylonian word for 'chalice'. The latter was probably a large bowl that was used in the service of Marduk.

18   Now if there is anything more degraded than a drunk man it is a drunk woman. So Zion — feminine — is drunk, too drunk to find her way home. Comes a sorrowful voice, pointing out that Zion has no sons left capable of performing the filial duty of guiding their mother home in her drunken state. For they themselves are all too drunk to help her.

19   Thus *two* pairs of evil, two acts of God, have befallen the exiles, two pairs because DI names those evils in doublets. His words moreover illustrate the inner and outer aspects of the situation. For they portray the moral collapse that accompanies the material distress that Israel had found herself in. Is this another reason why DI began his gospel by declaring that Zion had now suffered *double* for all her sins (40:2)?

20   All Israel has drunk from the cup of *the wrath of the Lord*. Israel has now reached the lowest ebb of her whole existence. Her whole being has been emptied out, and there is nothing left of her former self. Am I even able to console you? (v. 19, literally 'shake the head with you') asks the Almighty as he looks at the pitiful husk of her who was once his bride. Was there any point of contact left at all in Israel's bemused and befuddled mind which even God Almighty's words of comfort (40:1) could reach home to, and obtain a response? No, there was none at all, DI declares. Israel could not now even hear the words of comfort, far less make any movement to respond to them. For poor, stupid, egotistical Israel was now dead, and was even buried in her grave (cf. Ezek. 37:11 ff.). In fact, her descent into Babylon had become her descent into hell.

21   But it is just at that point when Zion needs God most that the God of all grace acts (cf. Hos. 2:14-15). Even though she is in a drunken stupor far more terrible than anything occasioned by wine, God remains her lover and her faithful husband. God says *listen to this, then, you poor soul*.

22   And then he acts, in the manner that a doctor may have to act to save an unconscious patient. What we now observe is the Word becoming act. God is now doing for Israel what she cannot do for herself: *Behold* ('look!') *I have taken from your hand the cup of staggering.* It is as her Advocate too that he does this, as one who stands beside her and *who pleads the cause of his people* (cf. John 14:16).

23 For in his infinite pity and compassion he has had to watch his beloved treated with all the brutality with which ancient peoples handled their prisoners of war. DI's choice of words at v. 23 possibly rests upon the last line of the so-called blessing of Moses (Deut. 33:29), 'And you shall tread upon their high places'. But from our recent study of the Ugaritic language we believe that the word *bamoth* (high places) should probably be translated as 'backs'. The Ugaritic sagas were already a thousand years old in DI's day. Such cruelty had evidently been the accepted thing ever since those far-off days.

DI has now brought us face to face with an amazing conception. It is that this virtual suicide, for an alcoholic is a suicide, this emaciated body of Israel now brought down to the point of death by her own deliberate decision and freely executed choice of loyalties, in God's eyes is still not merely his own beloved elected Servant but actually his suffering Servant. DI will soon expound this paradox in detail.

On the other hand, Israel was not the only sinful nation on God's earth. We have seen before (cf. 47) what Yahweh thought of Babylon, for example. Israel's tormentors had said 'Lie down flat, so that we can walk over you and step on your backs as if you were a street for walking on'. The justice of God demands that all the sinful nations of the earth should in their turn drink from the cup of staggering too. How this cup is finally snatched from their hands before it becomes too late only the NT can tell us, for only it can tell us who drank the cup in their stead (Matt. 26:39-42).

CHAPTER 52

1 The poem continues. God has to call upon Israel a second time (cf. 51:17) and tell her to wake up from the sleep of death, from the intoxication resulting from drinking the cup. DI's words are now clearly a theological interpretation of contemporary events, for they do not contain a prescription to the exiles of what they are to do when Babylon falls.

The poem is written in plain contrast with that to be found at 47:1 ff. There the queen of Babylon is doomed to destruction, for she is the personification of sinful pride. But here it is Zion that is addressed. She is Yahweh's Bride, and because of that she is to put on her wedding gown. She is to do this *before* she is rescued! This gown is not of course her own, for the gown is part of the dowry that the husband supplies to his bride. Zion's is a clean and beautiful gown; as such it is symbolic of purity and of sins forgiven (cf. Zech. 3:4). But what actually is this gown? It is nothing less that Yahweh's own strength. *Put on your strength, O Zion* does not refer to anything Zion herself possesses. Her strength is God himself (cf. Ps. 21:1; 27:1; 28:7; 46:1); *'oz* means both strength and glory at once. So her *strength* is defined by God's gift to her of her loveliest dresses.

Then two things will result: (1) She will move from the prison dungeon of Babylon into freedom, and so find herself moving from the death of the exile into the life of God. (2) She will become *holy*, even as God himself is holy, for all those who associate with him partake of his holiness (cf. Ex. 19:6; Isa. 48:2). That is why neither the uncircumcised nor the unclean will ever enter you again (cf. Rev. 21:27).

2 '*Qumi*, 'get up', *daughter of Zion*', says Yahweh to this poor girl bride who is now sitting in the dust into which Queen Babylon is about to descend. (When Jesus said '*Cumi*' to Jairus' daughter, it is clear that he saw her too as a daughter of Zion, Mark 5:41.) For dust represents all that is unclean, and one must *shake* it off before the clean new garment is put on. Yet Israel cannot raise herself any more than can Jairus' daughter. Only if she uses her divine Husband's strength will she be able to strike from her neck *the bonds* or fetters of servitude. In this verse there is a curious juxtaposition of genders. *Captive* in line *a* looks like a masculine form of the word; in line *b* it occurs as feminine. Probably DI is referring to the idea of the captivity of an Israel that is both Servant (masculine) and Bride (feminine) at the same time.

3-5 Till now Israel has been a useless Servant and a fruitless Bride. That is the essence of the rather obscure verses that follow. What DI is saying, as he looks back into the past, is that God's handling of his people till this time has been of no effect. The individuals who comprise Israel (the verbs are now second person plural) had learned nothing from Israel's stay in Egypt; and the Northern Kingdom had learned *nothing* from being overwhelmed by *the Assyrian* in 721 B.C. So God himself now explains why the exile that began in 587 B.C. has been necessary. The pain and suffering following upon the fall of Jerusalem have not been a pointless experience. Even when their Babylonian masters are mocking at the exiles in their bullying manner, and God's *name is despised*, God can weave all that into his plan. Even though Israel had been sold into Babylon's power *for nothing* (v. 3), that is, without effect, yet God of his own free sovereign grace will now redeem her *for nothing* too; but now the phrase means 'freely', 'without payment', 'from grace alone'.

6 Till now Israel has been only an empty shell of a Servant, has not even had the form of a Servant. But *in that day* the form will take on new content, for the name of God, God's very self, will dwell within that form. Remember that to *know my name* meant for DI's hearers to know his essential being. Thus to know God meant vastly more for DI than merely to know about him. It signified virtually that oneness of almost physical union that can produce new life (cf. Gen. 4:1 — new life, *'eth Yahweh*, from or by means of Yahweh). That is what Yahweh now promises, his actual presence, *Here am I* (cf. Ex. 3:12). Yet the ultimate union of God and Israel was not to coincide with the return to Jerusalem of the exiles rescued from the prisons of Babylon. It was to happen only *in that day*. This is the phrase used by the prophets to refer to the final outcome of the chain reaction that had been set in motion by God at the historical moment of which they are witnesses.

7 How thrilling it is to discover that, unimportant as man is in himself, he is a link in the great divine chain reaction. *In that day* an extraordinary thing is going to happen (v. 6). Yet that eventuality is dependent on DI's contemporary hearers as at this juncture they take their place in the evolution of the cosmic plan. Till now the exiles in Babylon had been utterly depressed, because the mainspring of their existence had gone. No man possesses any vital spark within him if he has lost purpose in life; in consequence he sees no reason to continue living. But he who learns that he is needed, that he has a necessary place in a mighty campaign whose outcome, if he is faithful, is assured (for God has spoken it) — that man gains an exhilaration of spirit that the world can never understand. So DI pictures this exhilaration in a form similar to a NT parable. He sees an exile who has been raised from the death of meaninglessness, of *tohu*, of negation, in the dungeons of Babylon, now bursting with the joy of one who has found that life has meaning and purpose, for he has discovered that God is alive and that he cares. Naturally this exile cannot keep the news of this new birth to himself. So he speeds over the intervening mountains to poor, ruined Jerusalem with this new song in his heart: 'God is not dead after all: he is reigning still, despite all appearances to the contrary' (cf. Rom. 10:15).

8 The excitement spreads. The watchmen on the ruined walls are the first to see this herald and so they catch the infection of his spirit themselves. The whole city as one man is moved to accept the news that is announced as the opposite of *tohu*, viz., *shalom*, fullness of being, salvation, the new creative life, the victory of the living God over *tohu* in all its forms, whether the latter is experienced as black despair in the human heart, or appears as the darkness of the prison cell that is symbolic of the Babylonian exile. Yahweh is of course present in his Word; so the people of God who are still living within the ruins now stand up 'all eyes', as the phrase seems to mean, and watch for the very presence of God himself.

9 DI's parable continues. Since the uttered Word of God bears within itself the power to fulfil itself, DI sees that it can inspire even the inanimate stones of the city to burst into song; for this is an otherworldly joy that has entered their midst by means of the human lips of a human messenger. And so he points to the mystery of God's total redemption who when he changed his plan (as *comforted* means) and *redeemed Jerusalem*, redeemed her very stones as well. Similarly with the mystery of the divine choice of vehicle for the Word. For the word 'messenger' means either a human being or an angelic agency. Here again DI obviously draws no line between them.

10   However, if *the Lord has bared his holy arm*, and the strength of that arm has in fact become visible *before the eyes of all the nations*, then this can have reality only if the invisible God reveals himself in his actions in and through the very visible and tangible agency known to us as the empirical people of God.

11   This empirical people is faced with an existential decision: whether or not to get out of Babylon when the city falls; whether to decide for freedom from servitude to a pagan empire and so to enter that service to Yahweh which alone is perfect freedom, or whether to remain in Babylon and thus to reveal more concern about mammon than about obedience. Yet here again the situation goes far beyond the moment of Israel's decision. For the Lord's vessels are primarily the implements used in the temple worship at Jerusalem, but which Nebuchadrezzar had stolen and which were still preserved in Babylon. As a matter of history, it was only many months after DI had told the exiles to *depart, depart,* 'get out of there' — his use of 'there', not 'here', shows he is not in the city itself but in some village nearby — that Cyrus finally gave orders to have the temple vessels restored (Ezra 1:7-8). DI could not be sure at the time of speaking whether Cyrus would do this or not. *The Lord's vessels* — the word is simply 'things' — could therefore refer also to any of the Israelites' possessions that were to be restored to Yahweh's holy city. All Israel had originally been called to be a 'kingdom of priests' to Yahweh (Ex. 19:6), even though there were in Israel men specially set apart to fulfil the office of priest. Thus it is all the exiles who are addressed here, and who are summoned to recognize their original calling to be 'a kingdom of priests and a holy nation'.

12   However, unlike the Exodus from Egypt, when things had to be done in a hurry, this second exodus is to be completed at leisure, for no one will prevent their leaving. Moreover God will be both before them and behind them. Just as he went before his people at the Exodus (Ex. 13:21), yet also came behind them in the form of the angel of the covenant (Ex. 14:19), so will he do again. Going both before and behind he will lose no stragglers on the way, but like the Good Shepherd, will finally bring home all his ewes and lambs to the fold of the holy city (40:10-11).

13-14   When *that day* (v. 6) finally arrives, as the ultimate outcome of
the redemption of the exiles from Babylon, what will the Servant look
like that Israel was chosen to embody? And how will his task appear to
the world?

It is not always possible to differentiate between God's messengers
in heaven and those on earth. DI draws no line between the task of the
Servant on earth and the nature of the divine plan for the whole of
creation. Or, to use another mixture of concepts, he can speak of the
Spirit's 'clothing itself' with a man (cf. Jud. 6:34), and, at the same
time, of a people putting on divine strength like clothing. In conformity with this type of thinking, we are therefore not surprised to find
that the Servant is here described in terms both of God and of man,
with no line of demarcation between the two.

Behold, says DI. That is to say, use your mental powers to delineate
the substance of the extraordinary theological picture I am about to
draw: *my servant shall prosper*, that is, will be *effective*. Man we know,
is never effective to the point of complete success in anything he
undertakes. Yet this verb here implies having the intelligence, insight,
and capability to bring to a successful conclusion what one plans to do.
As DI declares, it is only the Word of God and never the ephemeral
word of man which really endures, and which can therefore reach its
goal. Yet, some centuries later than DI, the book of Daniel actually
employs the active participle of this verb which is here translated as
prosper or succeed. There, at Dan. 12:3, we meet with it in the form of a
name, 'those who are wise', now describing Israel's function as Servant
of God. These 'wise' or 'prospering ones', then, shall (1) 'shine like the
brightness of the firmament'. But at once we find this word whose
meaning we are examining is linked with the idea of the resurrection
mentioned at Dan. 12:2; for (2) they shall be 'like the stars for ever and
ever'. Yet there is still another issue in this v. 3 in Daniel. 'Those who
are wise' shall inherit the resurrection because (3) they shall 'turn
many to righteousness'. This last phrase is built from another
participle used in parallel with the participial form 'those who are
wise'. As such each phrase explains and complements the other.
'Righteousness', as we have seen repeatedly now may mean (a) 'the
condition of having been put right, of having been saved or redeemed';
but also, and included in this doubly masculine-feminine noun, and
in consequence of having been 'put right', (b) to become com-
passionately concerned for the salvation of others.

Putting all these ideas together, then, we are to see that when *my servant shall prosper*, it means he will be effective in winning 'many' to righteousness and eternal life. We shall meet the word 'many' again at v. 14, and in ch. 53.

The Servant here is actually described in terms of divinity. The phrases *shall be exalted* and *lifted up* are representative expressions from earlier literature, such as Isaiah and the Psalms, used normally of God. (Note that we spend no time in this Commentary speculating on what personage this portrait represents, whether it be that of Abraham, Moses, Jeremiah, or DI himself, all of whom have had their champions. The 'scissors-and-paste' method of handling the text of previous generations compelled scholars to make such a search. But if we take the so-called 'Servant Poems' *in context*, then DI himself gives us his own dogmatic answer to our question.) Yet DI immediately couples these terms with others that can only be used of a man. For once again (cf. 50:5-6) he describes the Servant as a man whose face is *marred* by suffering. It is an interesting fact that the DSSI scroll vowels this word in such a manner that it means in English 'I have anointed' or even 'I have made Messiah'. But most scholars agree that the insertion of a *yod* (a small Hebrew letter) here to give this rendering has been done for dogmatic reasons, so it is to be rejected.

The word which is rendered as *many* occurs twice in this pericope, and it will appear again in the next chapter at a significant point. Both times it seems to mean, not 'the majority' of mankind, but 'virtually all' men. (If this translation is correct, then it has important consequences for our understanding of the words of Christ, as at Mark 10:45.) Our verse declares that once the masses of humanity see this Servant, they will be appalled at his marred mien, even though God does not seem to be appalled at it.

15 In fact, seeing him, nations will leap to their feet, quite other than the normal attitude toward the weak and helpless that unredeemed man naturally assumes. (Some scholars understand this last verb to mean 'sprinkled'. But this meaning does not fit the context well. Sprinkle is a word that belongs to the cult and so is inappropriate here.) The average man reveals himself as a bully at heart; he seems to take a sadistic delight in hurting the one who meekly accepts his cruelty (50:6). When Easterners *shut their mouths* under the influence of a powerful emotion, they show by their compressed lips and by drawing back the corners of the mouth that they are reacting with astonishment to a situation that has taken them unawares. Now, in those days a nation took its cue in its whole national life from its leader and his royal decrees. Thus, for example, if the king declared war, then all his subjects naturally fought for his cause. In like manner, if the king should be startled into new ways of thinking, the commoners of his realm would eventually follow suit. DI is obviously aware that the best strategy one can employ in the propagation of an idea is to begin with the man at the top.

The Servant's task is to give the masses a wholly new view of life, one that, as DI has already told us, is to be in accord with the Torah which God has already given (42:1). But the startling new element in its propagation is that it will be enunciated by one whose 'mien is inhumanly marred'. Such a thing is so utterly new that it is 'beyond all telling and quite unheard of'.

CHAPTER 53

---

1 The thing is so utterly new that it is 'beyond all telling and is quite unheard of' (52:15). The last words of comment in the previous chapter are repeated here to emphasize the unity of ch. 52 with ch. 53. For of course the chapter divisions in our English Bible are no part of the original text. And so the speaker continues: 'Who could have believed what we have heard? Whoever has had the Lord's arm revealed to him before?' (cf. 63:5; John 12:38; Rom. 10:16). One would have thought that Yahweh's arm would rend the heathen or tear asunder the hills, for 'arm' denotes power put forth in action. But when it was revealed, no one, neither heathen nor Israelite, could ever have imagined that this is what it would do.

2 A pest in all our gardens is the sucker which grows from the root of our rosebush, for it does not present us with a flower. Such a sucker develops when the ground is uncultivated and hard and dry; it grows straight up with thorns on its whole length; it has 'neither form nor charm, nor appearance to attract us to it'. The good gardener cuts it out and throws it away. The word sucker has two meanings in Hebrew. First, it can mean what its parallel implies, a sapling growing straight up out of the ground. But it can also mean one who sucks at his mother's breast, a little child. The LXX makes this second translation. It is interesting that by means of the parallel with *root*, DI reveals that he is making direct reference to the words of Isa. 11:1, spoken so long before his day: 'There shall come forth a shoot from the stump of Jesse, and a branch (sucker) shall grow out of his roots'. There the word for 'sucker' is *netser*, which means the same as *yoneq* here. Job 14:7 says 'For there is hope for a tree, if it be cut down, that it will sprout again, and that its *yoneq* will not cease'. A tree stump can appear to be dead. Not a leaf or a branch seems to have survived the felling. Yet months later, after the long reign of a winter's death, a *sucker* may appear through the ground several feet from the dead stump, but obviously from a root that is still alive. From that small beginning a tree will grow once again. In this way Isaiah of old had foreseen how one would arise, not necessarily as a physical son of David, whose tree would eventually be

169

cut down, but from David's roots in Jesse (Isa. 11:1). He would thus be the outcome not of flesh and blood but of the divine promise lying behind all that David was called upon to do and to be. Similarly the Israel to whom DI is now speaking is a vine that has been cut down to the ground (cf. Ps. 80:8-16) and is now lying dead on the dry soil of Mesopotamia. But the power of the Word of God is stronger than the destruction of Jerusalem and the felling of the vine Israel, for the Word of God endures for ever (40:8; cf. Ezek. 37). So the Servant grew up *before him*, which can mean only something like 'in the presence of Yahweh', 'under the eye of God', 'in conformity with the will and purpose of God'.

3 The portrait before us, however, is that of one whose rejection goes beyond even the humiliation and pain which the Servant people of God have had to suffer in Babylonia. It is the portrait of one who is wholly abject, who has encountered evil in its ultimate form.

Remember that for OT man, even more than for us, communal life was a *sine qua non*. No man at any period can develop to be truly human unless he lives in society; in fact a man goes mad if he is completely shunned by his kind. DI therefore puts his finger on the point of the greatest sacrifice of all which the perfect Servant has to make. He is to be utterly lonely. *We esteemed him not*; that is, 'we took no account of him'. We thought him an idiot in the Greek sense of the word: we regarded him as an isolated fanatic. In other words, the Servant's calling is to lead him to tread a completely lonely path, even as God himself must pursue the path of redemption alone (63:3).

4 The content of this line comes as a great shock. Normally man supposes that the only reason for suffering is penal. But DI has long since warned that a new thing is about to be revealed (cf. 48:6*b*, 16). He has declared that God has long been preparing his Servant people, first to understand this new thing, and then once they have accepted it, to live it out in the world (49:2; 51:16). It is thus neither wise nor possible, as we are now in the position to recognize, to isolate the so-called 'Servant passages' in the pages of DI from the rest of the text; for they contain the flowering of the slowly developing argument that runs through all of DI's sixteen chapters.

We, that is to say, humanity at large, had imagined that this Servant was suffering from a natural illness, so that his suffering was something that God had sent him as a punishment for his sins (cf. Jer.

170

10:19). If it was leprosy from which he was suffering, as some suggest, then he would have to be completely isolated from human society (Lev. 13:45-46). However, *we* might have gone as far as to suppose that God was making him suffer for the sins of his forefathers (cf. Lam. 5:7). Yet this chapter primarily paints a portrait or offers a theological picture of the historical situation in which empirical Israel had found herself. The Servant Israel was then meeting suffering which, while in part penal, was also just that ordinary suffering that all men must necessarily meet with in this fallen world.

5 But DI now makes the remarkable statement that it is *we*, humanity at large, free as we are to choose the evil as well as the good, who have chosen to pierce the Servant by *our transgressions*, that is rebelliousness, and crush him by *our iniquities*. It is understandable why DI should mention rebelliousness, *pesha*, as the first of all human sins. The man who, through pride, chooses to follow the dictates of his own ego and to disregard the Word of God has thereby rebelled against God's loving offer to him of fellowship and peace. Quite possibly DI had in mind here, as the type of all human rebellion, the disloyalty of the Bride Israel to the Lord and Husband who has never ceased to exhibit his *hesed* or 'steadfast loyal love' towards her, with the result that the pain she has caused him in her folly has pierced him to the heart (43:24; 50:1-2). For of course, as DI has already reported of God, you have made me into your servant at the cost of your sins, and you have made me suffer at the cost of your iniquities (43:24).

In both verses 4 and 5 there occurs what would appear to be an unnecessary use of the pronoun *hu'*, meaning 'he', in *he has borne* and *he was wounded*. This pronoun DI has already allocated for the self-revelation of the living God, when the Lord proclaims 'I am He' (43:10, 13). As we have said, therefore, this portrait of the Servant comprises two elements, that of a very human Israel, and that of 'God *in* Israel'. At this point one is not able to separate the two.

If it is indeed true, as many suggest, that DI borrowed some of his ideas and certain specific terms from Akkadian liturgical texts to which he would have access in Babylon, then it is all the more remarkable how much he has transformed them. For ideas belonging to very human documents, reflecting as they do a pagan cult, have now become vehicles of the deepest revelation of God that the Old Testament can offer. DI now emphatically declares that the suffering experienced by the Servant was not caused by a stroke, nor by the living death of leprosy, nor by his being reduced to poverty and shame from ruin or misfortune as was Job. Rather the Servant was voluntarily accepting the sufferings that had come upon him. At first glance it had looked indeed as if he were passively accepting his suffering in abject misery. In reality, however, his suffering was vicarious. His suffering was actually intended to effect the will of God. God's will, as DI has already told us, is no less than that all men should possess the full life in a covenant of peace (cf. Num. 25:12; Ezek. 37:26; and see Isa. 54:10), and so be healed of all their diseases (cf. Ex. 15:26; Ps. 103:3).

6   DI now connects the task of Israel with the historical picture of her that has been employed by the prophets before him, in fact, ever since the days of the shepherd king David. Ezekiel had newly painted the portrait of Israel as a forlorn flock of sheep, and had applied it to the exiles in their lost state in Babylon (Ezek. 34). Yet the *all we* of this verse must not be limited to the lost sheep of the house of Israel, but should embrace within its sweep the *many*, 'the masses' (see 52:14), that is to say, the whole world of men (cf. 52:15 and 53:11, 12); for this verse surely describes the manner in which humanity as such behaves.

For humanity is one and is bound together as one by a common guilt and a common fate (cf. Gen. 6:5; Isa.6:5). Man's common guilt is revealed as the innate desire in the individual human heart for each to turn *to his own way*, and thus to be wholly selfish and live a self-contained life. Moreover, it is this common guilt that unites all men, rather than rendering each man unique. It is this common guilt which *the Lord has laid on him*, and this means again that the guilt of the 'all-of-us' communally has fallen upon each individually. If two people, such as a husband and a wife, are so closely associated that they regard themselves as one (cf. Gen. 2:24), then each shares in the suffering of the other. DI has already explicitly stated at an earlier stage of his argument that God reveals himself as Israel's Husband. Therefore, when Israel suffered, God suffered too. Thus the extraordinary inference can be made that it was 'God in Israel' who became the Suffering Servant that Israel was elected to be, for Israel could not fulfil her calling alone (43:22 ff.). The Servant is a masculine and not a feminine figure. However, Israel herself continued to suffer. But in his grace the divine Husband accepted her deserved sufferings as if they were one with the vicarious sufferings he was undergoing in her. Thus, in his capacity as the Suffering Servant himself and by means of his union with his wife Israel, God had subsumed her justified and penal suffering into his own vicarious bearing of the 'rebelliousness' and the *iniquities* (v. 5) of *the many* (52:14).

7 DI would have before him as he wrote the words of Jeremiah 'But I was like a gentle lamb led to the slaughter' (11:19), a sentence which would only deepen his admiration for this ordinary sinful man who had had to bear so much suffering in his life. Yet Jeremiah complained bitterly at the suffering that came his way and never suggested that his suffering could bear away *the iniquity of us all* (v. 6). So the theme of this important verse presents at long last the content of the new thing which DI has kept reiterating that God has been about to reveal (cf. 42:9; 48:6). For the new thing is not just the return from Exile, as some suggest, although it is rooted in that historical situation. This is because the return is but part of the total action of God which, once he has initiated it in Babylon, comes to a head only as the outcome of this extraordinary revelation. The completely surprising thing here is the twice-repeated phrase 'he never opened his mouth' (cf. Acts 8:32). Yet why should this phrase give the surprise that it does? Surely suffering is part and parcel of this natural order and world in which we have to live. Yes, but to suffer vicariously, to bear unmerited suffering for another man, that is not normally considered an ethical action at all, unless of course the action is accepted voluntarily and spontaneously. Even then, the other man for whom one suffers also suffers, suffers as a consequence of his sin, and rightly so; for that is the penalty he must carry, the penalty of the burden of guilt.

However, the new situation revealed to us here is that it is the one who is rightly suffering for his own sins who becomes aware of a new and transforming reality in his own experience. It is that the other person is sharing the suffering with him which he ought to be carrying alone. This vicarious suffering on the part of the volunteer is therefore participative; it is neither substitutionary, nor yet is it penal. It reveals the act of enduring the pain that the other also suffers, so that it is endured, not *instead of* the other party, but *on his account*. In this way vicarious suffering actually becomes a remedial and redemptive force. How strange that it was Israel who was called to be this redemptive force by becoming a sheep or a lamb led to the slaughter, for of course she did not appreciate her calling. In fact DI believed that redemptive suffering had been God's plan for Israel from the very foundation of the world (51:16). Historically speaking, of course, there was no doubt that Israel had been led to the *slaughter* at the hands of evil men.

Consequently, it had now become evident that Israel, through her union with him whose Word endures forever, had been called to be 'the lamb slain from the foundation of the world' (51:16; cf. Rev. 13:8).

8   At this point scholars for centuries have felt it necesary to make countless emendations in the Hebrew text. Indeed vv. 8-12 are in places quite obscure. This state of things has arisen in all likelihood from the fact that the Church has always felt that this chapter is highly important, and that the subject matter is itself mysterious, and so is couched in suitably mysterious language. In consequence the cryptic and concise original language has always been regarded as a challenge by scholars as they have sought to interpret it, with the result that ever since the NT was penned, it has been easier to proffer some kind of an exegesis than to give a literal translation. The LXX varies from the Hebrew in a number of places. The Targum, containing the Jewish exposition of the chapter emanating from the time of the Fathers, yet set down in writing only about the seventh century A.D., deliberately takes the essential scandal out of these verses and renders them quite innocuous. It does so in evident reaction against the contemporary Christian interpretation. It is easy to make additional emendations, but then it becomes all too tempting to read the poor thought of man into what is the surprising new revelation of God. The Targum should remain for the modern scholar the awful warning of this possibility. Even at those points where the Hebrew is obviously not as it was left to us by DI, we should make every endeavour to translate the text as it stands.

The Hebrew text behind the first line may mean 'after arrest and sentencing he was taken away (unjustly)'; yet one essential emphasis comes home from the line, no matter how we translate it. That is the fact that the Servant is pictured as suffering unjustly. Some understand the oppression to be restraint *in* prison; others that he was taken *from* prison, unjustly — that is to say, without a proper trial — and so to death. Others translate by 'he was led to death' or even 'smitten to death'. However we read these words, we see that the Servant pays the ultimate penalty. If 'who gave a thought to his posterity' is correct (for some scholars prefer 'his fate') then we are given still another cause for suffering. For we are made to see a man dying before our eyes, knowing that no one is caring either for him or what he stands for.

9 *And they made his grave with the wicked* is not necessarily the best translation. For one thing the verb is in the singular, so unless *they* stands for 'one' in the sense of 'people', we must look for alternatives. 'He gave (himself freely to) his grave with the wicked' has been suggested, in which case the act of the Servant would be in parallel with *he poured out his soul to death* in v. 12. Others suggest 'He made the wicked his grave', meaning that he met them head on, so to speak, so that they killed him for his opposition to them. In parallel with this first line of v. 9 we have *and with a rich man in his death*. Curiously enough the word *death* here is in the plural. It may be so used to emphasise the horrible nature of his end — but that is only hypothetical. On the other hand, if we continue to recognize that the basis of the thought of this chapter is the existential experience of Israel, then the plural word 'deaths' might be understood to refer to the individuals who comprise the corporate body of the people of God. This is a likelier interpretation, since DI's mentor, the song of Moses, also makes use of this oscillation between the singular and the plural with reference to Israel (cf. Deut. 32:6, 21); and as we have already seen, this is a feature of DI's own thought (51:1-3). In this way Israel is accepted as both a corporate entity and a collection of separate persons at one and the same time.

Does *rich* refer to the wealth of the Babylonian empire and to the nations generally who are to serve Israel's God when they eventually behold his glory revealed *in* Israel? (cf. 49:23). In ancient times, however, it could be taken for granted that if a man unaccountably grew rich, then he must be wicked, that is to say he had gained his wealth by bribery and corruption. Such an idea may be suggested here in that the Hebrew word for 'rich' is merely 'wicked' written backwards.

Then again, some interpret *his grave* as 'his burial mound', or as 'his house of death'. In the Akkadian language of DI's day, the phrase 'to ascend one's mountain' had become a euphemism for the verb 'to die', the thing that all men wish to avoid; the same idiom appears as well in the Ras Shamra texts of the western coast of Syria. Such a conception may thus possibly be in the prophet's mind. The Masoretic (Hebrew) text may even contain two meanings in one word, a poetic device mentioned in the Introduction. Whatever the individual words mean, however, the main idea of the phrase is apparent. The Servant now accepts *violence* — and this word pictures rude excess and vicious spleen — so that he is brought down both to death and then to burial thereafter. In a passage which may be Jeremiah's but which could come from the exilic period, the action of Nebuchadrezzar in destroying Israel is likened to Israel's death; for in the vigorous words of the passage in question Israel is described as being swallowed by the monster of chaos, just as Jonah was swallowed by the monster of the deep (Jer. 51:34). Such a picture is in full conformity with that which Ezekiel envisaged, for he too regarded the destruction of Jerusalem and the deportation of Israel into exile as the death and burial of the people of God (Ezek. 37:11-12).

10 *Yet it was the will of the Lord* (cf. Mic. 6:13): this sentence holds in perfect balance the twin problems of divine predestination and human free will, the inter-relationship of which was as evident a reality to DI as it was to Peter centuries later (cf. Acts 2:23). 'It was the Lord who made him sick' (see RSV *ftn*).

The poet's swing from the third person to the second person in the next line need not disturb us, for this is a characteristic device of prophetic oracles generally.

We should note again from *ftn a* that the RSV rendering is not what the Hebrew says. The Hebrew runs 'If you make his *nephesh* an *asham*, he will see . . .'. These Hebrew words must be examined.

DI has inherited various theological ideas which we must bear in mind in seeking to understand this surprising statement. A man's 'person', *nephesh*, was his whole personality. To use for a moment the Greek trichotomy of the personality, his *nephesh* included all three parts of him, his body, soul, and spirit, though of course the Hebrews did not think in this way. So the *nephesh* included also the blood. One's blood was not merely nor even chiefly the vital stream in the veins of the body; it was actually regarded as the life itself (cf. Lev. 17:14). Death therefore meant for DI life that had been poured out in death. Now, since this concept arose from within the cult, DI saw it as the symbol of sacrificial death.

Then the word *asham*. RSV speaks of *an offering for sin*. This is all the one word, and again is a word taken from the cult. Its use is described at Lev. 5:14-19. There we read that the guilty man 'shall bring to the priest a ram without blemish (that is to say a very expensive animal), and the priest shall make atonement for him . . . It is a guilt offering' (vv. 18, 19). This guilt offering the Lord accepts as a substitute for the individual person presenting it. He represents and includes his whole family in himself. This offerer, as sinner, ought to die, for he has been adjudged as having committed a breach of faith (Lev. 5:14). The latter phrase demonstrates that type of disloyalty which marks the man, woman or family who has broken God's covenant of grace and has rebelled against it. By their act of disloyalty these people have freely put themselves beyond the pale, beyond the sphere of God's grace which is to be found in the covenant alone. Yet, paradoxically, by grace once again, God accepts the ram without blemish as a substitute offering in the place of the sinful family who have sacrificed it.

But here at 53:10 a new element appears, one not to be found in the Law of Moses. Here the offering of the *asham* is not for the salvation of the offerer: what we find instead is that God is making this innocent and obedient Servant into the *asham* himself, so that it is the latter, as the ram without blemish, who pours out his own blood, or life, even unto death.

Yet the purposes of God cannot be checkmated by death, especially when God fore-ordains that death. For when a seed falls into the ground and dies, that is not the end. *He shall see his offspring*, or as the Hebrew has it, his seed, in days to come. Does it mean that he will see generations to come with his own eyes, because he will be alive to see them? Then again, when the words run *he shall prolong his days*, does it mean that he shall do so *in* his seed, or does it mean that the seed will prolong its own days? Yet without doubt DI means that the *asham* carries within it its own inevitable outcome (cf. discussion at 46:10), and that therefore the self-offering of the Servant cannot be considered to have been in vain. Indeed, *the will of the Lord shall prosper in his hand*, just as, in the first line of the verse, it was *the will of the Lord to bruise him*. Prosper, *tsalah*, means 'to be effective, strong, of use, come to a successful conclusion'. This means that it is the power of the Lord's will which will make the Servant's voluntary self-giving successful. And it will be done *in his hand*. We saw that it was the hand or the arm of the Lord which revealed to the sight of man God's will actually being done, being seen to be effective in human life (51:9). As the gentiles had declared with astonishment at 53:1, *the arm of the Lord* was now being revealed in a way no one could even have imagined. So what we learn now is that the arm of the Lord was being revealed *in* the arm of the Servant, and that it was being effective before the eyes of the nations in the form of an *asham*. This was no less than a substitution for them in their rebellion, *in* the self-offering of the Servant. Thus the Lord's action and the Servant's action were, in some mysterious way, quite evidently one.

11a DI now expresses this new and astonishing truth in another fine poetic line. In it he brings to a head his promise to tell us about the 'new thing' that God was going to do in and through his servant people. Literally he says 'From the travail of his soul, his *nephesh*, he shall see — he shall be satisfied'. The LXX and the DSSI both help us here. They have both preserved the word 'light' after 'see'. Thus they have given us a still greater insight into the meaning of the new thing. Right in the midst of his personal torment, DI claims, the Servant will see the meaning of what he is doing; he will be certain that his self-offering will be effective for the salvation of mankind. This is because, as we have already been told, his self-offering is not his own, but is that of God Almighty working *in* him. And, as DI shows us later in his last chapter, our ch. 55, 'My word does not return to me empty, but prospers, *tsalah* (cf. 53:10) *in the thing for which I sent it'*.

11b *By his knowledge*: again, any idea that this refers to scientific knowledge must be dismissed. Hebrew has words for factual knowledge other than the word found here. We hear God saying to Israel at Amos 3:2 'You only have I known of all the families of the earth ...' We read at Gen. 4:1 'Now Adam knew Eve his wife, and she conceived ...' This verb *known* is used for the intimate knowing of love, of love between husband and wife, of love between the members of the Covenant for Him who bestowed it. Jeremiah, looking to the 'new covenant' that God will make with Israel, comparing it to the husband–wife experience, declares that 'they shall all know me'; the outcome of which will be that 'I will forgive their iniquity' (Jer. 31:31-34).

It is now God who is speaking. He says, Knowing Me (in this ultimate manner), he who is in a completely right relationship with Me (this is all one word), that is, My Servant, will now *make many to be accounted righteous* (see 52:13 and Dan. 12:3). This verb here does not mean, as some suggest, to declare another to be in the right in a forensic sense; rather it operates in the ethical realm, and so means to help another to attain a new quality of life. How will he do it? *He shall bear their iniquities*. The verb is used of carrying a load on your back. It means that *he* will carry, not his own load, but theirs for them. Who will do this? Once more we find the emphatic word *He* that DI likes to employ of God in particular (cf. 43:13). Thus, since God is speaking of his Servant, He must mean '*In* the Servant, *I* shall bear their iniquities'. Yet it is the body of the Servant, now accounted to be the arm of the Lord, that must bear the pain of the burden. DI has already made two statements, which we can now put together. One is mentioned at 45:14-15: 'God is in you only' . . . *truly, thou art a God who hidest thyself, O God of Israel, the Saviour*; and the other is to be found at 43:11: *I, I am the Lord, and besides me there is no saviour.*

12 So the Servant finally receives his reward. This reward is not to be understood in terms of selfish grasping at payment or of a boy receiving a prize at school. Rather, as in the case of the man who used his talents to good purpose (Matt. 25:29), the reward is shown to comprise sharing one's innate satisfaction with 'the masses of humanity' (rather than with *the great*). It is God who will share out this satisfaction between the Servant and humanity. Nor does the Servant grasp at his share, but, taking his cue from God, he continues to *divide the spoil with the strong*. God is the great Warrior. These here are the spoils of war; this is the great victory celebration that is to be held when God finally wins the war against the powers of evil. DI has already spoken of this eschatological joy at 41:16 and 49:13; see also 65:18-19. Isaiah of Jerusalem, in one short picture at 9:3, showed us the joy of ordinary men, of poverty stricken peasants rejoicing over harvest home or treasure trove that has unexpectedly come their way; or as in the NT, the joy of sitting down at a supper table together after having persevered to the end through the toils and tribulations of the life of obedience that marks the true Servant (cf. Rev. 19:9).

All this mighty consummation, this final victory, comes to pass (1) *because he poured out his soul to death*. The word *because* here, *tahat asher* means something like 'in reward for', and so makes a strong statement; and (2) because he *was numbered*, 'identified', *with the transgressors*, or better, 'with rebels' (there is no 'the' in the Hebrew), that is, with those who defy God's covenant of love. So the Servant actually put himself outside of the covenant in order to be *numbered* with those who had already done so. The verb *poured out*, or emptied out his *nephesh*, that is to say, his whole personality, was almost certainly before Paul's mind when he penned his vital 'kenosis' passage in Phil 2:7-8, where we read that he 'emptied himself, taking the form of a servant, being born in the likeness of men. . . . He humbled himself and became obedient unto death'.

And *He* (who? God? the Servant?) 'carried' (away) the sin of the masses. We read at 53:4 that 'He' *carried* (away) *our* 'sicknesses' — the same verb as here. The inference is that the sins of humanity are to be understood in terms of sickness (cf. Ps. 103:3). Moreover, this is the verb used at Lev. 16:22, where we read that, as part of the great Day of Atonement ceremony, 'the (scape) goat shall bear (carry away) all their iniquities ... (into) the wilderness' (the place of desolation and chaos where the Covenant God is not, 45:19).

Finally, he *made intercession for the transgressors*, or more exactly, 'he interposed himself for the rebels'. Long before, Moses had offered himself to God for that purpose (Ex. 32:32). But Moses was not wholly obedient to God, and so was not sinless. It is only one who is wholly obedient, therefore, who could be worthy to become the *asham* for the sins of the world.

CHAPTER 54

1 By setting the figure of the perfect Servant alongside the reality before his eyes, viz., the sinful, empirical Servant Israel, now bemoaning her fate as she is in Babylon, DI reveals with clarity the grace of Israel's God. For Israel now knows exactly what she has been called to do and be and must recognize at once that she is in fact totally unlike what she is meant to be. Even as the consciousness of this unlikeness enters her soul, God stoops, not to point the finger of scorn, but to show pity and to comfort his chosen one in her vexation of soul. So DI is here reiterating — but now with deepened content — the call to believe and proclaim the good news with which he began his narrative (40:1 ff.). At 40:6 he himself had asked *What shall I cry?* He has his answer at last. The new, deeper content of his message arises from the fact that Yahweh still loves Zion, not only when her failure has been shown up in relief, but also now that the perfect Servant has been delineated. What the Lord has to say to Zion now is therefore spoken in a setting very different from that of ch. 40. And yet Yahweh himself has not changed — he is the same Yahweh; for *the Word of our God will stand for ever*, (40:8).

No wonder Zion is to jump for joy, and even cheer. This is an extraordinary word for DI to use. The NT uses the word 'hilarity' to seek to express the eschatological joy which can be known now that the Church has received the gift of the Holy Spirit. Yet in classical Greek 'hilarity' was used of one who was unbalanced in mind. For the point is that *cry aloud* really means to neigh! Here too the joy of Yahweh that sinful Israel can share is so strange an experience that only strange words can seek to describe it. We are to remember that Yahweh has now revealed his love for Israel. He has shown her how he himself, in the form of Israel, will be the Servant that she is called to be herself. He has shown her how he can bear away the sin of the world, provided he can be united with the body which he had planned to use from the foundation of the world (51:16). When this happens, God will have revealed his glory as he had promised he would (40:5), in Israel (42:8; 44:23).

The occasion of Israel's joy is the revelation of the coming successful effect of God's action in the Servant. We read of it in 53:10: *He shall see his offspring, he shall prolong his days* (into the future). 'The masses' whom the Servant is to receive as his portion, we remember, are to be his own children. These are to be born from the reunion of Yahweh and Israel; for Yahweh has now brought home his Bride in triumphant love.

2 So Zion is to make more and more room for her children yet unborn. 'Don't stop making room', says God, 'but do with faith what Elisha commanded the widow to do when pouring out her oil' (1 Kings 17:14).

3 The returning exiles are to receive from *the nations* the countryside of Judah which they have overrun and whose *cities* are now *desolate*. But since DI is now speaking in eschatological terms, this very factual recovery of Israel's ancient territory is only the historical basis for a far wider hope. The hope for the future that the Bible offers never hangs in the air, so to speak. It is always based on, though not limited to, the factual experience of Israel in this life that is set within space and time. *Your descendants will possess the nations*. This includes within it the miracle of the masses of the world sharing in the benefits of the Servant's self-offering (44:3-5; cf. Gal. 4:27). No wonder Jerusalem is not just to grow larger quietly and naturally; she is to 'burst forth' *to the right and to the left* as her population explosion forces her children to find their homes far afield. The promise made to the patriarchs thus continues to be valid.

4 Once again, as at every eschatological moment throughout the whole Bible, there sounds the command 'Don't be afraid!' What might Israel be afraid of? Primarily of the consequences of her sin. When Hosea took home his licentious wife, she had just cause to be afraid of what he might do to her (Hos. 3). Israel had been fornicating with other lords by giving her loyalty to anything except Yahweh. She had originally promised to be faithful to him at that time when Yahweh, her true Lord, took her to himself at the foot of Sinai (Ex. 19:1-6). But *the shame of your youth*, her experiments in extramarital relations, was now a thing of the past. Israel would now no longer remember them with a sense of guilt. This was because she had just been given a vision into the very heart of God. There she had seen how, as the true Servant himself, God had now borne her guilt away. Therefore her recollection of her sins can now affect her not with a sense of guilt but only with a deep knowledge of the grace and love of her faithful God. Then again, her period of being put away in exile (50:1), when she could bear no children because she was not in contact with her divine Husband, will also turn from evil into good.

5-6 This is because her whole existence depends upon who her Husband is. Yahweh is no god such as the heathen worship, one who exhibits all the vices and failings of mortal man. Who is he then? In awed wonder and adoration DI now applies to Yahweh four transcendental names that no heathen god could ever bear. *Husband* and *Maker* are both written in the plural to show that they refer to *'elohim*, the Hebrew plural word for God. This all-holy One had actually claimed Israel as his Bride when she was an attractive young woman in the days of the wilderness wanderings (Hos. 2:14; Jer. 2:2). What honourable husband could ever forget the girl he had loved when they were both young together, *a wife of youth*? Then how much more will Yahweh love Israel if she is deserted and broken hearted, and thus all the more in need of the love and loyalty of her Husband. Yet imagine being married to Almighty God, the Creator of the stars — and having children of the union! The language of the biblical revelation is scandalous indeed (cf. 62:4).

7 How God must then have hated to let you be *cast off*. God even says so. Note that, as in 50:1, he did not divorce her; yet he had to find some way of making her discover the blessedness of the married state. For centuries she had played fast and loose with her divine Husband. But now at last she knew his love for her as never before. In his wisdom God had made her taste the death of separation from him, though only *for a brief moment*. This had been essential if Israel was ever to learn that God Almighty was in earnest about her election.

8 *In overflowing wrath* — the words are highly onomatopoeic in the original Hebrew. Could we say that God allowed the dam to burst that held back the wrath he eternally feels toward the evil in his world? Was his beloved Bride then suddenly overwhelmed in the great waters over which he rules (cf. Ps. 46:1-3)? Yet his wrath is but a necessary expression of the everlasting covenant-love, *hesed* which he had laid upon Israel at the marriage which he had contracted with her at Sinai (see commentary at 49:20). Even within the covenant, Israel had had to experience alienation from God before reconciliation could be possible. Satan must first lead Job to the dunghill, where he curses his day, before Job can understand the joy of life in God.

But God's love never changes even when his wrath flows as a flood. So, as when the time of the flood was past, says the divine Husband, so 'I have had compassion on you'. We notice that it is not only DI's transcendent themes which are expressed in scandalous language: so also is his imagery of love. *'Compassion'* here is virtually 'I have hugged you close like a mother'. DI knows that no line can be drawn between the two types of love that the Greeks call *agape* and *eros*. The physical passion that is the basis of true love between man and woman DI actually regards as the basis of the transcendent love of him who is the Holy One of Israel, and whose nature is utterly other than that of mortal man. (It is interesting to note that the old Károli version of the Bible in Hungarian uses the word for physical love to represent the love of God even in the NT.)

9   The picture of the dam bursting reminds DI of the flood in the days of Noah, and so he puts this simile into Yahweh's mouth. He wants it to be clear to Israel that if she had never known a period of separation from her Husband, she would never have believed in the reality of a time of wrath. The word *this* refers here to the whole experience of the exile.

10   *Mountains* and *hills* were naturally the most permanent things that Israel knew. But someday, DI declares for Yahweh, these are going to *be removed* and *depart*. On the other hand, Yahweh's *hesed*, his *steadfast* or covenant-*love* will remain, for it is the expression of his *compassion* for his bride — Israel is still addressed as 'she'. So the corollary of this statement must be that she who is the object of God's covenant love will also remain forever before him; or, to put this truth in other language, that experience which Israel thinks of as physical death will never be able to end the covenant relationship or disrupt the marriage which Yahweh has sworn to uphold to all eternity. This is now the second time (cf. 40:8) that DI has made use of this particular argument to claim the reality of the life beyond. It is the same argument that Jesus used in discussion with the Sadducees (Mark 12:18-27).

The Lord is a God who likes making covenants. He made one with Noah and then with the patriarchs. He made the 'ancient' (rather than 'old') covenant with Israel at Mt. Sinai. This meaning of 'old' leaves

God room to update his ancient covenant as he wills when new circumstances arise. Of course he will never rescind it (Rom. 9 – 11). At Jer. 31:31-34 we read of Jeremiah's expectation of just such an updating and fulfilment of the ancient covenant. DI would know this passage. Again, when Jeremiah's covenant is referred to in the NT it is described by the Greek word *kainos* for 'new'. *Kainos* means newness in the sense of the refurbishing and completion of the old. There is a second word for 'new' in Greek, viz. *neos*. But *neos* means new in the sense of 'different'.

Parallel now with *my steadfast* (or 'covenant') *love, hesed*, we meet the phrase *my covenant of peace, shalom. Shalom*, as we recall, can mean very much more than peace in the newspaper sense of the word. The root of the verb from which it derives means to be whole, complete, finished. The noun may thus mean wholeness and completeness, though it may also include the ideas of welfare, prosperity and security, not to speak of peace from war. Here 'my covenant of *shalom*' presumably means something like 'my all-embracing covenant offering you wholeness of life, prosperity and peace'. 'This wholeness', says the Lord, 'has been obtained through my steadfast love revealing itself in you, Israel, as the Suffering Servant; yet in you also as my Victorious Servant. For it is I, the warrior God, who have revealed *myself* in Israel's calling to be the Servant'.

The reader will recognize that other scholars have placed other interpretations upon the person of the Servant than the one portrayed here. The above one is what I have drawn from all that God has revealed of himself in the preceding fourteen chapters. I have tried to be consistent in my exegesis of the person of the Servant, even as DI has spoken of him bit by bit, recognizing that the picture we receive in ch. 53 is but the culmination of DI's cumulative argument from ch. 40 onwards. Thus it may well be that this reference to *my covenant of peace* becomes the coping-stone of this particular line of exegesis. For this promise of God that we meet with here is made only after, and in fact out of, the pain, sorrow and final death of the Servant; so that it is really one with God's promise that the Servant would *see the fruit of the travail of his soul and be satisfied* (53:11).

11 Our eyes have newly been directed to the ultimate outcome — beyond the age of the hills — of God's covenantal love (v. 10). So the Jerusalem that DI paints for us here is no longer the poor, ruined capital city of Judah on her forlorn hilltop. Yet this picture is based upon the empirical city to which the exiles were soon to return (see v. 3). We need not pause to identify the precious stones, for it is their significance that invites our attention, not their chemical composition. The motif that is in this picture of the new Jerusalem is what scholars of Near Eastern thought have called Urzeit = Endzeit, 'The beginning of time = the end of time'. The belief of many ancient peoples was that in the beginning the ultimate purpose of 'God' had been expressed in a perfect creation. Israel too believed this and described that perfection in terms of the precious stones of the earth (cf. Gen. 2:11-12). But DI has now asked us to lift our eyes, not to the beginning this time, but rather to the end of the city of Jerusalem. This end must of course necessarily emerge from events that have already taken place in the empirical city of Jerusalem; for Jerusalem is the 'holy city' (52:1), 'the city of our God', the 'centre or navel of the earth' as Ezekiel had said (38:12), that spot in fact where 'God has put his name to dwell' (Deut. 12, *passim*); so it is that place where ultimate events must surely come to pass (cf. Luke 9:51-53; 13:33-35; 18:31; 24:47, 49). Yet they will come to pass only after the completion of the self-offering of the perfect Servant. Otherwise, of course, DI would have placed his present picture of the lady Zion alongside that which he had painted of the lady Babylon (47:1 ff.), the wicked city that epitomized the reverse of the self-emptying of the Servant.

Once again the sex motif unashamedly obtrudes. Antimony is the *kohl*, powder, which an Arab girl employs today to make her eyes attractive to the opposite sex. Zion of course needs to be adorned, for she has lost her attractive power in her dejection of spirit. So God himself will give her back the attractiveness she needs in order to make him love her. She is an 'uncomforted one'. This is the negative of the word that DI used in the beginning of his message — *Comfort my people* (40:1) — and we are also reminded of the name of one of Hosea's children, *Lo-ruhamah*, '*not pitied*' (Hos. 1:6), which rhymes with our word *lo-nuhamah, not comforted.*

12 The precious stones therefore are just the ordinary limestone blocks in Jerusalem's walls, yet now glorified to be the precious stones of the new Jerusalem glinting in the sunshine of the love of God (cf. Rev. 21:2, 18-21). The coming of the new Jerusalem is of course a miracle; but that miracle is only consequent upon the still greater miracle of the resurrection of the Servant, which in the sequence of DI's argument is now a future certainty.

13   Then he declares that Jerusalem's 'builders' will be taught by the Lord (see comments at 50:4). RSV's *sons* employs the same consonants in Hebrew as 'builders'. It is not possible to declare which reading DI had in mind, for vowels were not known or used in his day. But in the next line it seems quite appropriate to translate with the RSV *and great shall be the prosperity, shalom, of your sons*, as this follows from v. 10. This too, of course will be a miracle of grace.

14   But along with privilege goes responsibility. *Righteousness* here is that feminine noun *tsedaqah* which we have seen describes the creative love and compassion of God which Israel must pass on to others. Then, and only then, *you shall be far from oppression ... and from terror*. It is as if DI knew the words 'For whoever would save his life will lose it, and whoever loses his life (pours it out, as at 53:12) for my sake will find it' (Matt. 16:25).

15   On the other hand, as we have clearly seen in ch. 53, oppression can come unprovoked, for man is quarrelsome by nature. So DI asks Israel not to put the blame on God for the iniquities of man. In fact, since God is *in* Israel, he who falls upon Israel falls upon the wrath of God.

16   We are reminded of DI's categorical statement in 45:7 about the nature of God: *I form light and create darkness, I make weal (shalom) and create woe (ra')*. His illustration now of the blacksmith is interesting, for by it he is again showing that God is ultimately responsible for evil, that is, God is responsible if people make *weapons* of destruction: *fire*, sword, or, in our day, the nuclear bomb.

17   But that does not mean that God is responsible for the sin in the heart of man, leading him to oppress his brother with the sword that he has made. In fact, it is the way of the *servants of the Lord* that wins in the end, not the sword. If Israel, then, the people of God were to be the 'form' of the Servant, as DI declares they are called to be, then it will be their *heritage*, their 'share', even their divine calling, to accept the oppression of violent men. These they need never fear, however, for the creative love that they are to show has its source in Me — the noun *tsedaqah* once again, the feminine noun. The passage ends with a very emphatic phrase. It is not the usual '*says the Lord*' of the RSV, but 'is the veritable Word of the Lord'. There are those who decry such a

187

translation of the mysterious Hebrew word *ne'um*, declaring that this kind of English exaggerates DI's thought; just as there are those who are nonplussed at finding the great emphasis our theologian (rather than 'prophet'!) lays upon the reality and power of the Word — a reality I point to by consistently using a capital W whenever it occurs. In the same way, still others dislike it when exegetes find in DI, as they suppose, the 'neo-orthodox' 'Theology of the Word' of a modern theologian like Karl Barth! I leave the reader to make his own judgment upon these issues.

CHAPTER 55

1 We now reach the climax of DI's great thesis. Chapter 53 seemed at the time to form the peak of his message to the world with its description of the Servant. There he was God's arm revealed, God's instrument for the redemption of the world. Yet ch. 54, standing on the shoulders of ch. 53 as it does, rose to an even loftier peak of revelation. For it demonstrated what the love of God actually is. It showed how, through the *perfect* Servant, God reveals his love for the *sinful* Servant. It showed how by grace God has identified the empirical, sinful Israel with the Servant who is here revealed as his own almighty 'arm'. But in this last chapter the outcome of God's purpose in the Servant is at last revealed. That purpose is the redemption not only of Israel herself but of all mankind, including even the earth on which mankind takes his stand. That surely is good news and the climax to all that DI has to say.

Whose voice do we hear at this point? Is it DI's or is it God's? Obviously the answer is meant to remain open. The prophet has now become so completely the mouthpiece of God himself that the word he speaks is not his own but the Word of God.

This message takes the form of a gracious invitation. As such the speaker does not compel his hearers to come. He respects their personality and leaves them room to refuse. This of course is wholly unlike the manner in which man is accustomed to summon his fellow man (cf. 53:7).

Notice the eschatological provenance of the whole chapter. We can take it for granted that normally the exiles in Babylon would not lack for food or water. But once in the desert on the way home to Zion they would become completely dependent upon God for their daily needs. Moreover God had already promised to open pools of water for them alongside the highway home (41:18). Such a figure of speech therefore removes DI's words from the historical moment in which he is speaking and turns them into an eternal invitation. However, in conformity with the holy materialism of the biblical manner of revelation in general, this eternal Word that DI is uttering is not to be understood as a mere philosophical or metaphysical idea. For it arises from an existential situation.

We recall that the summons to Israel to enter the promised land of Canaan in the days of Moses had been bound up with the very material action of eating and drinking. For example, the covenant between God and Israel had been sealed with such a mundane thing as a feast (Ex. 24:11). As Deut. 8:3 asserts, God's intention in feeding Israel had a sacramental import: 'That he might make you know that man does not live by bread alone, but that man lives by everything that proceeds out of the mouth of the Lord'. Thus when Canaan's delights are eventually visible to the itinerant Israelites, and the new land is described as 'a land flowing with milk and honey', the eschatological overtones of the phrase become abundantly clear. For milk and honey were the traditional food of the gods throughout the whole Fertile Crescent in Moses' day. Thus, just as the land of Canaan had been God's free gift to Israel, with its milk and honey, so now Israel is invited to sup, for free, on bread and wine and milk with the Lord of the land of Canaan, viz. Yahweh, in a sense that went beyond the eating of material food.

And so we come to DI's day when Israel was facing a new exodus that was to begin at any moment. Surely with a knowledge of her whole past history in mind, Israel would readily discover that it was the bread of 'life', in the eschatological sense of the word, that she is here invited to come and get and eat and live (cf. Pss. 42:2; 63:1; Prov. 9:5). These verbs all occur in the plural, so that the invitation is to the individuals who comprise the people of God. Elsewhere, but in the same manner, it is the *water* of life (cf. Isa. 12:3) that Israel is summoned to come and drink, that water of which Ezekiel too in days of exile had spoken and which he had described as the river of life (Ezek. 47:1-12; cf. John 4:10; 7:37-38). As for *wine*, it was the symbol of joy, for it was in wine that a wedding toast was drunk and it was wine which made a dinner a merry occasion, and of course, *bread* is the staff of life. The imagery which DI uses here then is that of a banquet spread by Yahweh himself to which he invites his Bride, the sinful Israel. For we have learned that Yahweh loves her still, and that she has now been brought back, proleptically speaking, to where she belongs in her divine Husband's home. It is from this and similar verses that so much of the later imagery of the Bible is taken, where Israel's hope for the future is pictured (cf. 25:6 — a passage later than DI — Matt. 22:2 ff.; Rev. 19:9). The Qumran community, even before the advent of Christ, evidently understood their own sacred meal partly in the light of this passage. For their banquet and their song were concerned with the celebration of the mighty acts of God's deliverance of Israel in the future as well as in the past.

2   Unless he eats this spiritual bread, man's life is vain. Getting and spending we lay waste our powers, that is to say our *labour*, or energy *for that which does not satisfy*. Normally man seeks to live on what the Hebrew calls here 'non-food', that is, the gratification of his own selfish desires. The result is that in the end he is left hungry and unsatisfied. Why should man be such a fool? *Why* indeed, asks DI with emphasis. (1) This food is free. (2) It is for all — the verbs are plural. (3) Yet it is offered to each individual person one at a time. (4) This food is the whole answer to human need, viz., it satisfies. To *delight yourselves in fatness* meant enjoying what, to the easterner, was the best of the meat, the fatty parts of the fatted calf or sheep, or else any food that has been cooked in olive oil. For these were both considered the greatest delicacies of which a humble farm worker or artisan could hope to partake (cf. 25:6; Pss. 36:8; 63:5; and see Jeremiah's introduction to his 'new covenant' passage, 31:12-14).

3   If a man then will but *come to me* and eat this bread and drink this cup, he will *live* in the sense that only divine food can enable a man to live. Moreover, God's will is not that men should just eat and drink once only and then return to their old and stupid ways. His will is that this new experience of fullness of life should remain as man's eternal heritage. Consequently, God now offers to pledge this eternal life to Israel within the bonds of the covenant, that is to say to an Israel that has now tasted the bitterness of death and the descent into hell.

This new and exciting fullness of life is understood, first, to be rooted in the historical moment of the 'resurrection' of Israel from the grave of the exile (Ezek. 37: 12-14); and second, to be one with the eschatological outcome of this historical experience of Israel's resurrection. That is to say, it is to be understood in terms of the final moment in the chain reaction set off by the events of 538 B.C. when Cyrus issued his famous decree. For while the chain reaction is going off, the Word is in the process of becoming 'flesh'. Third, since sinful Israel shares by grace in the action of the Servant, this new fullness of life is the reward that the Servant is offered; for the Servant is to share with 'the masses' the spoils he has seized when he rescues them from the bonds of evil and from death (53:12).

This *everlasting covenant* is now given a surprising new content and

191

direction. This is because it is defined in terms of the unshakable
covenant love that 'I bestowed on David'. We must first look to see
what such an idea meant for DI himself. DI was well aware that
Yahweh had chosen David in an earlier century even as he had chosen
Israel as a whole (2 Sam. 7:8). Moreover, David himself had recognized his election to be set within the larger covenant. So it had been
ordered in all things and made 'secure' (2 Sam. 23:5), or 'established'
(2 Sam. 7:16), where we find the same word as is translated here as *sure*
(cf. Ps. 89:28-29). The election of David was rooted in eternity, even
as Israel as a whole was to be God's Servant people to all eternity.

4 Yahweh had *made*, or rather 'appointed' David, as DI says here,
and along with David there was included of course his house or
dynasty. Together they were appointed to be *a witness to the peoples*.
How often do we think of the reason for the existence of the line of
David to be just that? They were to witness to the reliability of God and
to his loving concern for all peoples. That was the meaning of the
covenant which God had made with David, this God who does not
change. This calling of David is explained in the two terms that follow.
For David had been called to be *a leader and commander for the peoples*. But
'leader' (the word *nagid*) can also mean 'expositor', deriving from the
verb *higgid*, that is, one who announces or tells forth (in this case, the
good news of God's great invitation to the world). As for the word
commander, the Hebrew can also mean something else: it can mean one
who expresses the orders (of God, in this case). Later OT writers
certainly idealized David in this way, or else they would not have
attributed to him the authorship of so many psalms. Probably they
based their belief on 1 Sam. 16:13, amongst other passages: 'Then
Samuel took the horn of oil, and anointed him in the midst of his
brothers; and the Spirit of the Lord came mightily upon David from
that day forward'.

Yahweh's covenant with David would never have been made if the
prior covenant with all Israel at Mount Sinai had not been entered
into first. David himself was an Israelite and was thus king over the
covenant people. He could not have been the man he was, had he not
been born within the covenant, and had his whole life and thoughts
not been shaped by its content and force. Thus the Davidic covenant is
the lesser of the two covenants, and is dependent upon the greater for
its validity. On the other hand, David was the head of Israel. The king
in Jerusalem was both the representative of his people in the sight of

God and the mouthpiece of God to all the people. The Davidic line, in other words, was encouraged by the prophets to see itself as the apex of a triangle. The base of that triangle was the people of Israel. The king, placed at the top of the triangle, represented in himself all those who were contained within the three sides. The people for their part were all summed up in him, took their direction from him, and lived their whole life in him. Thus what happened to David happened to them; and what Israel as a whole suffered, David too felt in his soul. For David was the epitome, the essence, the representation, of all Israel; he was 'the breath of our nostrils, . . . of whom we said, "Under his shadow we shall live among the nations"', in the Babylonian exile (Lam. 4:20).

The king was thus both singular and plural at the same time, depending on whether one regarded him as the apex of the triangle, or as the whole of the triangle: he included within himself all the people of God who were sheltering under his wing. In fact, he was the head of a living body. As such he guided and directed its life; but at the same time he suffered pain too when the members of this his own body felt the pains of life upon their individual hearts. The Gospel writers are clearly aware of this representative function of King David (cf. Matt. 2:2; 21:5; Mark 15:2, 9, 12, 18, 26, 32; John 1:49; 18:37).

The content, as well as the meaning and purpose of the old covenant which God had made with David (and in consequence with all Israel) and to which God had been absolutely loyal, God was now promising to continue with the new Israel whom he had 'resurrected' from their grave in Babylon. God had appointed David to be *a witness to the peoples*. But God had told his Servant people to be his witnesses. Consequently, it would seem that the new Israel was to be God's expositor to the world, for God's Spirit now rested on the Servant people (42:1; 44:3; 48:16; and cf. Num. 11:29). Israel, then, was now being called in covenant to be God's teacher to the nations and to be the one who gave God's *mishpat*, or the words of the revelation in the *Torah*, to the world (42:4; cf. Matt 16:19). In a word, the basic reason for the very existence of the new covenant that God was now offering was one of mission, and that alone. Commentaries on Luke's Gospel, such as that by E. J. Tinsley (*The Cambridge Bible Commentary*), show how this reality was clearly in the mind of Jesus.

Finally we should note an interesting grammatical question. The word for *steadfast love* here is written in the plural in the Hebrew. This is an unusual form. Most expositors regard it as an intensive plural. It may very well be such. Yet it may also be what grammarians call a distributive plural. If so, then by means of it DI declares the oneness of God's covenant love, first, between himself and David and, second, between himself and each and every member of Israel as the people of God. Moreover, this covenant love God will give to Israel as a gift — *lachem*, 'to you', and not the usual *'immachem*, 'with you' — since it is something she cannot possibly earn.

5   Now comes a swing from the plural back to the masculine singular. This change is not visible in the RSV. But the original Hebrew suddenly abandons the plural of the verbs that have been used since v. 1 and startles us by declaring *'you shall'*. Evidently 'David' is now Israel epitomized. But this is not difficult to understand, for we have seen that he is the whole body even while he is its head: to use the language of Ps. 80, he is both the vine and the branches at once. At 43:10 DI could say *You* (plural) *are my witnesses . . . and my Servant* (singular) *whom I have chosen*. Yet now, addressing Israel in the singular, he declares *you shall call nations* 'unknown to you', virtually employing words that occur in Ps. 18:43 in connection with the individual King David. What DI wishes us to understand is that the call of the perfect Servant, who has now subsumed sinful Israel within himself, could well be fulfilled in a single 'David' yet to come. The identification of 'David' with the perfect Servant, and so with Israel, is expressed still more clearly in the next two lines. *Nations that knew you not shall run to you* is an echo of what was said of the sinful Servant Israel at 42:4; yet it was not said at that point for Israel's own sake, for of herself Israel is nothing. It was pointed out then that Yahweh's glory is to appear *in* Israel (40:5; 42:8; 43:7; 45:25; 46:13; 48:11). Consequently and at last we have been shown explicitly what the new thing is that DI was looking for. It is that the glory of God is to be revealed when the arm of the Lord offers himself as an *asham* (see commentary at 53:10) that the masses may be saved. As we saw at 53:1, the only answer we can give to a questioner about this act of God could be 'Who could have believed what we have heard?' DI is thus in the position now to sum up his whole argument with the words *Because of the Lord your God, and of the Holy One of Israel, for he has glorified you*. In other words, the glory of Yahweh, revealed as it is in the perfect Servant, is now to be made manifest in the empirical Israel by that David to come who will sum up in himself the calling of Israel.

To make this final point clear, DI does two simple things with language. First, he recapitulates the idea of running 'to' (*'el*) *you* by employing the preposition *le* to mean the same thing before *the Holy One of Israel*. (The RSV does not show this usage.) There he declares that if the nations run to Israel, then they are in fact running to the Lord of Israel. He will be known to them only as they see him *in* Israel. Second, DI suddenly and unexpectedly employs the feminine form of the word *you*. In this context, *you* can naturally be no other than Zion, the people whom God has chosen to be his Servant and his Bride at once. How the paradox 'God was in Israel, reconciling the world unto himself' is to be understood is the theme only of the next section of his argument.

6-7   Though to *incline your ear, and come to me* (v. 3) is only the first step in God's plan for sinful humanity, yet it is basic to all else.

We notice that DI does not identify the crass nonsense of idol worship with sin. In an earlier chapter he had laughed it and the idol makers out of court. Sin is something far more terrible than idolatry, now that we have been shown what man will do to the Servant if left to his own devices. For sin is quite simply planning one's own plans and going ahead with one's own course in self-centred disregard for the plan of Yahweh that has now been revealed. This line of verse reads strangely when we recall all the heinous sins that man can commit. Yet DI makes no mention of what we call the flagrant sins, which all derive ultimately from the one fundamental concept that the human mind is so prone to entertain: a man believes that he knows better than God his maker what he is meant to do with his life (cf. Gen. 3:5). In the Garden of Eden story, however, we read that God takes fallen man even as he is in all his pitiable emptiness, and with compassionate love gives him clothes to cover his nakedness. DI's gospel is that God offers forgiveness to man at the very moment when man is committing the fundamental sin from which all others issue. God will forgive him completely ('multiply to forgive', literally, *abundantly pardon*), because such full and total forgiveness is the expression of a love which is willing to empty out its *nephesh*, its total personality, even unto death. The 'arm' of God that has now been revealed is his forgiving and renewing love.

DI has already declared that Yahweh forgives sinners even *before* they are able to repent. Nowhere therefore does he affirm that repentance is a condition of forgiveness. Forgiveness is in fact offered free to all men even before they are aware that they are sinners (43:25). The awareness of that forgiving love, however, and of man's tremendous need for it must be brought home to sinful man. Of his own free will man must *shub*, that is, turn round and 'come home' to Yahweh. The Israelites had an initial advantage in this regard, for Yahweh chose and redeemed his Servant people even before they were able to make a conscious choice of him. In fact, every little Israelite boy on the eighth day was circumcised in order to reveal scramentally that the grace of God precedes any statement of faith he may later wish to make, for this circumcision was the sign that he belonged to the already redeemed community. Thus in coming back to Yahweh, who will *abundantly pardon*, the Israelite was but coming back to the home where he originally belonged.

Seek the Lord while he may be found, however, is not a good rendering of the Hebrew, which may equally well be translated '*where* he may be found'. God is surely ready at any time to receive home the returning prodigal. It is into his 'home', however, that the Father welcomes his son, that is, back into the covenant fellowship which he maintains with the people of God. In today's language, then, it is primarily within the fellowship of the Church that the sinner finds the mercy of God.

8   These well-known lines are each introduced by the particle *ki*. This particle can mean 'for' or 'because', but it can also introduce direct speech or even represent the two together. This means that a verb of strong asseveration is to be understood before the clause of direct speech, such as 'I swear' or 'realize!' Next, note that the usual translation of *thoughts* is not quite adequate here, for the reference is to what immediately precedes. We have seen that the wicked man's thoughts issue in wicked plans. God's loving thoughts must therefore issue in loving, creative plans and then actions. The word *plans* consequently is to be understood in a theological sense. It does not mean that God as creator has many scientifically discernible marvels still up his sleeve for men to wonder at thousands of years from now. Rather, as we see from Jer. 29:11, the emphasis is that God's purposes, which transcend what any human being could ever have thought out — 'my plans are not your plans' — have now been revealed. In fact they are now in process of becoming 'flesh' through the ideal of self-offering of the Servant.

9   To DI such a plan is a far more astonishing reality than the mysteries still hidden in the wonders of God's natural world. In fact, man cannot even begin to comprehend the depths and heights of the love of God and of his plans of salvation that embrace the whole of creation. How sordid were the ways of the proletariat of Babylon —

bowed down with superstition as they were, riddled with jealousies and fears, their homes cramped and mean, their morals bestial and repulsive — compared with the self-emptying of the Holy One of Israel in his Servant for the redemption of the world.

10 Yet a vital element in the good news is that God's way of salvation will win in the end over the sordid ways of men. In fact this is inevitable. This verse contains the longest sustained simile that DI employs. In it we are reminded that God is in full control of the processes of nature. Moreover, these processes are orderly, and they work together according to natural law. Interestingly enough, they are creative and are not merely mechanically conditioned. As such they form the sacramental woof and web of man's life under God. For man lives on bread (55:2), and cannot hope to find fullness of life unless he first sustains his body on meat and drink. Thus the food that grows out of the ground is the inevitable outcome of the movement of God's loving purpose for man in the processes of nature. Moreover, this movement cannot reverse itself. It must go forward according to the pattern that God has first created, a good pattern, for it is a pattern that reveals a purpose of love. In other words, it is an effective pattern, for it results in the fulfilment of the divine plan.

11 This is DI's analogy by which he declares the effectiveness of the divine plan of redemption. His choice of language rests upon the generally held ancient concepts of the potency of the word and its substantive existence once it has been uttered. As we have seen in the commentary at 44:24, this view is basic to DI's argument. When God speaks, he naturally speaks with intent. For he is the faithful God.

So shall my word be that goes forth from my mouth; it shall not return to me empty, that is to say, without hitting the target at which God has aimed. Once his Word is uttered, therefore, it necessarily becomes effective to save, even though it may be deflected from its course for a time by the resistance of the free will of man. In the end, however, God's Word must inevitably reach its target: *By myself I have sworn* (for there is nothing greater than God by which to swear), *from my mouth* 'creative love' (*tsedaqah*) *has gone forth*; (it is) *a word that shall not return: 'To me every knee shall bow, every tongue shall swear'* (45:23). 53:10 had ended with the words: *The will of the Lord shall prosper in his hand*. We saw there that this verb means 'to come to an effective conclusion'. DI now uses it once again, at the end of v. 11, to make the same claim for the Word.

12   This extraordinary news is world-shattering. Even *the mountains and the hills ... shall break forth into singing, and all the trees of the field shall clap their hands.* So Nature is to share in the joy of the Lord! In place of harmful plants God will give trees useful to man. Even the physical is to experience resurrection. DI's disciple, whom we call Trito-Isaiah for convenience, brings this whole issue to its logical conclusion. For, in chs. 65 and 66 he declares that in the end God will actually create new heavens and a new earth. Then the eschatological significance of this present world, amalgam as it is now of both matter and spirit, will be finally revealed.

'Realize then', we read, 'when you poor, dispirited Israelite exiles *go out* from Babylon, you will go forth from the city with the *joy* of God in your hearts'. He, of course, dwells in joy, since he knows the end from the beginning (41:4; 44:6; 48:12). Yours will be the inestimable joy of discovering that you are sharing in, even acting as the trigger of, the greatest of all divine activities. This movement will now go on like the inevitable linked, progressive, onward movement of a chain reaction, or more properly, like the inevitable, linked, forward movement that proceeds from promise to fulfilment.

13   Right at the end of his thesis, then, our prophet-theologian returns to the subject with which he began in ch. 40. There the new exodus was seen to be composed of very ordinary people, trudging along a very ordinary road as they returned from Babylon to Jerusalem. He does not suggest that these poor straggling sheep could be said *per se* to constitute revelation. What he is emphasising is that God has now uttered his Word. This Word has gone forth and therefore cannot return to him *empty*. But since it has been uttered within the form and framework of this particular depressed group of people, this people has therefore become in reality the very form of the Servant, and so of divine revelation. And this Servant people had already been summed up in the person of one individual, David the king.

So it is that our author's last and highly significant words come as a completely fitting climax to his whole message. It is that being *led forth in peace, shalom*, or 'fullness of life', will be but one aspect of the rebirth of the whole creation. For this rebirth leads to the conclusion of God's comprehensive (*shalom* again) Plan. Here we are witnessing the power of his *hesed*, the 'loyal-love of God', expressed in his comprehensive covenant made with Israel, a love that can best be described in the words 'O love that wilt not let me go'.

DI is clearly the greatest theologian that has ever arisen. Paul was his humble disciple. For DI did not deal with metaphysical speculation like Plato, or the philosophers of Islam, or the medieval disputants, or the Neo-Platonists of the present day. He dealt with facts. In these 16 chapters he has given us a total theology of God's redemptive plan for his world, and he has done so basing his statements wholly upon history. He has handled (1) the fact of Israel; (2) the fact of the Exodus in the days of Moses; (3) the fact of the *Torah*, the revelation teaching of God to be found in the Pentateuch; (4) the fact of the destruction of the city of Jerusalem in 587 B.C.; (5) the fact of the Exile in Babylon with all its accompanying horrors; (6) the fact of the rise of king Cyrus of Persia. But there was one more fact of history that eventuated only after DI's death. He looked forward to it in faith, building his certainty upon the reliability of God and the nature of God's covenant-love. This was the fact that Cyrus issued an edict in 538 B.C. which permitted the displaced persons of Israel to return home to Zion, and thus to repossess their Land. Moreover, armed with this certainty of the one action of God still to come, he could express his absolute certainty of all that God was doing in and through Israel.

Out of these factual events of history DI has produced a thesis which he believes is rooted in eternity, that is completely true as revelatory writing (55:13). He believes God has given it to him to 'mediate' (43:27) for mankind. Using history as the structure of his argument, he has produced a theology of the creative and redemptive love of God. God has used the body of Israel to that end as a whole. But he also invites individuals to share in his redemptive task with him in covenant. DI believes in what he has written (and remember it is all in poetry, like the words of Milton and Dante) because it has come to him through the Spirit of God (48:16).

Why should we, with our centuries of cumulative knowledge ever since his day, smile at him for not possessing in his native Hebrew the words for 'theological thesis', and for imagining that he could never have written one because he does not possess our technical terms? We forget that DI made full use of those concepts available to him half a millenium before the birth of Christ.

He now completes his thesis by declaring emphatically first that *it shall be to the Lord for a memorial*. This last word is *shem*, 'name'. The name that a person bore sought to describe the nature of its owner. This, as we have seen more than once. DI believed to be true of God (cf. 47:4; 48:1-2; 50:10). Consequently DI is stating that the thesis he has just concluded *shall be for* 'a revelation of the nature and purpose of God'. Second, it shall become *a sign*, 'belonging in eternity', which shall never become invalid or be done away with. A sign, *oth*, to his way of thinking was virtually what a sacrament means to us today, and evidently meant to Jesus. For he too, having accepted DI's thesis in all its fullness, declared categorically 'We worship what we *know*, for salvation is from the Jews' (John 4:22). Or, as Professor Karl Barth put it in his *Dogmatics in Outline*, 1949, p. 80: 'Israel is not a sick man who was allowed to recover, but One risen from the dead'.

SELECTED BIBLIOGRAPHY

Anderson, Bernard W. *Understanding the Old Testament*. Englewood Cliffs, N.J.: Prentice-Hall, 1957.

Aytoun, R. A. 'The Servant of the Lord in the Targum', *Journal of Theological Studies*, XXIII (1922), 172-80.

Barnes, W. E. 'Cyrus, the "Servant of Jehovah"', *Journal of Theological Studies*, XXXII (1931), 32-39.

Bentzen, Aage. *King and Messiah*. London: Lutterworth Press, 1955.

————. 'On the Ideas of "the Old" and "the New" in Deutero-Isaiah', *Studia Theologia*, I (1947), 183-87.

Boer, P. A. H., de, editor. *Second Isaiah's Message*. (*Oudtestamentische Studiën*, Vol. XI), Leiden: E. J. Brill, 1950.

Brownlee, William H. 'The Servant of the Lord in the Qumran Scrolls', *Bulletin of the American Schools of Oriental Research*, 132 (1953); 135 (1954).

Buber, Martin. *The Prophetic Faith*. New York: The Macmillan Co., 1949.

Clines, D. J. A. *I, He, We, and They*. Journal of the Study of the Old Testament, Suppl. Series 1, 1976.

Danell, G. *Studies in the Name Israel in the Old Testament*. Uppsala: Appelberg, 1946.

Driver, G. R. 'Isaiah 52:13–53:12: The Servant of the Lord', in M. Black and G. Fohrer, ed., *In Memoriam Paul Kahle* (BZAW 103), 1968, pp. 90-105.

Driver, S. R. and Neubauer, A. *The Fifty-third Chapter of Isaiah According to the Jewish Interpreters*. Oxford: J. Parker & Co., 1876-77.

Eaton, J. H. *Festal Drama in Deutero-Isaiah*. S.P.C.K., n.d.

Eissfeldt, Otto. 'The Ebed-Jahwe in Isaiah xl-lv, in the Light of the Israelite Conceptions of the Community and the Individual, the Ideal and the Real', *Expository Times*, XLIV (1933), 261-68.

————. 'The Promise of Grace to David in Isa. 55:1-5', *Israel's Prophetic Heritage*, ed. Bernhard W. Anderson. New York: Harper & Row, 1962, pp. 196 ff.

Engell, Ivan. 'The Ebed Yahweh Song and the Suffering Messiah in Deutero-Isaiah', *Bulletin of the John Rylands Library*, XXXI (1948).

————. *Studies in Divine Kingship in the Ancient Near East*. Uppsala: Almquist & Wiksells, 1953.

Ginsberg, H. L. 'The Oldest Interpretation of the Suffering Servant', *Vetus Testamentum*, 3 (1953), pp. 400-404.

Gottwald, Norman. *A Light to the Nations*. New York: Harper & Row, 1959.

Herbert, A. S. *Isaiah 40-66*. (*Cambridge Bible Commentaries*), 1975.

Holmgren, F. *With Wings as Eagles — Isaiah 40-55, an Interpretation* (BSP), 1973.

Hooker, Morna D. *Jesus and the Servant*. London: S.P.C.K., 1959.

Jastrow, Morris. *Aspects of Religious Belief and Practice in Babylonia and Assyria*. New York: G. P. Putnam's Sons, 1911.

Jocz, Jakob. *A Theology of Election*. London: S.P.C.K., 1958.

Johnson, A. R. *The One and the Many in the Israelite Conception of God*. Cardiff: University of Wales Press Board, 1942.

————. *Sacral Kingship in Ancient Israel*. Cardiff: University of Wales Press Board, 1955.

Klein, Ralph W. *Israel in Exile: A Theological Interpretation*. Overtures to Biblical Theology, Philadelphia: Fortress Press, 1979.

Knight, G. A. F. *A Christian Theology of the Old Testament*. London: S.C.M. and Richmond: John Knox Press, 1959, 1964.

Lambert, W. *Babylonian Wisdom Literature*. London: Oxford at the Clarendon Press, 1960.

Lindblom, Johannes. *The Servant-Songs in Deutero-Isaiah*. Lund: Lund University Press, 1951.

Lindhagen, Curt. *The Servant Motif in the Old Testament*. Uppsala: Lundequistska Bokhandeln, 1950.

Lofthouse, W. F. 'Some Reflections on the Servant Songs', *Journal of Theological Studies*, XLVIII (1947), 169-70.

Manson, T. W. *The Servant-Messiah*. London: Cambridge University Press, 1953.

Martin-Achard, R. *De la mort à la resurrection d'après l'Ancien Testament*. (Bibliothèque Théologique), 1959.

Melugin, Roy F. *The Formation of Isaiah 40-55*. de Gruyter, 1976.

Morgenstern, Julian. 'The Message of Deutero-Isaiah in its Sequential Unfolding', *Hebrew Union College Annual*, XXX (1939).

————. 'The Suffering Servant — A New Solution', *Vetus Testamentum*, 11 (1961), 292-320.

Mowinckel, Sigmund. *He That Cometh*. Oxford: Basil Blackwell, Nashville: Abingdon, 1956, 1959.

Muilenburg, James. Introduction to 'The Book of Isaiah, Chapters 40-66', *The Interpreter's Bible*, Vol. V. Nashville: Abingdon, 1956.

Newsome, James D. Jr. *By the Waters of Babylon*. Atlanta: John Knox Press, 1979.

North, Christopher. 'The "Former Things" and the "New Things" in Deutero-Isaiah', *Studies in Old Testament Prophecy*, ed. H. H. Rowley. Edinburgh: T. & T. Clark, 1950.

—————. *The Suffering Servant in Deutero-Isaiah*. Rev. ed. New York: Oxford University Press, 1956.

—————. *The Second Isaiah*. London and New York: Oxford University Press, 1964.

Orlinsky, Harry M. 'Studies in St. Mark's Isaiah Scroll, II', *Journal of Near Eastern Studies*, XI (1952), 153-56.

—————. 'The So-called "Servant of the Lord" and "Suffering Servant" in Second Isaiah', *Vetus Testamentum*, Suppl. 14, 1967, pp. 1-133.

Peake, Arthur S. *The Problem of Suffering in the Old Testament*. London: Robert Bryant and C. H. Kelly, 1904.

Pritchard, James B. *Ancient Near Eastern Texts Relating to the Old Testament*, 2nd ed. Princeton University Press, 1955.

Rignell, Lars G. *A Study of Isaiah 40-55*. Lund: Gleerup, 1956.

Robinson, Henry W. *The Cross in the Old Testament*. London: S.C.M. Press, 1955, Philadelphia: Westminster Press, 1956.

—————. 'The Hebrew Conception of Corporate Personality', in 'Werden und Wesen' des Alten Testaments, *Beiheft zur Zeitschrift für die alttestamentliche Wissenschaft*, LXVI (1936).

Rosin, H. *The Lord is God*. Leiden: 1956.

Rowley, H. H. *The Servant of the Lord, and Other Essays on the Old Testament*. London: Lutterworth Press, 1952.

Scharbert, J. 'The Vicarious Suffering in the Ebed Yahweh Songs', *Biblische Zeitschrift*, 1958.

Schoors, Anton. *I am God your Saviour*. Leiden: E. J. Brill, 1973.

Seeligman, Isaac L. *The Septuagint Version of Isaiah*. Leiden: E. J. Brill, 1948.

Simon, Ulrich E. *A Theology of Salvation*. London: S.P.C.K., 1953.

Simundson, Daniel J. *Faith under Fire*. Minneapolis: Augsburg Publishing House, 1980.

Skinner, John. *The Book of the Prophet Isaiah*, Chapters XL-LXVI. Rev. ed. (*Cambridge Bible*), 1917.

Smart, J. D. *History and Theology in Second Isaiah*. Westminster, 1965.

Smith, George A. *The Book of Isaiah, Vol. II (Expositor's Bible)*. London: Hodder & Stoughton, 1890.

Smith, Sidney. *Isaiah Chapters XL-LV: Literary Criticism and History*. Oxford University Press, 1940, 1944.

Snaith, Norman H. 'The Servant of the Lord in Deutero-Isaiah', *Studies in Old Testament Prophecy*, ed. H. H. Rowley. Edinburgh: T. & T. Clark, 1950.

Stuhlmueller, C. 'The Theology of Creation in Second Isaias', *Catholic Biblical Quarterly*, **XXI** (1959), 429-67.

——. *Creative Redemption in Deutero-Isaiah*. Rome: Biblical Institute Press, 1970.

Thomas, D. Winton. *Documents from Old Testament Times*. London: Thomas Nelson & Sons, 1958.

Westermann, Claus. *Isaiah 40-66 (Old Testament Library)*. London: S.C.M. Press, 1969.

Whitehouse, Owen C. *Isaiah XL-LXVI (Century Bible)*. London: T. C. & E. C. Jack, 1931.

Whybray, R. N. *Isaiah 40-66 (New Century Bible)*. 1981 (1975).

——. 'The Heavenly Counsellor in Isaiah XL:13-14', *Society of Old Testament Studies Monograph Series I*. Cambridge, 1971.

——. 'Thanksgiving for a Liberated Prophet', *Journal of the Study of the Old Testament*, Supplementary Series 4. Sheffield, 1978.